An American Booksellers Association Indies Introduce Featured Title

Praise for *A Clean Hell*

"Eric King spent ten years in some of the worst prisons the world has ever seen. And lived to tell the story. *A Clean Hell* is a haunting, harrowing journey through hell and back, told with unflinching honesty and a crooked smile. Like Alexander Berkman and Martin Sostre before him, King keeps the anarchist flame burning—prison be damned."
—Dan Berger, author of *Stayed on Freedom: The Long History of Black Power Through One Family's Journey*

"*A Clean Hell* is an unflinching, harrowing account of state violence. King exposes the brutal realities of federal prison—offering rare, deeply personal insights into the hidden world of ADX—where he was imprisoned in retaliation for his acts of resistance and solidarity with the Ferguson Uprising in 2014. Through his testimony, he challenges us to cultivate compassion, extend empathy to ourselves, and commit to collective struggle—because revolution is not just about survival, but about building a world where we all thrive."
—Zane McNeill, editor of *Y'all Means All: The Emerging Voices Queering Appalachia* and *Vegan Entanglements: Dismantling Racial and Carceral Capitalism*

"*A Clean Hell* is a raw and unfiltered recounting of a life inside the American gulag. As abolitionists challenge the prison-industrial complex, Eric King's brutal firsthand experience of every federal security level will be crucial knowledge for the fight ahead."
—Josh Harper, former US political prisoner and SHAC 7 defendant

"Eric King's *A Clean Hell* vividly takes us into the bowels of the most repressive prisons in the country. The reader experiences the beatdowns by gangs of guards, the strip search designed to be a sexual humiliation, the twenty-four-hour-a-day lockdowns, the worry about the anguish of one's family, as well as ways people resist. These prisons are designed to break one's spirit, and there's the added hostility toward Eric as a 'traitor to the white race.' What makes this book particularly inspiring is that it's written by someone who not only came out of prison unbroken but who also continues to be a fireball of activism for social justice."
—David Gilbert, former US political prisoner and author of *No Surrender* and *Love and Struggle*

"Eric King's an antifascist, antiracist political activist who spent over a decade in the worst US federal prisons, including solitary confinement, and ADX, the most extreme and repressive prison in the world. *A Clean Hell* is a searing exposé and indictment of the Federal Bureau of Prisons, the Department of Justice, and the US government. The use of violence, physical and mental torture, and retaliation by the authorities all fuel Eric's fight against the slow death of politically motivated imprisonment. For any activist, organizer, resister, or anyone studying American history, this is a guide to understanding the viciousness of intended death by incarceration."
—Susan Rosenberg, former US political prisoner, writer, and teacher

"King's visceral account of his political imprisonment within America's supermax torture chambers will grab you by the throat and force you to bear witness to the antihuman violence and irrationality at the core of the prison system. But that's not all. The grounded analysis of this self-proclaimed 'race traitor' allows us to reflect on antiracist, abolitionist, and anarchist approaches to fighting fascism at a time when such analysis is more critical than ever."
—Orisanmi Burton, author of *Tip of the Spear: Black Radicalism, Prison Repression, and the Long Attica Revolt*

"It is so necessary for any movement to have an accurate and complete documentation of its own history and struggle—to avoid being erased, or worse, misrepresented by the shrieking sirens of the Empire. Eric King's excellent new book about the hidden world of the ADX in Florence is a part of that tradition of griots, those ones who help us remember and know the truth about ourselves. Gandhi once said that you could see the true nature of any society by witnessing the treatment of its prisoners and animals. By that rubric, this society fails. King's condemnation is powerful and is a timely call to action. King has been a reliable and principled reporter on state repression for years. Having this antifascist and antiauthoritarian 'insider's' view of the carceral state is an inspirational personal account of survival and triumph."
—Marius Mason, US political prisoner and artist

"In this heartbreaking debut, Eric King takes us on a rage-inducing journey into the life of a political prisoner abused by the system at every turn. From manipulative lawyers to sexually deviant cops, King is subjected to the worst that humanity has to offer. However, through it all, King clenches his fists, opens his heart, and solidifies his opposition to the forces that oppress us. His descriptions of prison will leave you breathless. Your jaw will hurt from clenching at the depictions of brutality and violence at the hands of the state. Yet the little flickers of joy in King's dogged rebellion radiate with the possibility of hope and revolution. King's prose burns like a gas-soaked rag in the mouth of a Molotov."
—Josh Fernandez, author of *The Hands That Crafted the Bomb*

"Sentenced to the US's most repressive 'supermax' prison, Eric King defied the government's unrelenting attempts to crush his spirit through years of isolation and physical and mental attacks. His profound dignity shines through this account of survival and resistance, offering lessons to everyone committed to fighting the forces of repression."
—Donna Willmott, former US political prisoner

"I can attest to the words of my brother Eric King, who knows the dehumanizing use of 23/7 lockdown prisons, built to destroy you, kill your spirit, and crush your mind. These are places no man wants to be. Eric knows firsthand, since they sent him there as punishment for winning his case against staff who brutalized him at FCI Florence. Eric is not a criminal, he is a fighter for justice. When you stand up for yourself and humane treatment in the face of a corrupt system, you can suffer as my brother did, getting locked down in a supermax. We all must stand up and bring an end to these prisons. Eric was there, and he has no fear of telling the truth. That takes a lot of guts."
—Oso Blanco, Indigenous artist, author,
musician, and US political prisoner

"The federal prison, ADX Florence, is but the more modern version of Alcatraz, Marion, or Guantánamo. To understand the justification for violence and torture of human beings by the state, one needs to take a deep look at how imprisonment impacts real people. Eric King is one of a long list of people who not only survived but is dedicated to expose and oppose the endemic nature and inhumanity taking place in these shadows of the Bureau of Prisons. *A Clean Hell* is a must-read."
—Claude Marks, former US political prisoner and
cofounder and codirector of the Freedom Archives

"Eric's story sticks with you long after you put his book down. It's a brutal read, and a nakedly honest one, never varnishing over the monstrous violence of the prison system, intimately experienced by Eric. At the same time, his truth-telling ability is all heart, burning with a radical love in defense of empathy, dignity, and freedom that not only aided him in the one 'victory that matters in prison,' which is 'getting out alive,' but also in passing along hard-won wisdom about how we can solidaristically fight to keep each other alive. *A Clean Hell* is a timely, immensely powerful gift!"
—Cindy Barukh Milstein, author of *Constellations
of Care: Anarcha-Feminism in Practice*

"They tried to bury Eric King alive, but he achieved the near-impossible: He got out. *A Clean Hell* is a rare look into a place that the US government doesn't want you to see—the darkest corners of the federal prison-industrial complex. A place where officers act with impunity, kangaroo courts run rampant, and inmates are left to wither away in underground cells. Eric's story isn't one of survival, but radical resistance. And a reminder that indeed, those they try to bury actually are seeds."
—Jake Conroy, former US political prisoner, SHAC 7 defendant, and host of the podcast *Radicals and Revolutionaries*

"Eric's new work detailing his experiences in the ADX, along with the voices of others—some still trapped inside—is powerful and compelling. *A Clean Hell* is a must-read for everyone interested in the support of prisoners and the complete destruction of prisons and the state who maintains them."
—N.O. Bonzo, anarchist illustrator, printmaker, and muralist

"As I sat in prison myself, I followed Eric's story. He offered the hope, joy, and inspiration I needed to get through my own bid. I am forever grateful for his resistance."
—Pepe Bandit, founder of Stay Free Coffee, music producer, and creator and host of the podcast *Back on the Grind*

A Clean Hell

Anarchy and Abolition Inside America's Most Notorious Dungeon

Eric King

Edited by Josh Davidson

Foreword by Ray Luc Levasseur

A Clean Hell: Anarchy and Abolition Inside America's Most Notorious Dungeon
© 2026 Eric King
This edition © 2026 PM Press

All rights reserved. No part of this book may be transmitted by any means without permission in writing from the publisher.

ISBN: 979-8-88744-159-7 (paperback)
ISBN: 979-8-88744-160-3 (ebook)
Library of Congress Control Number: 2025935654

Cover design by Courtney Davis and John Yates / stealworks.com
Interior design by briandesign

10 9 8 7 6 5 4 3 2 1

PM Press
PO Box 23912
Oakland, CA 94623
www.pmpress.org

Printed in the USA.

The ADX is a far more stark environment than any other prison I've ever seen, and I've been to all of the federal prisons. When I call it a clean version of hell, I mean that it's squeaky clean and quiet, because everyone there is locked down. It's a very abnormal environment. This place is not designed for humanity. When it's twenty-three hours a day in a room with a slit of a window where you can't even see the Rocky Mountains—let's be candid here. It's not designed for rehabilitation. Period. End of story.
—Robert Hood, ADX warden from 2002 to 2005

The obligation of anyone who thinks of himself as responsible is to examine society and try to change it and to fight it—at no matter what the risk. This is the only hope society has. This is the only way societies change.
—James Baldwin, "A Talk to Teachers"

Contents

FOREWORD	*Ray Luc Levasseur*	xiii
INTRODUCTION	It Started with a Joke, or How I Ended Up in ADX	1
PROLOGUE	A Brief History of ADX and Supermax Confinement	8
CHAPTER 1	Taking the Stand: The Reality of Trial	13
CHAPTER 2	The Scariest Ride of My Life	34
CHAPTER 3	Nothing but Neglect: Canteen and Medical	55
CHAPTER 4	A New Type of Institutionalization	72
CHAPTER 5	How Did I Get Here?	79
CHAPTER 6	Stolen Moments of Freedom	85
CHAPTER 7	Who's in Here? A Breakdown of Demographics	92
CHAPTER 8	When the Fascists Hold the Keys: A Look at the Guards	121
CHAPTER 9	Support Saves Lives	129
CHAPTER 10	Antifascists and Political Prisoners	137
CHAPTER 11	Resistance and Consequences: Standing Up to Repression	150
CHAPTER 12	The Control Unit	171

CHAPTER 13	**Little Guantánamo**	178
CHAPTER 14	**Those Who Stay and Those Who Go**	190
CHAPTER 15	**Before the Devil Knows You're Gone: Walking Out of Hell**	202
CHAPTER 16	**First Breath of Freedom**	211
CHAPTER 17	**When One Door Closes**	213
	ACKNOWLEDGMENTS	223
	GLOSSARY	226
	ABBREVIATIONS	229
	ABOUT THE CONTRIBUTORS	230

Foreword

Ray Luc Levasseur

There are many pipelines leading to hell. In an unpublished autobiography, Gus Heald, good friend and jailhouse lawyer par excellence, wrote:

> My first horrific disillusionment with the correctional system came as a result of my being committed to the boys' reformatory in Portland, Maine. It set the terrible pattern which haunted me half a lifetime. It was not the end of a criminal career, as it should have been, but the beginning. All it took was a broken nose, two cracked ribs, the loss of one-third of the vision in my left eye, and one horrendous night filled with stark terror that no boy of fourteen should ever experience.

Gus had been committed to this youth prison not for a crime but for a status offense—truancy. On through the pipeline went Gus, becoming a jailhouse lawyer along the way, which is what punched his ticket to the US Penitentiary Marion, supermax and precursor to ADX (Administrative Maximum). From skipping school to "the worst of the worst." Gus died of hypothermia on the streets in 1992.

My own gateway to supermax opened with my first taste of political activism with the Southern Student Organizing Committee and its antiwar, prolabor, and civil rights agenda. Following a police raid and marijuana conviction, I was slapped with a five-year prison sentence.

County jail conditions were atrocious. Black and white prisoners unified and went on a food strike. The following day, I was carted off to the Tennessee State Prison, jacketed as a "troublemaker." At TSP, the "problem of the color line" manifested itself through de facto racial segregation. When I defied that vestige of Jim Crow, I was classified as a "radical and racial agitator" and transferred to the end of the line—Brushy Mountain State Penitentiary.

In 1970, Brushy was an early version of supermax. Had I arrived five years earlier, I would have been forced to work in a coal mine, as Brushy was originally part of the "worse than slavery" convict leasing system, which was followed by a decades-long period when the state operated the mine using prison labor. After many deaths and injuries, the mine closed in 1966, and Brushy converted to a lockdown regimen. An all-white guard force watched the rest of us, half being Black, including death row, while we sat idle in our cells.

The US has the largest prison population in the world. America's colonial project used murder, punishment, and detention to control and expand. The embedded roots of today's prisons reach back to the decimation of Indigenous people and chattel slavery. The confluence of race and class in the prison system demonstrates that for many the pipeline begins when they leave the womb.

Prisons are the fruit of the poisonous tree, and prisons like ADX are the most toxic. The system is not broken, nor can it be derailed with reforms. The system works just as ruling-class flunkies designed it—as a powerful tool of social control that commands submission and aims to incapacitate.

The entire criminal legal system is capitalism's first line of defense against the noncompliant.

My next encounter with supermax also began with political activism. During stints with Vietnam Veterans Against the War and SCAR (Statewide Correctional Alliance for Reform, a prisoners' rights organization), and after too many negative encounters with police, I took my activism clandestine with the hope of building a revolutionary resistance movement. Ten years later, I was a captive enemy of the state. At the conclusion of my trials, I was sent directly to USP Marion based on my "political beliefs and associations." ADX was still in the planning stage.

As is well documented by many, Marion was "hell in a very small space." Condemned by Amnesty International, cited for violating the UN Standard Minimum Rules for the Treatment of Prisoners, dogged by the Committee to End the Marion Lockdown, and criticized by a federal court for conditions that were "horrible and sordid," the government's response was that Marion was not horrible enough. So they built a monstrosity they named the ADX.

Marion had a design flaw that the BOP (Bureau of Prisons) sought to rectify. Marion's physical structure was built primarily for small-group isolation, with standard steel-barred cells and other drawbacks.

With ADX, college-educated architects designed a prison from the ground up that imposed extreme isolation on captives. Using boxcar cells as the starting point, the walls became shackles. (In 1978, a federal court judge ruled that the use of boxcar cells at Marion was unconstitutional. At the time, Marion had only six boxcar cells, each located in the segregation unit. However, at ADX "cruel and unusual punishment" was acceptable practice.)

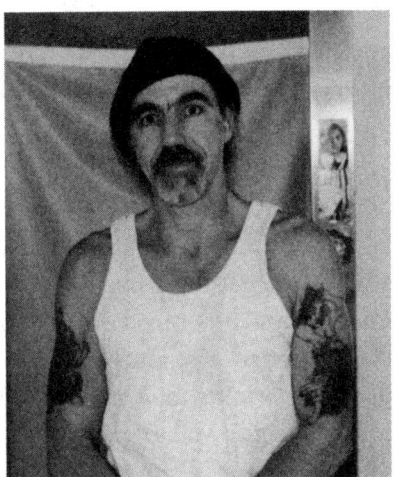

Ray Luc Levasseur during his time at ADX.

Marion prisoners were the first to fill ADX cells. My last day at Marion and my first day in ADX exemplify the decade I spent in both. Shackled, chained, cuffed, black-boxed, I was taken to Marion's dispensary, where I was X-rayed. I was then shown a Regional BOP document authorizing an anal probe. My pants were pulled down, and I was bent over a stainless steel table, where I was thoroughly probed. Hours later, I arrived at ADX, ate the mystery food slid into my cell, and spent the night vomiting in the toilet, the sound reverberating off the walls.

Sexual assault, food poisoning, degradation—but I had little recourse, as the power to abuse and harm the captive knows no restraints, has no checks and balances, no conscience.

A boxcar cell is like a cage within a box. The design places severe limitations on what you can see, hear, and touch, slowly grating on your senses. Between the bars of the cage and the steel door of the box is the "trap," a fitting name for the condition of one confined in a boxcar. I often thought of the proverbial fox or coyote caught in a leghold trap who chews through flesh and bone to free itself. All it got me was envy—the animals were not in ADX. Leghold traps do not discriminate between species, and boxcar cells respect no ideology, race, religion, IQ, or mental condition. You are fair game for cruel, unusual, and degrading punishment.

In late 1995, ADX received new blood. The "crack riots" rocked the federal prison system, causing the most extensive property damage in BOP history. Youngsters in their twenties tagged as instigators and leaders of the rebellion were transferred to ADX and got a beatdown in the segregation unit when they arrived. ADX was moving on to the next generation.

Supermax prisons and the expanded use of solitary confinement are part of the state's master plan developed in response to the Attica uprising and other prison rebellions of the 1960s and 1970s. They took the movement slogan "Attica Means Fight Back!" literally. While the prisoners' rights movement from that era slowly receded, the entire criminal legal system ramped up its capacity to imprison and control millions.

Eric King has provided us with a powerful lens through which to feel up close and personal the effects of solitary confinement on the mind and body, families and communities. To see the concentrated effects of state-orchestrated violence and the desperate resistance of those subjected to it, as well as the inevitable internecine violence that roars like a wounded animal from a cave.

Eric enables the silent screams of captives to serve as a public indictment of a dehumanizing system that is beyond salvageable.

This long-overdue book has now arrived, written in the true spirit of a caring human being and unrepentant antifascist. May there be no speech nor language where their voice is not heard.

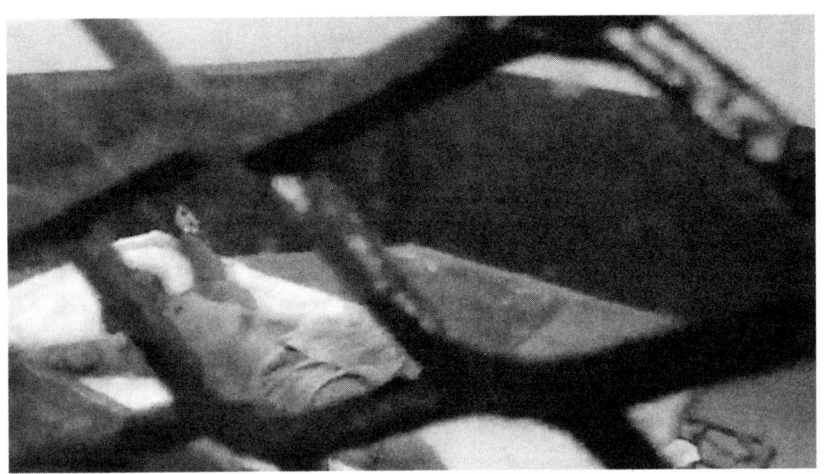

III INTRODUCTION

It Started with a Joke, or How I Ended Up in ADX

There is a time when nine guards are beating you mercilessly that you may ponder, *Am I going to survive this?* When you start blacking out from their knees being pressed deeply into your lungs, you might think, *I may not ever take another breath.* When you are strapped to a chair and carried down a flight of stairs leading to the basement chamber, you will be justified in fearing, *They are going to throw me down these stairs.* When they stand you up against a wall and use metal shears to slice off all your clothing, you will certainly think, *These motherfuckers are going to rape and kill me.* Finally, you are forced onto a metal bed, your legs forcefully stretched as far as they can go, chained to the corners of a steel mattress. Your shaking arms are cuffed above your head, pulled so violently you know for sure they will get wrenched out of their sockets. Your body is now a vulnerable human X, completely and totally at the whims of your attackers. Your hands numb, your feet numb, your chest and back radiating pain in ways you cannot describe or have ever imagined feeling. While being brutalized, you may think, *This is actual torture. This is literal torture. I may not make it out of this.*

When the FCI and ADX captains come in to tell you that they plan on having you raped, beaten, and destroyed at your next location, oddly proclaiming, "This is street justice," when those same captains place a plastic shield over your face and torso and push on it, forcing all the air out of your lungs, suffocating you, and when one of those same captains places his hand over your mouth for twenty seconds that feel like twenty hours, you will know for sure that you are going to die here. What happened to me is called four-pointing, because your legs and arms are chained to the four points of a steel frame. In the past, it was called quartering. Seven and a half hours of not moving a single muscle, of staring at a fluorescent light bulb, of trying to find

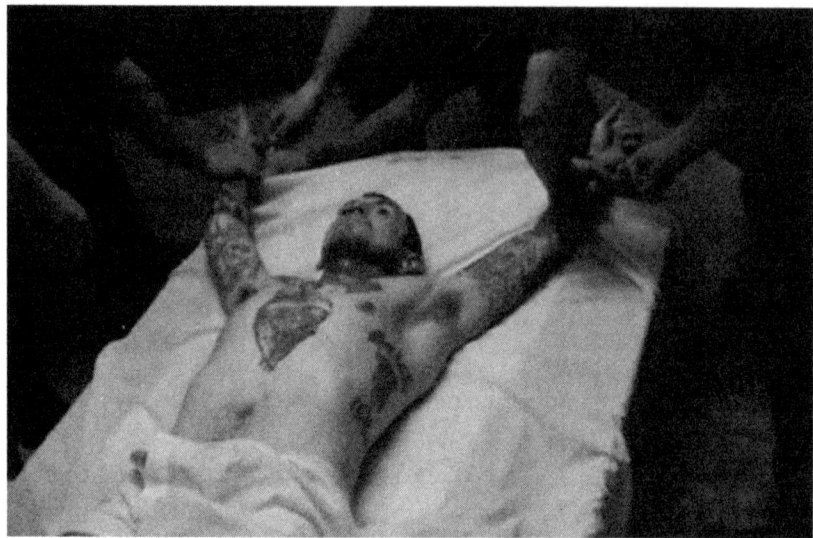
Eric King being handcuffed by seven guards while being four-pointed.

any sort of peace within the agony. There is nothing you can do but feel it. Screaming will make no difference. No one who cares will ever hear your pleas.

You will urinate on yourself. You will lie in a puddle of your own piss and know that your torturer is doing this to break you. They want to degrade you, humiliate you. Everything in prison is about breaking our bodies or spirits. Struggle all you like, but that will only stretch and pull the muscles farther. Every minor movement causes fire to race through your body. All you can do is come to peace with your misery. *This is my life now, nothing but unstoppable pain.* Years later, you still won't be able to feel parts of your hands. You will still have pain in your shoulders, back, and neck. You will still cry when you think of the powerlessness. When you reflect on your inability to stop the attack, you will feel panic in your chest, tears racing down your face. It wasn't your fault. You didn't do this to yourself. It is their crime, their inhumanity. You will come to understand that later, but at the time all you can do is suffer and feel it.

Michael Brown was eighteen years old when Officer Darren Wilson murdered him. He was barely old enough to vote, yet he was old enough to frighten the officer into pulling out his pistol and opening

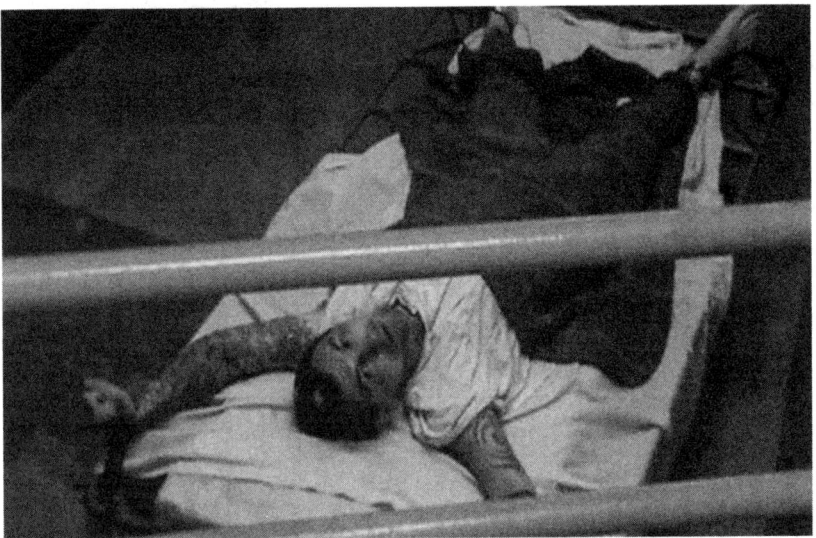

Looking up at the camera while being four-pointed. The blanket was added hours into the session.

fire. Michael Brown had committed the unforgivable crime of walking down the street while young and Black. Officer Wilson found him guilty, and the sentence was six bullets into his young body.

The streets erupted, justifiably so. The people of Ferguson forced the world to see and experience their sorrow and anger. What are you supposed to do when children in your community are being murdered and no one is being held accountable? I don't know what you're supposed to do when you see this sort of heart-wrenching drama play out, but for me and many others, the only option was action.

Countless people from Kansas City made the four-hour drive across Missouri to the battle zone. Some went to observe the wreckage, making uprisings a spectator sport, the tragedy less interesting than the spectacle. Others went to take control, treating the community like a group of children to be patronized and led. Many, though, went to offer a hand. To pass out water, to bring supplies, to be another body on the front lines. Not as leaders or warriors, but as allies and comrades. That was my brief experience. Carpooling with three strangers, listening to "Shake It Off" to calm our nerves. We needed to counterbalance the force of the state. The National Guard was there. The cops were there. The militias were there to support the cops. All brothers-in-arms.

While there, witnessing the hatred displayed by the authorities, I'd seen enough. When I returned to Kansas City, I couldn't shake the unforgiving guilt I felt. While I was sleeping peacefully, they were mourning and battling. There were no stun grenades going off on Charlotte Street in KC. There were no armed militias in downtown Westport. Our privilege sickened me, and it was hard to swallow. Our streets didn't smell like tear gas, and that didn't seem right. Who were we to have such peace? Kansas City was sleeping with angels while Ferguson was battling with demons.

My actions started small. I didn't want to lead a mass movement; for me, this was a personal revolution. I saw myself as a serious revolutionary. There are a thousand ways to sabotage the police state, and I thought I was Alexander Berkman. I was not clever. I knew nothing about security culture outside of wearing masks and gloves. On September 11, 2014, I wanted the people of Ferguson to know that someone, somewhere in Kansas City, remembered them and was in solidarity with them. They deserved to be fought for. If their lives and freedom were on the line, didn't my solidarity demand the same of me? My life was not more valuable than theirs. My freedom was not more precious than theirs.

Bottles filled with Styrofoam, lighter fluid, and gasoline changed everything for me. They didn't burn the brick building down, but they did turn my life to ash. Those two Molotovs and my lack of any precautions led to me being arrested and sent to a private jail in Leavenworth, Kansas. I wanted to go to trial but others convinced me it was the wrong idea. Signing the guilty plea was one of the worst feelings I've ever experienced. Total surrender and defeat. That led to me being sentenced to 120 months in the Federal Bureau of Prisons. I was sent to one of the easiest and weirdest yards in the BOP, FCI Englewood (FCI stands for Federal Correctional Institution), a low-security prison in Littleton, Colorado. This was a very short engagement. Within months, I was transferred up a custody level to the medium-security FCI Florence. I had drawn stick-figure cartoons the administration found threatening.

I never knew how bad it could get. I thought I knew. I thought I was prepared. I had no clue. I knew I would face repression. I knew there would be restrictions and cruel cops. But what came was something entirely different. I was a naive child, but reality has a way of teaching cruel truths, and I would learn them the hard way.

On August 17, 2018, my life changed forever. At around 1 p.m. at FCI Florence, I was called down to the lieutenants' office to discuss an email I had sent to my wife. Instead of going into the office to talk over threat assessments, I was escorted into a mop closet. There are no cameras in mop closets. There are no windows in mop closets. This is a place to carry out violence. While in the camera-less closet, I was confronted by an enraged Lieutenant Wilcox. I was shouted at, spit on, threatened. I made a decision, a decision that has affected me ever since. I laughed in his face. I laughed at the veiny-necked, juiced-up, overconfident, sewage-breathed lieutenant who was actively threatening to batter me. His response was something I had never expected to happen, though I should have. I was pushed, I was punched, and then I was punched again.

Our lives are made up of massive moments that are birthed from tiny, insignificant ones. I sent an email, I laughed, I threw three punches to his bulbous face. I fought back. I struck down a member of the federal government. A chain of events that led me to the hardest times you can possibly imagine.

When you are in prison, there are times you may be challenged by an officer. You will have a personal feud, and the guard will have to prove how big of a man he is. He will take off his work utility belt, put down his walkie-talkie, and give you a "fair one." This is usually a one-on-one fight, and after it's over, the beef is over—no write-ups, no discipline, you just move on. These are rare, but they happen. Sadly, this wasn't that. Florence cops are well-known badged thugs. They have been sued countless times for gang-beating, sexually assaulting, and torturing prisoners. They are cowards. They are petty, they are schemers, and they have as much dignity as a puddle of mud.

There are also times in prison when you learn that you cannot let yourself be a victim. You learn that you can't appeal to pacifism when people plan on crushing you. Any holier-than-thou, I'm-above-it-all morality needs to be checked at the door. You cannot let someone push you, punch you, or attack you. After all, your life is on the line. People die in prison. The only person who will fight for your existence is you. You have to make split-second decisions, or your inactivity could be the end of you. There is no time to ponder the consequences of your actions. You must just survive. The only way to win at prison is to get out of prison. *You have to survive.*

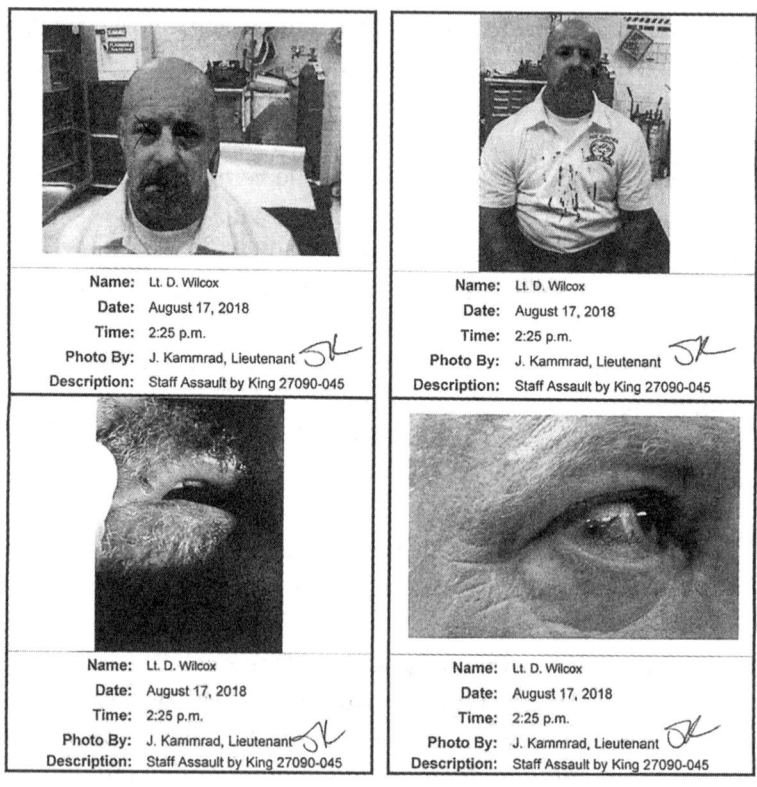

Photo sheet showing injuries caused to Lieutenant Wilcox in the mop closet.

    The three punches I put all my might into busted Lieutenant Wilcox's face to bits. His nose sprayed blood, his head shot back, and his body collapsed onto me and then onto the floor. He had picked the wrong one. I'm not the victim type. A blink of an eye after he collapsed, I knew this had only one ending. Slammed on the floor, stomped to oblivion, chained to a steel bed, suffocated, tortured. This is the price someone pays for defending themselves in the Bureau of Prisons, an institution where you are expected to lie down and let people who outweigh you by fifty pounds batter you. You are expected to be the ultimate victim. Take your abuse and humble yourself before us. I was not prepared for the next six months, the next five and a half years of continual segregation. A half decade of constant transfers, of absolute restricted communication, of violence upon violence. I should have seen what was coming around the bend. I was very naive then.

Almost a year to the day after the attack, I was flown to FCI Englewood and immediately placed in a six-foot-by-eight-foot cell within the SHU (Special Housing Unit). Two days later, I was taken to court. I was being prosecuted. The FBI had taken up the case and charged me with assaulting a federal employee and causing serious bodily injury. The prosecutor was asking for the highest possible punishment: twenty additional years within the Federal Bureau of Prisons. My assault was an attack on them, and they wouldn't stand for it. Any self-determination within the walls is seen as a bad thing, but standing up for yourself physically is the most dangerous game. They didn't want to choose a misdemeanor, they wanted blood. They wanted my future. They wanted to ruin my wife's life, my kids' lives.

I would not claim any guilt for the horrendous crime of not letting a federal thug beat my head in. I would not entertain any plea deals, and there weren't any offered. I was going to trial.

III PROLOGUE

A Brief History of ADX and Supermax Confinement

> The ADX is like a living beast that feeds off pain and misery. This place is made to break the soul. They walk by and see us as animals. The world should know prison is not the solution. Being locked in a cage twenty-four hours a day for years really fucks people up.
>
> —Randy Platt, ADX prisoner as of 2025

> Marion is simply a "warehouse" for human beings, used as an experiment to deny human rights under the guise of modifying behavior defects in alleged criminals. When the propaganda machine of the U.S. Justice Department departs with statements such as "the worst of the worst, bunch of rotten apples, hardnose criminals," etc., it allows the bureau of prisons to exact any type of punishment upon men incarcerated there with impunity.
>
> —Kojo Bomani Sababu, former Black Liberation Army political prisoner who spent years at the ADX; he is still imprisoned as of 2025, now at FMC Butner

The ADX was not created in a vacuum. This prison was created while the BOP was in the midst of a situation they could not handle. It was created out of desperation and fear. They had seen how powerful the prisoners could be when they had had enough. They had seen what mass mobilization by activists could do to the public opinion of the prison system. The BOP honchos needed a solution. They needed to quell any future prisoner solidarity movements and stop the amount of influence that revolutionaries had within the BOP. They needed to convince the public and Congress that the prison system was full of people so dangerous that there was no other option besides burying

Aerial view of the Florence Federal Correctional Complex, where the minimum-security Florence Camp (lower left), high-security US penitentiary (upper left), supermax ADX (upper right), and medium-security FCI (lower right) are located.

them. Out of sight, out of mind. And the ADX achieved every one of these goals.

In 1934, the US government transferred control of its island military prison in the San Francisco Bay over to the Federal Bureau of Prisons. This was Alcatraz. Alcatraz was built to convince the public that the BOP took crime very seriously—so seriously that they would isolate and hide away anyone deemed worthy enough of this prison. "The Rock," as it was known, was not a lockdown facility but a hideaway facility. Its purpose was to separate high-profile prisoners and troublemakers from the rest of the prison community and from their comrades in the free world. When Alcatraz opened, it had unbelievable restrictions. Access to any sort of media or entertainment was severely curtailed. There were times when prisoners were not allowed to speak to each other or to anyone else.

Although Alcatraz is known for caging people like Al Capone and Machine Gun Kelly, most of its prisoners were just regular people who were tired of following the BOP's commands. They could not be broken by restrictions or SHU time, so they were sent to the Rock. This is similar to how the ADX is used now. The big names become the face of the prison, but the vast majority of prisoners are just people who insisted on living by their own standards within the prison system.

Alcatraz closed in 1963 and became a museum. That same year, the BOP opened USP Marion in Marion, Illinois, as its replacement. USP Marion would serve as the new federal maximum-security prison, and in the 1980s it housed the first control unit in the United States, paving the way for the ADX.

In the 1970s and 1980s, USP Marion was a very serious prison. There were a handful of escapes, staff assaults, riots, and all the things generally associated with a rowdy facility. USP Marion housed countless radicals, such as Leonard Peltier, Ray Luc Levasseur, Bill Dunne, and Kojo Bomani Sababu, as well as several Puerto Rican independence fighters, such as Oscar López Rivera and Rafael Cancel Miranda, who was one of the participants in the attack on the House of Representatives in 1954. It was not just revolutionaries at Marion, however. The 1960s and 1970s also saw the rise of federal prison gangs. Prison revolutionary gangs like the Black Guerrilla Family terrified both the prison system and racist white prisoners. In response to this terror came gangs like the Aryan Brotherhood (AB).

By the 1980s, the AB was dominant. They had evolved from a white supremacist gang into a white supremacist criminal organization. It was this gang, in conjunction with radical inside/outside organizing, that would lead to Marion finally closing its doors. In 1983, the unthinkable, yet inevitable, happened at USP Marion. Two guards, who were either in the wrong place at the wrong time or who had the wrong attitude in the wrong place, were both murdered within hours of each other by members of the Brand (how the federal Aryan Brotherhood refers to itself). In today's prison world, this sort of action is inconceivable. A guard being murdered would result in the entire prison being locked down for months or years. At Marion, after the first murder, committed by Thomas Silverstein, they were not even locked down for hours.

The second murder of a guard came ten hours later, and after that Marion went into a total lockdown, with all prisoners locked in their cells. Marion thus became the first control unit prison and the first federal supermax. Prisoners were locked in their cells twenty-three hours a day, seven days a week. They faced harsh conditions and an enraged staff. Every prisoner in that prison paid the price for those murders, either directly or indirectly. Silverstein spent the next thirty-six years in twenty-three-hour lockdown facilities, dying in ADX custody in 2019.

In 1994, the BOP opened the United States Penitentiary Administrative Maximum Facility located in Florence, Colorado: the ADX, its opus, its crowning achievement. A prison that was designed and built entirely to hold prisoners in twenty-four-hour lockdown. A prison that could not be escaped from or overtaken by prisoners. It would hold up to 450 prisoners, and the BOP would never be humiliated by incidents like the double officer deaths or protestors lining the streets in Illinois ever again. Although ADX opened in 1994, Marion did not lower its custody level to medium until 2006. For a brief period, there were two supermaxes, though by the 2000s there were less restrictions at Marion. ADX was sold to the public and to Congress as a prison designed entirely to secure the worst of the worst. The public was not safe as long as these prisoners remained in normal custody facilities. Although this clearly signaled the BOP's inability to maintain its own facilities, the public and the government bought this propaganda.

As of 2025, ADX still has this reputation. It is commonly believed to be housing the worst, most dangerous prisoners in the United States. The general public is filled with misconceptions about this place, and that is by design. I hear "prison experts" proclaim that our showers are wheeled up to our cell doors and then slid under the door. I hear that the prison is both underground and rotates, discombobulating the prisoner population. What I do not hear is that maybe ADX is a money-laundering scheme. Much like how the FBI creates scenarios and then entraps Muslims and activists—thus creating the illusion that they need more funds to combat terrorism—the BOP creates the idea of the worst prisoners, likewise to ensure increased funding.

There are dangerous people in ADX. There are dangerous people in the White House and in the Capitol building. There are dangerous people in our neighborhoods. To isolate one group of humans and proclaim them to be the "worst" is propaganda. The absolute worst, most murderous prisoner inside ADX has killed significantly fewer people than any health care CEO. Billionaires kill tens of thousands by refusing to relinquish a tiny portion of their wealth to housing or feeding people in need. Lawmakers kill countless women every year by stripping away their bodily autonomy and health care rights. While these ruthless murderers are given privileged positions in society and held up as kings, a young man born into dire circumstances, behaving in ways he was taught from a young age to survive, will spend decades in ADX, demonized and criminalized.

We know who the worst of the worst is, and it is not the men at Marion or ADX.

III CHAPTER 1

Taking the Stand: The Reality of Trial

Many people assume that prison is a lawless place where hordes of angry villains roam the halls with no fear or consequences. This is far from the truth. Every year, countless people are prosecuted for assaults, stabbings, possession of weapons, having phones, committing rape, bringing in contraband, and a variety of other offenses. When you are charged with an additional crime within prison, the institution will place you in the SHU and transfer you to a pretrial facility, where you will attempt to fight your case. If you are lucky, you will be "on the yard" (around other prisoners, with regular prison hours and not twenty-four-hour lockdown) and not placed in the SHU for the entirety of your pretrial period. You will be able to make friends, share food, go out to rec, and have unlimited communication with your loved ones and law team.

    I was not lucky. I was overwhelmingly unlucky. Having a serious assault on staff as your new case will almost always get you placed in the SHU. They do not like that charge. FDC Englewood (Federal Detention Center, with federal pretrial facilities) is one of those locations. FDC Englewood was staffed with the same bastards who were responsible for sending me to Florence when, two years prior, I had drawn an "antigovernment" cartoon to let off some of the mental steam that was fogging up my brain. The guards at Englewood had taken this drawing, given it to the FBI, placed me in the SHU, and driven me immediately to FCI Florence to face a custody level increase and an FBI referral.

    Trials in the federal system are outlandishly rare. According to the Pew Research Center, only approximately 2 percent of federal cases go to trial. An outrageous 90 percent of cases are resolved with plea bargains, and another 8 percent are dismissed. In 2022, only 0.4

Stick-figure cartoon by Eric that led to an FBI referral and a transfer to FCI Florence.

percent of federal cases went to trial and were acquitted. The reasons for this vary but mostly revolve around the loose and low standards that are needed for a guilty verdict, laws that are written to favor the government in insurmountable ways, and the terrifying consequences of losing.

Federal sentencing laws are life destroying. So many crimes are accompanied by decades in prison. Many decide to strike a plea deal, and many more decide to cooperate with the government to get even more time off. Most defendants have overworked public defenders who do not have the time or resources available to give every case the attention it deserves. Most people would prefer to see the free world again someday. When people hear that you are going to trial, they will give you the side eye and mutter under their breath what a moron you are. "Who do you think you are to go to trial? You think you're better than us?" At the same time, *everyone* will encourage you to your face to "take it to the box!" Prisoners want to fight their cases; they want to show the world how corrupt and insidious this government is. Then they get offered that first plea deal and make the decision that is best for them, which 90 percent of the time is accepting that plea. The weight of the sentence is not worth the effort when you know that if you lose you may never see the free world again.

Pretrial
The pretrial process is a long, drawn-out nightmare. I was pretrial for two and a half years. Two and a half years of sitting in a six-foot-by-eight-foot cell hoping that my team had enough to beat the government. Two and a half years of dealing with prison staff who felt I had attacked one of their colleagues, a friend of theirs. Many officers would confront me throughout my pretrial, making sure that I knew how pathetic I was and how pissed they were. Many of the officers at FCI Englewood once worked at the Florence prison complex, and they were all close. They hated me, and I made it easy for them. I gave them hell all the way down. I wasn't the only one, either. Many other prisoners facing new cases from Florence and the FCI Englewood Camp joined me in making these pigs' lives as hard as we could. No easy days for the badges.

My pretrial was fraught with problems, restrictions, and violence. This isn't often the norm, but it was our norm. While I was pretrial, fascist leader Donald Trump declared antifa to be an enemy to the sacred American way of life. He spoke out about antifascism and made all of us a target for his brownshirt goons. In federal prison at that time, I was the only openly antifascist prisoner, and therefore I got the brunt of the rage and indignation. Being open about your ethics inside federal prison can have dire consequences. If you are at a lower custody level, you will most likely skate by and not have any problems (except for the harassment from the guards). The higher up in custody you go, the more race matters, and the more problems you can have. The guards hate race traitors, the prisoners hate racial solidarity, and they both hate LGBTQ folks. They deeply hate queer folks, obsessively hate queer people of any kind. If you stand for something leftist, you will face many challenges.

During my pretrial, there was never a time when I was allowed to send a TRULINCS email to my wife, Rochelle. Even during COVID, when people were given two or three calls per week *for free*, I was not allowed to hear her voice. I would have killed to hear her voice and know how she was doing and if she and our family were safe. I was *never* allowed a contact (touching) visit with my wife. There were only three months when I was allowed visits with family during this time, and all of them were live monitored, planned weeks in advance, noncontact, and only one hour long behind a Plexiglas window. Over the course of the most stressful period of our lives, I was allowed to see my wife for one hour every other week, at most. It was hard. It was stressful beyond explanation. My life was on the line; all my dreams were on the line. They kept family and friends away on purpose. The more you see your loved ones, the more hope you have, and they don't want us to have any hope. They want to crush our spirits first, and if that doesn't work then they move on to our bodies.

Mail, as usual, was used as a means of torture. At the best of times, my letters would take three to six weeks, even from family in Denver. At its worst, mail would take months or never show up at all. In 2020, local comrades decided to have a New Year's Eve noise demo outside the prison in solidarity with me and all political prisoners. This was live streamed by the radical media collective Unicorn Riot and viewed by the BOP hierarchy. On January 6, four days after the noise demo, I was taken into the lieutenants' office, where a member of the Regional Office, the captain of the prison (Sapp), the Special Investigative Services lieutenant (Garza), the SHU lieutenant, and three officers were waiting. I was told that I would no longer be receiving mail and that I would be placed on a Correspondence Restriction Ban, meaning the only people I was allowed to write to or receive mail from were my wife and my lawyer. They made sure to throw away, delay, and reject as many letters from both of them as possible. It got bad. The only tool they could use to hurt me was my family, and they wielded this means of abuse freely. This destroyed me mentally. Having to face the world

> NOTICE TO: Inmate Eric King, Reg. No. 27090-045
>
> FROM: B. Grellick, Warden
>
> SUBJECT: **General Correspondence Restriction Status**
>
> The purpose of this memorandum is to notify you that you are to be placed on restricted general correspondence, pursuant to 28 C.F.R. § 540.15. Based upon your recent use of general correspondence, you are to be placed on Restricted General Correspondence Status as a matter of classification pursuant to 28 C.F.R. §§ 540.14(d) and 15(a). Your continued access to unfettered general correspondence privileges might pose a threat to the security and good order of the institution and the protection of the public.
>
> Accordingly, your general correspondence (incoming and outgoing) is limited to verifiable immediate family members only (spouse, mother, father, children, and siblings), as well as the following individuals: (wife), ▚▚▚▚▚▚▚▚▚▚, and ▚▚▚▚▚▚ (mother), ▚▚▚▚▚▚▚▚▚. This change in status does not effect your special mail privileges.
>
> This decision will be reviewed in six months to determine if it should be renewed. Before this status takes effect, you may respond to this determination, either orally or in writing. You may consider this an attempt at informal resolution under the Bureau's Administrative Remedy Program. In addition, you may seek a formal review of this decision through the Bureau's Administrative Remedy Program.
>
> Received: May __, 2020   _refused to sign_
>   Eric King, Register Number 27090-045

General Correspondence Restriction form, used to legally ban all of Eric's mail except to and from his lawyer, wife, and mother.

without hearing Rochelle's voice or reading her words was the worst thing they could have done to me. And they knew this, which is why they did it. This mail ban, which everyone assured me was illegal, and which none of us thought was real or possible, lasted almost two years.

Fighting your case behind bars is annoying and stressful, and even more so when you are constantly being prevented from speaking with your family and loved ones. When you are isolated and in abnormally harsh conditions, waiting for trial feels like an impossibility. The prison wants you to plead guilty. The DA wants you to plead guilty. Everyone pleads guilty. I was continually reminded of my race traitor status, told that I was an N-word lover for my original charges and for my antifascist beliefs. I was continually reminded that if I just took a plea deal, all my suffering would come to an end. All the beautiful promises made were all nothing but lies to trick me into giving up. I would not fall for their bullshit.

One of the more difficult aspects of facing trial within the SHU is dealing with lawyers. The prison makes it incredibly difficult to have legal calls, which are unmonitored calls with your lawyers. For over a year, I was allowed only one fifteen-minute legal phone call per week.

Legal visits are difficult to arrange and are made to be as uncomfortable as possible. They are held in an asbestos-covered room, behind a filthy Plexiglas wall, without any bathrooms or water fountains. The prisoner sits on a concrete stump, the lawyer on a lumpy rolling chair. My first lawyer was a comrade named S. They agreed to stand by me and my family to fight against the BOP. They understood the difficulty of fighting the federal government, and they understood that I would not be taking a plea deal by any means. Trial was our only option.

Of all my trial lawyers, S was the best, and the only one I ever felt safe with. They spent countless hours and countless dollars visiting me, calling me, speaking with my family, putting together our files, doing everything they could to help me secure my freedom. S often passed messages between Rochelle and I, and they were often the only free-world person I would have any contact with for months at a time. S brought other people to the team and did the best they could with the vast array of responsibilities needed to fight a federal trial.

To my dismay, six months into the pretrial, S contracted Lyme disease, which was crushing news. Switching lawyers is a frightening prospect. It means starting over completely. You have to explain everything again, convince them again, review all the discovery again, and formulate the plan anew. It is the ultimate burden. You have no idea if the new lawyer is going to come to visit you or if you will have legal calls. Are they going to be receptive to your ideas and ideologies? Are they going to respect, include, and listen to your partner? This was so important to me, because Rochelle understood this case. She knew all the little holes and all the small nuances. She wasn't a burden to overcome, but a massive asset who knew me and this case better than anyone.

Ultimately, I ended up with a "radical" law firm. I am not going to dive much into this, except to say I wish I hadn't. I wish I'd gone with a local public defender. There were good times with the lawyer from this firm and their coworkers, but also shockingly bad times.

Eventually, S was able to rejoin the team, and I am grateful for it, even though they also had problems with the firm. An unhealthy culture can affect everyone involved in the team, not just the prisoner.

Prison torture was enough to deal with, let alone lawyers I didn't feel I could trust any longer. I knew this was a dead relationship, and there was nothing I could do about it. It is quite a powerless feeling to know you can't step away without jeopardizing your future. With the trial fast approaching, timing and fear were the only things that kept me in this relationship.

As the trial grew near, the lawyer brought in a local attorney to help with trial prep. He would grill me with questions so that I would know what to expect and how to be best prepared for taking the stand on my own behalf. Toward the end of our session, he asked me how I was physically capable of dropping the lieutenant. He said that with me being so little and the lieutenant being so big, the only excuse he could find was that I had sucker punched him, which is the claim the government's story relied on. I explained to him that I was a boxer, that I had boxed essentially my entire teenage and adult life, that I had sparred with world champions and fought successfully in national tournaments. I don't know much, but I know how to punch.

He said we had to lean into that. That we *must* talk about my boxing history. Otherwise the jury would have no reason to believe I was able to hurt him like that. He was able to convince my lawyer to change our entire strategy. We would focus on my boxing past, on his advice. This was the thing I had been begging for, the thing I was told was stupid and would only make me look bad. I was told that under no circumstances could we bring up my boxing past. This was an important reminder that my opinion meant nothing. Rochelle's opinion meant less than nothing. We were charity cases, nothing more.

Trial

Believe it or not, despite what you may have heard, trial is not a fun experience. It tests every ounce of resolve you have. After almost four years of continual isolation, physical and mental torture, COVID, multiple lawyers, and a couple of hospitalizations due to staff brutality, I was going to be in a room larger than my bathroom-sized cell. I was going to wear real-world clothes and sit at a wooden desk with a comfortable chair. More importantly, though, I was going to go before a jury and try to convince twelve people from Colorado that I had a right to defend myself against a federal agent.

Trial is brutal on your body and your mind. Every day between 5:30 and 6:00 a.m., two guards meet at your door. They cuff you behind your back and walk you down to R&D (Receiving and Discharge). You sit in this cold room by yourself for at least an hour and a half. They bring you breakfast, which is typically an apple and a bologna sandwich. After an hour and a half, they bring you what are called "bus clothes." These are beige elastic-waist pants, underwear, socks, and a beige jail shirt. Once you've changed, you will be rushed into another room to sit and wait some more.

At around 7:15 to 7:30 a.m., you'll be fully shackled, loaded onto a prison transport vehicle, and driven to the courthouse, where you will be escorted to a holding cell on the same floor as your trial. This room is frigid, with only a stainless steel bench to sit on. It is incredibly unpleasant, as usual. Everywhere a prisoner or accused person is given seating, it is always the most uncomfortable place they will ever sit. My lawyers were able to bring me the clothes Rochelle had brought to the courthouse prior to trial, all of which had to be searched and approved. You are told to pick out which outfit you are wearing before they place it in the holding cell, put you in there, and tell you to get dressed.

This was my first time in six years wearing formal clothes, and it felt fantastic. Truly wonderful. Rochelle got me comfy underwear, silly socks, shoes without laces, and dress clothes that were nice but also a little gaudy, exactly what I needed. Peacocking into the courtroom. Feeling confident and ready to fight. Sadly and slightly embarrassingly, the US marshals had to tie my tie. Then I had to wait. Everyone will experience this differently, but I wasn't nervous. There wasn't a doubt in my mind that we would win this trial due to the work that S, Rochelle, Badger, and others had done, as well as knowing that I would take the stand to defend myself. There is seldom a time when I do not trust in my own ability.

Trial is not like on TV. There isn't an air of the dramatic, or people shouting and charging into the room. You cannot bring in surprise witnesses or last-minute evidence, and I have never heard a jury gasp in exhilaration. I have seen them nod off, slight snores echoing from their noses. Every day is the same dull nonsense. Every day you arrive, get dressed, and get stared down by the marshals. They despise you and can't wait for you to be found guilty. At 8 a.m., you go into the courtroom and try to look at your family while being told to turn around. The marshals treat family eye contact like a criminal act. The first day is entirely spent on voir dire, which is where you attempt to weed out the potential jurors you don't feel good about while trying to keep the ones the prosecution hates. This is hours and hours of asking jurors

The mop closet at FCI Florence where Eric was attacked. The prosecutor argued this space was an office.

different questions related to the case: "Do you agree with self-defense laws?" "Do you have family in law enforcement?" "Could you ever rule against someone in law enforcement if the evidence showed they weren't being honest?" Over and over we asked dozens and dozens of potential jurors these questions. After about seven hours, if you're lucky, you'll have a jury that *might* give you a decent chance.

Once trial starts, the adrenaline stops and real life sets in. This isn't a boring movie, it's your boring real life. This repetitive theater will determine the next decades of your life. You listen to the prosecutor as they prompt lie after lie from their witnesses, and you listen to your lawyer try to discredit them. You have an hour lunch where you are fed a ham sandwich (which I didn't eat). Lunch breaks are more of a chore than a break. Your tie must be taken off (because you may hang yourself with it), and you have to take your belt off too (same reason). You are quietly by yourself with your thoughts, with the events of the past couple hours twirling in your brain. Every word spoken against you. Every lie meant to ensure you spend the next twenty years in prison. You try to pass the time as calmly as possible. You are alone, and just like being in the SHU, you have to deal with this on your own. No one is going to come and comfort you and pat you on the back and make sure you're doing okay. Your suffering is your own, and you must manage it. The marshals do not care if you are scared or crippled with doubt and anxiety. They are not your friends. Then you are ushered back into the courtroom to repeat this process until 5 p.m. After that, you are taken back into the holding cell, stripped out and placed back into bus clothes, and taken back to jail, hopefully to find your dinner tray sitting in your cell. If it is there at all, it will be freezing. Most likely, though, you will go to bed to hungry. I lost a lot of weight during trial.

The prosecution called officers who had photographed the mop closet and were claiming there were not any mops or buckets in the room. They presented photos showing a cleaned-up, organized room. When they were then shown the original photos, taken prior to their meticulous cleanup, photos *they* had taken, photos that contradicted their entire argument, they had no explanation. The sworn-in federal agents could not explain how their own pictures showed things that contradicted their own verbal testimony. Officers can't say, "I'm a well-known obvious liar," so they just keep it going until shown otherwise. They "couldn't recall" why the rooms looked so different. Why they

Blood smeared on the floor of the mop closet.

hadn't submitted the original photos. Why they had neglected to discuss those photos.

S asked one cop if I was attacked in a closet or in an office. The sworn-in officer looked S straight in the face and stated clearly that it was obviously an office. The officer was then shown her own documents, paperwork she had personally filled out, documents that were given to the court and to the FBI. It said the incident transpired in a "storage room." Unsurprisingly, the FBI doesn't mind as much when the cops lie under oath, or when they falsify documents. They have no shame in their pursuit of repression. Only a fool believes in the morality or decency of their cagers.

One of the wildest witnesses was the prison nurse who saw me after the assault, Nurse Baroney. This nurse saw me with my face bruised, my head swollen, my heart racing. At the time, she asked me where I was hurting, and I told her that my face and head were in bad shape, that I had been attacked and I was hurting. She checked my pulse and checked my heart rate. Then she said I was good to go. As in, I was good to now be four-pointed by these officers. S made her look like a goddamn fool on the stand. S asked her if at any point she had checked my head or my face for injury. Whether I had told her I was feeling pain on a level of seven out of ten. Nurse Baroney said that no, she had never touched or reviewed my skull or face. When S asked why, Nurse Baroney stated, under oath, that it wasn't "relevant." Again, she stated that in her professional opinion any pain I had was not relevant. A human being had told a professional nurse that he had just been attacked and was having serious issues, and the nurse never spent a single second checking on it. I cannot overstate how little they care for prisoners' lives.

This exposed a lot about my treatment—and the treatment of all prisoners who have had to deal with prison nurses in this capacity—and called into doubt the government's honesty and credibility. I was seen with a swollen eye and lumps on my head, complaining of severe pain, and the nurse took absolutely no interest in checking on my well-being. She only checked me to make sure I wouldn't die during the upcoming torture. I was then four-pointed for over seven hours, and she never checked on me once. We are not humans in their eyes. Never for a second think that they see you as a human. They will watch you slowly die a painful death and not make a single move to eradicate that suffering. If you asked Nurse Baroney why she didn't do her job or even pretend to care about us, she would tell you the truth: She is a cop first and a nurse second.

Despite interesting moments like Nurse Baroney being exposed as disgracefully unprofessional, the trial was mostly just exhausting. You are tired, upset, overheated, and dehydrated, and you have to listen to people lie about you all day. People who swore an oath to never lie, to uphold the Constitution, were lying without pause. The officer who kicked my head in swore he never put a hand on me, then swore I was throwing wild haymakers at him, then claimed he wasn't even in the room when I was taken down. Rambling, incoherent, and contradictory. This is the Thin Blue Line—the oath to always protect and uphold each other, even when the other officer is clearly in the wrong. Lying, attacking, planting evidence, killing—all these things are acceptable in upholding this code. Acceptable and demanded. Demanded and expected.

This is what "All Cops Are Bastards" (ACAB) means. It is an acknowledgment of their loyalty to each other and their disdain for actual people. Whether a specific officer is the one pulling the trigger means nothing, because they will all 100 percent lie and protect the officer who did. There are no innocent officers. Every single person wearing a badge is complicit in this attack on humanity and should be seen and treated as such. If the bank decides you no longer deserve a home, it is the cops who will do their bidding. If the president gets tired of leftist protesters, he will call in the BOP officers to crack our heads open. When the officer's knee is on your neck and lungs and you dream of one last breath, it's the entire police force that will protect them and blame you. They will look right in the cameras and declare you a thug, a monster, a raging bull that needed to be taken down for the benefit and safety of the community.

One of the more shocking aspects of the trial was when the prosecution brought in officers from FCI Englewood to prove I had a pattern of abusing staff. This included Officer Gustafson, who had placed me in the hospital after slamming my head directly on the concrete floor. The same pig who was six foot four and over three hundred pounds and had claimed that I had assaulted and really hurt him—despite my hands being handcuffed behind my back. (I was later found innocent of this assault at a prison disciplinary hearing.) This officer who had

```
From:           Robert Cordova
Sent:           Friday, August 17, 2018 2:31 PM
To:             Clay Cook; Cronan, Amber K. (DN) (FBI)
Subject:        Fwd: IM King Email
Attachments:    GlobalInmateSearchReport.pdf


>>> Robert Cordova 8/17/2018 1:28 PM >>>
King, Eric, Reg. No. 27090-045, OA Unit cell 607

>>> Jose Morales 8/17/2018 1:22 PM >>>

FROM: 27090045 KING, ERIC G

TO: "Rochelle          <                    >

SUBJECT: RE: 10:37

DATE: 08/17/2018 01:13 PM

I got thjis after our phone call, so did you end up hanging out with the girls? I bet they were so happy to see you and know that

you are ok (hearing and seeing are different, at least for me).

Your voice sounds so damn raspy and cute, it always sounds that way post-surgery, and probably always will sound that way

during your upcoming 23423 surgeries lol..

So you want to hear great news?! A newer Paisa ROCKED A LT!! That's why we were locked down for a little bit lolol! One for

the home team! I hope that the weight of every prisoner who has been disrespected, felt belittled, felt less than human by any

guard or Lt ever was behind that punch. Wish I would have gotten to see it or hear it or experience it via VR. This is a win for

every prisoner ever. Hard to stop smiling thinking about it.

I love you so much and am so happy that the surgery went well. You are the most.

----
```

J. Morales
Special Investigative Services

The email Eric sent to his wife that led to his attack in the mop closet.

cracked my head open while my hands were cuffed behind my back, who could've killed me if I had landed the wrong way on the concrete, took the witness stand and swore under oath that I was a threat to him, that I had hurt him. This is the Thin Blue Line.

Prosecutor Aaron Teitelbaum showed my drawings from five years prior, which were done at the direction of the psychology department as a part of an anger management program during my first stay at FCI Englewood. The same inflammatory and dangerous stick-figure drawings that had gotten me transferred to Florence in the first place. They showed the jury the email to my wife that had led to the lieutenant calling me to the mop closet, an email in which I celebrate every assault on every officer ever. They claimed this email proved that I was a violent sociopath who couldn't wait to hurt them, who had been waiting to hurt them for years. What was said in that email I believed then with all my heart. Now, seven years later, I believe it even more.

Taking the Stand

One of the things you hardly ever see in federal trials is someone testifying on their own behalf. Some inside consider this to be snitching. Some don't do it because their lawyers feel it would hurt their case. Others just don't want to, because they don't care or don't have anything to say. I was different.

I told my lawyers from the jump that we would be taking this case to trial and that I would be testifying. I didn't bother myself with prison politics or the negative impact it could have on the case. My lawyers weren't going to continually silence me like the prison had. I'd been silenced for four straight years, and I wasn't going to self-inflict the Bureau's muzzle. I would be telling the jury my side of the story. I would explain prison life and politics to them. I would explain the sorrow, grimness, and inhumanity. I would face these twelve people and tell them that the federal agents who had sworn to tell the truth were disgraceful liars. A Thin Blue gang that would say and do anything to protect one another. I would point out how three of the four officers had told literally exact opposite stories. I would tell them that I *never* have to be a victim and that they wouldn't want to be either. The same officers who throw away your mail while you are at recreation will take the witness stand and lament how disgraceful you are. How you are a bully, a monster. Their shamelessness is unparalleled.

I took the stand on Wednesday, March 17, 2022. St. Paddy's Day, a very good omen. I wore green and pink and felt that nothing could stop me. They weren't going to get a goddamn win off of me. I would share every single horror that they were trying to keep secret and buried. Teitelbaum's entire cross-examination of me was built to make me angry. He was desperate to make me look like a raging lunatic who couldn't control his violence. A walking volcano who is a hothead filled with bitterness and anger. *Look at how quickly he reacts! Look at how desperately he hates officers!*

I had practiced testimony all evening in my cell. Teitelbaum was rattled when I wouldn't take his bait, flustered when I refused to go down his rabbit hole. At one point he asked me four or five times in a row whether the mop closet was actually an office. He pointed out that there was a chair and, in the very back, covered with paint cans, a desk. A single desk. Weren't desks inside offices? Therefore, logically, wasn't this in fact an office? No. No, you incompetent moron. Although irritated at first, by the second day I was able to respond in ways that clearly upset him and made him look aggressive and kind of stupid.

Not many things feel better at trial than seeing the prosecutor lose their composure. At one point Teitelbaum asked me if I was happy to see officers get assaulted, if it was an us-versus-them situation. I told him absolutely yes. Without question, yes. Yes, every day of the week. The abuse they thrived in dishing out meant that they were always our enemies. It was their choice. They decided to brutalize us. They decided to torment us when we were at our most powerless. This isn't a naturally occurring thing. It is trained behavior. They are taught to smash us, implored to rule with an iron fist. When, occasionally, the tide turns and one of us goes off on them, it is a moment to celebrate. Put a candle in the cake.

I finished testifying on March 18, a Thursday. The anniversary of my deceased father's birthday. He would have been seventy-three. I knew my story front and back, because it was truly what had happened to me, and I was able to explain everything to the jury: my years of boxing, my abilities, my years inside prison. I was able to look these strangers in the face and tell them *why* I hated the police, *why* I was so adamant in my resistance. I told these twelve strangers how the guards belittle us and steal every ounce of dignity we have. I allowed myself to be vulnerable and explained to them how the guards do everything possible to make our families feel horrible about themselves and feel even worse about their relationships with us.

The jury heard how the rat bastards would tear up photos, attack you in your sleep, pepper-spray your food, piss on your floors. I looked them in the face and explained how the guards treat our joy like an affront to them. I spared no emotion. I cried, I shouted, I stood up and demonstrated how to throw a punch. I showed them that I would *never* throw a wild haymaker like the officers were claiming. I was too good at boxing for that horseplay. I cussed, I was sarcastic, I was emotional—I spoke as Eric. I let them feel it all, and they were actively listening. They were not sleeping anymore; they were captivated. My testimony is one of the proudest moments of my life. Being vulnerable is scary. Opening your heart and soul to people you've never met is a dangerous feeling. It was the absolute right choice. The prosecution decided not to recross me. The case was over. In a room packed with officers, state lawyers, and captains, I got to speak my truth and the truth of countless other prisoners. Their visceral hatred warmed me like a nice weighted blanket. I felt true joy.

I finished testifying around 10 a.m. From 10 a.m. until 5 p.m., the jury deliberated. They went into their chambers and tried to figure out whether to believe the nine federal agents or the heavily tattooed convicted felon. Less than 1 percent of defendants in federal criminal cases are acquitted. Less than 1 percent. Without a verdict at 5 p.m., the judge decided to send us all home for the day, with the process to be repeated the next day.

On Friday, March 19, I returned to the courthouse, got completely dressed, and sat in the holding cell for the next eight hours. In this cold, barren, uncomfortable room, I had to find my peace of mind. What can you do when you are alone with your thoughts and your entire future is on the line? It is the strangest feeling. You are all alone. No one can comfort you; no one will hold your hand or tell you it will be all right. Not to worry. You find peace or you don't; it's all on you. For me there was lots of pacing, singing any songs I could remember. Lots of trying and failing to sleep on the metal bench. Lots of counting my steps. Seven steps forward, two steps to the side, seven steps back. Whatever would occupy my mind, forcing it to focus on anything except the verdict. You have no control; you do not have any power over what is happening. You can't make the jury vote for you; you can't make them hurry. The pigs do not care if you fall apart. It is on you to find ways to hold it together for those hours. Whatever gives you peace of mind and comfort during that period, you cling to that.

The jury's first question came around 4:30 that afternoon. The jury had written down their question for the judge: "What if we can't come to a unanimous verdict?" The jury couldn't come to a decision. Someone in that room would not budge one way or the other. The judge sent word back to them that they would find a unanimous verdict or they would be back in the courtroom after the weekend. They would absolutely find a verdict. We were supposed to be finished at five o'clock, but the judge was giving them extra time to get it done.

At 5:50, the marshals came to get me. The jury wanted to know whether it was still self-defense if I *thought* I was in danger, as opposed to actually having been assaulted. Can you respond with reasonable force if you truly believe that someone is about to assault you or harm you? The question came from one juror. One juror didn't believe that I had been assaulted by the lieutenant but felt that I may have *perceived* the threat. My black eyes had formed because of the perceived fist, not the physical one. The judge sent them back with directions, and I was led back to the holding cell. We had ten minutes. If they didn't have a verdict by six o'clock, we would be coming back on Monday.

At 5:56, the marshals came to get me again. We had a decision. The judge received the verdict from the bailiff and read, "We, the jury, find the defendant, Eric King, *innocent* of one count of assault on a federal agent causing serious bodily injury."

Inconceivable. Surely this was a dream I would sorrowfully wake up from. I wept. All the trauma and sadness and rage spilled out of me. I couldn't stop. I looked to see my wife sobbing and our comrade Badger crying. The people who had stayed were all crying. It felt like I was a champagne bottle just waiting for the right celebration so it could explode. This was that celebration, and my emotions were shooting out.

I would not receive twenty extra years in prison. I would (presumably) make it home to my family. I'd get to see my kiddos go through high school and have their big moments. I'd finally get to support my wife after the decade of her supporting me. I felt hope, pure hope. Something I hadn't felt in so damn long. Hope had eluded me, had shaken me off at every turn. Now I could grasp it and cling to it. I don't think you can duplicate that feeling. Prison is unique, because it fills you with the utmost despair and tragedy, which rarely leads to the utmost joy and relief. I have never felt that way before or since.

The prosecution looked pathetic and defeated, because that's exactly what they were. The marshals looked enraged, because they were. I hugged my lawyers, smiled at my wife, and was led away by the marshals. I foolishly thought it was all over. I foolishly thought I would be returning to a medium-security prison to finish my bid. The jury said I was innocent; the court system that the prison relied on to find justice had ruled that I had done nothing wrong. The prison *surely* had to respect and honor that. I thought I would be out of the SHU, removed from my restrictions. I was a naive fool. Even after all I had been through. Even after watching the Bureau violate their own laws over and over in their treatment of me and others, I still stupidly thought that the court's decision would make things right. I feel like an absolute prat when I think back on that brief period before reality set in.

I was fortunate to have support in the courtroom. My best friend, Devo, and our great friend Annie came out, and Badger was there every day with Rochelle. There were many supporters I had never met. Another lawyer, comrade Joey, was there seemingly every day. Getting any support at a midweek trial feels huge. To be able to leave work and spend all day in a courtroom in the middle of downtown Denver is not easy. The parking alone would've bankrupted most people I know. I would meet many of those strangers once I was free. I would never forget how safe they made me feel. There was also a slight sadness. Dozens of people were listening to the live stream, but I had really felt like the courtroom would have more people in it. It's an ego thing, and I had significantly more support than many. But there was a part of me that was kind of shocked that it wasn't at least partially full. I had folks there who had driven from out of state, so why couldn't others come from Denver or Colorado Springs? I don't feel that way anymore, but at the time it hit me right in the feelings.

The most difficult part of the trial was not turning around and staring at Rochelle all day. I was desperate to see her, but the marshals would only let me turn my head slightly for a few seconds at a time. I was worried about how she was doing, and I had no way to get word to her. There were many times I would write notes for the lawyers to pass to her, and every time they told me they had passed them. Later I found out that despite what they said, not a single note was given to my family or friends. This was one of many things I found out after trial that made me further distrust my main lawyer and not want to associate with them any longer. My family isn't a burden; they are my everything. My lawyers went out of their way to isolate the one person I fully trusted and could absolutely count on. They assisted the government in isolating me further from my family. They did the cops' jobs for them. When you're facing time, your family is facing time right along with you. You cannot separate the two.

Rochelle felt scared and alone, because she was scared and alone. She was not receiving any info or kindness from our legal team. It hurt. It is common decency to let the partner of someone on trial know they aren't alone and that they are supported and loved. This shouldn't have been an issue. These complications spoiled the victory for me. A tantalizing-looking meal will still taste horrible if the ingredients are rotten. When you've felt lied to and disrespected during the most difficult moments of your life, it is not easy to come back from that.

When I had my first call ever with my lawyer, their secondary told me, "Yeah, we've decided to take on this case. It's either us or a public defender, and you know how they are, so..." I thought I had no other options. I was hopeless and foolishly thought that they would care about me as a person and honor my wishes and ideas. That wasn't what occurred, and it still hurts. If I could go back in time, I would not have expected them to care or understand. I would've expected them to be all business and no solidarity. If I could go back, I would've accepted that public defender, because I know how they are.

Trial Aftermath

To believe that things would get better after the trial was childishly foolish. I was placed right back in the SHU at FCI Englewood. I was kept on communication restrictions and was told they were going to transfer me to ADX or the CMU (Communications Management Unit). When I relayed this to my lawyer, it was scoffed at. They thought I was trying to beg for attention. They saw repression as status and didn't feel I deserved that status.

For the next two weeks, I was held at the FCI Englewood SHU until I was unceremoniously sent back to USP Lee in Virginia, a place of nightmares. I had already spent fourteen days there on layover status before being sent to Englewood for the trial. I still have trauma from my time at USP Lee. I still cringe when I see ants because of all the nights I awoke with dozens of them all over my sweaty body, nibbling all over me. I would be held there until the BOP decided what to do with me. I prayed that I would be redesignated to a medium-custody-level facility. Sadly, the jury's verdict had meant nothing. The Bureau had been embarrassed by Unicorn Riot's hilarious coverage of the 2020

New Year's Eve noise demo, they had been embarrassed by the phone call-in campaigns, and now they had been humiliated by the not-guilty verdict. These are people used to having power and enforcing that power. They were not accustomed to taking losses. They would get their revenge. They would do everything they could to extinguish my spirit and annihilate my family. It's only what I deserved. Street justice.

||| CHAPTER 2

The Scariest Ride of My Life

I've lost count of the number of times I've been left in cells for hours while black-box handcuffed and leg ironed; spending as much as 17 and 20 hours in such restraints during transport and waiting delays, with no water and no toilet access. I have numb areas on my hands, wrists and ankles, from this treatment, and from being kept in control unit prisons for years, locked down for 23 hours or more a day.

—Thomas Manning, former political prisoner who spent years at ADX; he died in prison in 2019 after thirty years of federal imprisonment

Year after year alone in a cage affects the strongest mind. This is why I tell you death is more humane. I'd never take my own life, but I'm not at all in fear of death. This, what I'm living in, is torture. Believe that. Words do nothing in explaining the truth of it.

—J, former ADX prisoner

At the ADX, you can't see nothing, not a highway out in the distance, not the sky. You know the minute you get there you won't see any of that, not for years and years. You're just shut off from the world. You feel it. It sinks in, this dread feeling. It's just the harshest place you've ever seen. Nothing living, not so much as a blade of grass anywhere.

—Travis Dusenbury, former ADX prisoner

Arrival

On my second day at USP Lee, I was informed by the psychology department that I would most likely be sent to ADX. The paperwork had been started at Englewood and would be finished there. I would do my ADX process in the Lee SHU. After waiting two months at USP Lee while pending acceptance into ADX, I was finally given the approval letter—a simple piece of paper that said "Approved." The transfer process is long and arduous and began with two weeks at the USP Atlanta transfer center SHU. Everyone being sent to or from the ADX or CMU is held in the SHU while transporting. This was followed by one week at the SHU at a federal transfer center, FTC Oklahoma City, before I was shuttled away to my final destination.

When you are designated to the supermax, no matter what jail or prison you're being held at, you'll be placed in segregation. You will be alone in a cell at all times. Anytime you want to go to SHU recreation, they will use two guards and a lieutenant to walk you there, and you'll be in a rec cage by yourself. The second you are approved for ADX, you are treated like an ADX prisoner. Even at USP Lee—where they would rather beat you to death mercilessly than give you a solo cell—you are kept by yourself.

On the day of my exit, I was already awake when, immediately following breakfast, a voice came over the intercom in my cell telling me that it was time to get dressed. I was transferring. Immediately I felt the avalanche in my tummy. The butterflies turned to boulders. Transferring is an unnerving process. You have no control; you are at the whim of people who hate everything about you. At every turn, you are placed around people who could be enemies. They could leave you handcuffed next to someone looking to get a cheap shot. They could do a thousand things. It's a highly stressful situation; the entire process is exhausting and takes all the emotional energy one can muster.

When leaving OKC on an ADX transfer, you are walked into a room by several guards and given bus clothes: fresh elastic-waist khaki pants, new boxers, and a new white shirt. Then the belly chain is placed around you and your wrists are put in the "black box"—a horrible contraption that is clamped around the handcuff chain that prevents you from rolling your wrists at all or adjusting the cuffs, very painful—and your ankles are shackled together, so that you are totally contained. Shuffling down the hallway filled with long benches and gawking prisoners, you finally make your way to the bench closest to the exit door. This is where they place all the black-box transfers. Here you will sit in discomfort and mental misery for about an hour while waiting to be loaded onto the plane.

There were two other people headed to ADX. One was a state prisoner from South Carolina, the other a Native with severe mental health issues and deep, thick scars up and down his arms. He was headed to the mental health unit at USP Florence. This is essentially the ADX for people with extreme self-harm issues, and this would be his second stay. Annoyingly, he spent the next four hours explaining how I and South Carolina weren't *actually* going to ADX, we were *actually* only going to the USP, and that *actually* the whole referral process we went through was a scam. He was so sure that I couldn't be going with only two years left on my bid. This is a common thing among know-it-all-bastards. They are certain they know more about your situation than you do; they are certain they know more about everything than you do. They yak it up for everyone, anything to gain status as some sort of expert. The most annoying people in the prison system are the need-to-be-an-experts.

The flight lasted two and a half hours before landing in Colorado. When the plane finally touched down and the doors opened, the marshals began reading off names. Once your name is called, you stand up, make your way down the aisle while awkwardly bumping into everyone still sitting, shuffle to the door, and walk down the steps of the plane. Walking down twenty steps while having your ankles and wrists shackled is an incredibly unenjoyable experience that I would not recommend. There are multiple federal prisons in Colorado, and each one has a bus there to pick up new people and drop off those being transferred. For the Florence Federal Correctional Complex, there is the minimum-security Florence Camp bus, the medium-security FCI Florence bus, and then the USP Florence bus, which takes those going to the high-security penitentiary and those headed to ADX. The Native, SC, and I were ushered onto the USP bus.

The Ride to Hell

Prison is a scary place. We can posture like it isn't and pretend that nothing fazes us, but that's all show. There isn't a single facility where you don't face potential danger or hostility. This was new, though. This was the scariest bus ride of my entire life, and maybe the only time I've truly felt my life was in danger in a way where I could do nothing about it. Native had gotten into my head. His entire dialogue was about the ADX Step-Down Program. When people are being transitioned out of ADX, after spending a year in J-Unit showing they can behave, those who make it are sent to the Step-Down Unit at USP Florence. In this unit, you are around people, you go to rec with people, and you eventually eat and live with other people. Native was certain that we were going to the Step-Down Unit, not the actual ADX.

The thought of going to the Step-Down Unit ripped me to shreds. Being in a confined unit with all the white power dudes would be a true nightmare. I have "ANTIFA" tattooed on my face, and they know that they're the "FA." I understood how prison works, I understood how violence works, and I understood that walking into that situation with that many potential enemies without any allies would be a reckless, dangerous task.

My fear was that I was being sent to be massacred. That the BOP was getting their vengeance for Lieutenant Wilcox. They couldn't get the conviction to stand, so they would get the gangs to do their job for them.

I've never felt my heart do the things it was doing on that bus ride. Fear was like electricity coursing through me, making me both more alert and more dissociated than I could stand. I had to pee, I had to puke, I had to cry. I was staring out the window while every terrible thing I could possibly imagine ran laps around my brain.

Focusing wasn't easy to do. I was staring out the windows of the bus, watching fields and neighborhoods soar past us, wondering if this would be the last bus ride of my life. Wondering if I would ever get to hold Rochelle again. I had been on dangerous transfers before, but with those I could typically find a way to avoid instant violence. I could navigate the choppy waters and find a smooth landing spot. This was different. My mouth was dry and my eyes watery. Nothing felt right and nothing felt peaceful. I was trying to figure out what options I had to prevent this impending massacre from happening. It is a truly disorienting and horrible feeling believing with all your heart that you are being sent to your death.

I think at some point I may have had a minor heart attack. Or maybe that's what real-deal panic attacks feel like. At different stages,

The visitor and staff entrance to the ADX facility.

my hands and arms went numb and my vision went blurry. I was begging the universe, pleading with the goddesses: *Don't let this cursed bus drop me off at the penitentiary. Don't let these bastards send me to that specific program in that specific prison. After surviving so many different attacks, please don't let these bastards get me in this way.* As we got closer, I visualized how the news would get to Rochelle, how she would react, how the kids would feel. My chest hurt in a way I'd never experienced and hope to never experience again. This was bad, and I couldn't get the images in my mind to stop.

After what felt like two lifetimes but was really two hours, we pulled into the Florence complex. Somehow things got even more intense. This was it. Would I be dropped off at the Step-Down Unit in the penitentiary to be a sitting duck, or would I be dropped off at the actual ADX? And if I did get dropped off there, what would the reception be like? These same people were all friends with Wilcox; these same people had kicked my face off and four-point-tortured me. Which trap was I walking into?

The bus drove into the compound and past the medium-security facility—where I had been attacked by Lieutenant Wilcox—and past the camp before pulling over to allow the officers to take off their guns and place them in storage. We then slowly pulled right past the ADX, and my heart felt like it was imploding on itself in slow motion. My face was freezing, my body was shaking violently, my joints all felt stiff and overworked. It was hard to wrap my head around what was about to happen. As we drove past the ADX, I tried to make mental peace with what I was facing. This was my reality now. I was alone and would have to handle whatever situation they threw at me.

I was forced to sit and wait with uncertainty as the bus lingered. I couldn't weep in front of the other convicts, but I wanted to. I'd had enough of the hard times. I'd faced enough violence. The pressure inside me was so intense that I didn't know if I would ever take another breath again. *Please, goddesses, please don't send me to my coffin. Please don't do this to Rochelle.* With what felt like a miraculous intervention, the bus slowly began to back up again. This couldn't be real. We backed up until we were catty-corner with the ADX, certain to carry me to safety—or at least more safety? My relief was agonizingly brief, and this twisted mind-melt took another turn when the bus began to pull forward *again*. All my demons working against me to pull the bus toward my doom.

We parked near an entrance of the penitentiary, the driver turned off the engine, and then some smug-faced pig bastard stood up, cleared his throat, and said, "When I call your name, stand up and exit the vehicle." This was it; this was the real deal. There was no wishing or hoping my way out of this. No peace visited me; no calmness arrived within me. All heart attack, all fight-or-flight. I needed to take off first. I needed to get the first shot off and pray the guards didn't let four or five others jump in and smash my head in. I needed to do whatever it would take to ensure that I had the best possible chance of making it home, even if that chance was slim. If I could get the cuffs off first, then I would know what to do; I knew I couldn't waste a single second.

The cop started to read the names, all in alphabetical order by last name. The first name they called was Briggs, the second name Deacons. My whole world was coming to a standstill; there was no avoiding this reality. Third name Heath, which was Native. So goddamn smug, this bastard, smirking to me and SC: "I'll see you guys down there!" This is who I would attack. Fourth name . . .

There was no chance my spinning head or thunderous heart were going to let me stand up and walk off this godforsaken bus. There was no chance my legs would carry me down that aisle and down those steps.

The other men were lined up outside of the bus directly in front of the prison. Bored, exhausted, ready to finally be on the yard. Outwardly showing the exact opposite of how I was feeling. Then the pig called out, "Madison." No way. Did mercy just bless my name by hiding it from the officer's eyes? Did I hear that right? Was I losing it and just hearing what I needed to hear? They had skipped my name. Was this a typo on the roster? Was it a trick? A ball of joy, or relief, swelled in my throat and chest. I've never felt lighter in my life. SC was skipped next. We both knew at that point that Native was not as knowledgeable as we had expected. SC voiced what I was thinking: "Looks like that clown was a fucking know-nothing."

Everyone was off the bus except for SC and me. I waited to see if the guards would come back and start the bus to drive off, or if it really was a trick and they were waiting to get everyone else inside before taking us to the Step-Down Unit. I trusted nothing. Everything in prison feels like a trick or a scam. Never once have I believed something was going to happen until it was happening. It's the hope that kills you.

The guards did come back, though, started the bus, and headed to the most secure prison in the country. A prison I had heard about my entire bid, a prison where my best inside friend, Smiles, was located. A place I had heard a thousand rumors about, a thousand mistruths. A place that spins on an axle, a place built underground, a place I had never imagined in a million years I would be sent. And we were now headed there.

ADX is surrounded by several layers of razor wire and multiple spiked fences. There are also multiple checkpoints before entering the grounds. Guards check underneath the bus, clear names of the transport staff, confirm our names, get radioed in. It took five minutes to make it through the first gate. We then slowly rolled around the prison, guards with weapons walking in front of and behind the bus. All of this was over the top, as there was clearly no threat and no possible way for a threat to spontaneously arise. This was for their own benefit. This was to prove how secure and serious this prison is, not for any actual safety. They were all playing a role in this political theater. This prison is sold as *the prison* in America, and the staff buy into that personification. The media buys into it as propaganda. The politicians and administrators buy into it and perpetuate it as a security necessity. It's all theater. We could have just driven to the entrance and been done with it, but it would have robbed these guards of their performance.

The bus wrapped around the prison fence and pulled up to a large garage in the back. The garage doors opened, and we slid in. There were five officers waiting inside for us, and once the doors closed, one of the guards entered the bus and flippantly said, "Well, head on out, guys, no rush." I'm not entirely sure what I expected, but it wasn't this. I had pictured guards lined up on both sides, maybe guard dogs barking at us to strike terror into any thought of resisting. That's how we were taught to believe this prison operates, to strike terror into the prison population. That's the level of myth that surrounds this dungeon. Instead, there were a handful of guards waiting for us. They didn't even assist us in walking off the bus. There was more security walking off the bus at FCI Englewood, the lowest of low-security prisons.

SC was off the bus first and was immediately led into R&D. I was next, and it felt wildly surreal. Following directly behind SC, I was placed in a small green holding cell. I was bewildered. Was this really happening? Was this the real deal? This prison holds and has held the most powerful people in the BOP, the most infamous prisoners, the most violent, most resistant, most wild, most revolutionary. Ray Luc Levasseur had been here. Dr. Mutulu Shakur had been here. Tom Manning was once behind these walls. Now it was me. Now it was holding me. I had never killed anyone, never stabbed anyone, never escaped, never led a gang. What was happening? My heroes had walked these halls for their unrepentant revolutionary actions. I would gain strength knowing that these combatants had been here and survived, that they had refused to be broken. I knew that my placement here was in direct response to my resistance. They want us to be quiet and scared. I hadn't fulfilled their desire, and now I was filling the left-wing quota in this dump. Part of me really thought that this was a scam. Was I only here so the guards could set me up again? How in the world does someone with medium-security points end up in a supermax facility? They fear strong leftist resistance. Look at what they've done to our elders and our peers. If you speak up enough, fight back enough, they will find ways to deal with you. Our elders paved the way, and I would walk their trail.

After about ten minutes of sitting in the holding cell, the guards came and opened the door. They didn't cuff me up nor tell me to walk out backward—things that are normal procedure at just about every institution. This dude just opened the door and led me to a small cell

Eric's ADX mug shot when first arriving.

so that I could change out of my bus clothes and into ADX clothes (which are the same). I had to show them under my armpits, inside my mouth, underneath my penis, and the bottom of my feet, along with doing the entirely unnecessary "squat and cough" routine. They make you literally go through an X-ray machine, yet squatting while naked is still on their menu. This is their R&D intro. At a normal yard, this would take hours, as every single person transferring with you would need to be stripped and questioned by the different departments. This time, though, it took about fifteen minutes.

Medical came and asked if I had any emergencies, any urgent matters, and then they took my blood pressure and heart rate and kicked rocks. Psych came next and asked if I had the urge to hurt myself or commit suicide. (Trick question, of course. If you are foolish enough to say yes, you will be placed in a suicide cell, which is an empty cell void of all things including your clothes. You will wear a "turtle suit," which is a tear-proof body wrap, and you will stay there for at least three days.) I've never known anyone not attempting PC (protective custody) to say yes to the suicide question. Next came a unit manager, who gave me the forms to sign to accept the TV in the cell. Forms saying that I would have to purchase a new one if I broke it and that if I broke it four times in a year, I would be suspended from TV use. They had me fill out my clothing sizes so that the laundry department could give me my weekly supply of clothes.

Next came the Special Investigative Services (SIS)—the FBI within the prison system, who reads your mail and listens to your calls. They are a nasty, bitter bunch. There were two officers, one of which had been my SIS officer at FCI Florence. At the medium-security FCI Florence, this officer had given me a lot of leeway regarding receiving and sending out radical writings. Would it be the same here? Along with them was an older officer who informed me that they were close friends with Lieutenant Wilcox. "But I'm a professional, it won't affect you in any way." This meeting went much better than I'd expected. I was fed the usual company line that things would be different here, that I would be allowed mail, that I would be allowed books, that over time I would even be able to get phone calls back and be able to have actual visits (noncontact, of course). None of the restrictions from the previous institutions had followed me here. They assured me that I would not be censored but that if I was passing messages or "giving orders," they would crack down on me. They really thought that I had ordered the noise demo that had humiliated the Bureau three years earlier. They were not going to ban anarchist or radical literature and even said, "In fact, we prefer you to have it, helps us build a profile." ADX works directly with the FBI. They want to know who is reading what, thinking what, who they are talking to, what they are talking about, what they should investigate more, what they should refer to local police, how they should treat us in the future. This is serious business.

This is where I learned I would be dumped into C-Unit, a miserable unit that was once the SHU and was now the discipline unit. I asked how it was possible I was being placed in a discipline unit when I hadn't even stepped foot in the prison yet. Apparently, it was a mood check. I had a history of "bucking" (resisting) and pushing the line, and this was for them to see where I was at, what my plans were. If I were to lie low and relax, I would be given phone calls back (eventually) and would be moved to a different range (eventually). I wound up on C-Unit for a year.

Once they were done with their spiel, it was time to move, to head into the belly of the beast. The R&D officers took my picture for my door ID and had me stand on the X-ray machine to see what I was hiding inside me, and then it was go time. This is all standard procedure. When you enter a prison, they make it as invasive as possible. They want to show you who is in control not just of the prison but of your body. You belong to them. If they want to see inside your rectum, they will (whether you want it or not). If they want to see inside your whole body, they can and will. I've been full-body X-rayed more times than I can count. They pretend it's to see if you are smuggling in contraband, yet somehow they never actually catch the contraband (because they aren't X-raying their coworkers). That's because they want the contraband in, and they also want to demoralize prisoners—to set the tone the second you walk into the prison that you are not in control.

Two guards grabbed my arms and walked me off the X-ray. One of the guards had his baton out, and the other had a hand on my arm and a hand on my shoulder. We walked out of R&D into a black-and-white-checkered hallway. We took a corner and were standing at the top of another hallway, this one incredibly long and sloping. I took in my surroundings as we made the long hike down to my unit. Everything was on the left: A-Unit, B-Unit (which was now the control unit), the kitchen where "prisoners" from the Florence Camp came to cook our meals. (They are the same bootlickers who do all the cooking and maintenance when a prison is locked down, thus allowing that same prison to stay locked down longer.) There was the room where the commissary was sorted. This hallway's steep decline is the source of the rumor or conception that the prison is underground. We cannot see dirt out of our windows; there aren't worms squirming by us. But the entire prison is built *into* the ground. We are below ground level. If I had tried to drill out of my cell through all the concrete and steel, I would've wound up face to face with dirt. Every prisoner who has stepped into ADX has gone through this process. Every person has faced the reality that there is no getting out, that there is no hope.

I was exhausted by the time we reached C-Unit. All the adrenaline from the day was turning off, and I crashed. All my energy depleted. At the very end of that oddly long hallway was my unit. I walked past the "guard bubble," where the guards sit monitoring the cameras and intercoms, took a left down a small flight of stairs, waited for the guards to electronically open the gate, and then walked down the range to my first ADX cell. I'd thought the range would be longer. I'd thought the units would be packed and full. I'd thought there would be screaming and rage and resistance and violence and disorder. I hadn't realized how empty the units would be. I hadn't realized it was a tomb. I hadn't realized that this was where spirits were stolen and destroyed. Two hundred years of trial and error had led to this hellhole.

My cell was the second on the range. The guards opened the outside door and had me walk into the cell, where I was faced with bland nothingness. You are alone. You will face this battle on your own. No one can help you here. The inside cell door closed electronically. I backed up to the door, and the guards took off my handcuffs through the "bean slot," where food trays are passed. They then stepped out and closed the outside steel door, containing all the hopes and dreams and defiance of the humans inside. This was it. I was here. These cells had held Tom Manning and Ray Luc, Mutulu Shakur and Oscar López Rivera. Now I joined my elders in maintaining my resistance while buried in the Rockies. This was where I would do my last sixteen months. This was where I would finish my long fight against the BOP. All the bucking, protesting, resisting, fighting, starving, and struggling had led to this. When they can't handle your presence, they try to erase it. When that doesn't work, they bury it.

Early Days

At one point, despite already being a twenty-four-hour lockdown facility, ADX had a SHU, also known as Seg, the Hole, the Box. At the time, this unit was called Z-Unit. I'm not sure why. When I arrived at ADX, Z-Unit was no longer the SHU, and it was no longer called Z-Unit. It was instead known as the "disciplinary range" and was called C-Unit. A disciplinary range is typically for people who are not behaving according to the standards of the administration. It is supposed to

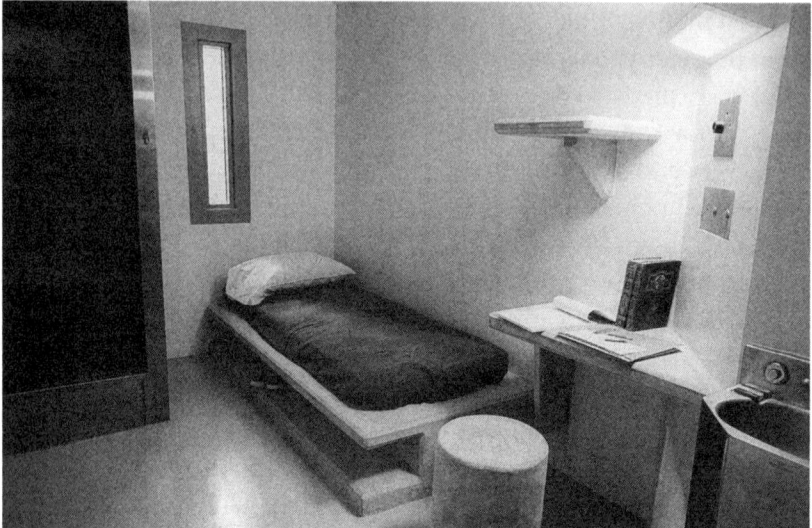

The view facing into an ADX cell. Not every cell has a stool or a desk on that wall.

be a temporary location, with a stay usually shorter than six months and never longer than eighteen months, unless you continue to resist. C-Unit is like every ADX unit. It is small. There is C-A Upper and C-A Lower, and then C-B Upper and C-B Lower. Four total ranges make up this tiny unit. Most of the time, at least half of these cells are empty (thankfully).

Each of the ranges have only eight to ten cells. While in C-Unit, as in any other unit, you never see the men on the other ranges. There are no ways to communicate with other ranges unless you sign up for inside recreation and the guards take you to another range. This usually only happens if your range is full already. Each range is one short hallway. All the cells are on the left side, and two inside recreation cells are on the right. You cannot see into anyone else's cell. The only way to communicate with the other people on your range is to stand at your inside door and yell at the top of your lungs. If they aren't busy, they may scream back and you can try to have a conversation. You may also try to chat through the toilet/sink combo. If you'd like to try this out, use a toilet paper roll as a funnel, hold it to the holes in the bottom of the sink where the water drains, and blow into it as hard as you can. This will enable you to talk with the cell next to you, but you must blow every ten seconds, and it isn't guaranteed to work. The

The view of an ADX cell facing toward the entrance. Two doors separate each prisoner from the hallway.

other person also has to blow into their sink to get their water and air bubbles cleared up. This is a lot of work for minimal gain. I sink-spoke approximately twice, and both times it felt completely useless.

At the end of the hallway, there is a cell that is empty of everything except a concrete desk, a huge black legal book, and a computer. The computer is built into the surface of a steel desk so that you have to hover over it to see the screen. This is the law library. If you are fighting a case or trying to sue the BOP, this is your only resource unless you have outside lawyers. If you want to go to the law library, you must write a "cop-out" (a written request) with the date and time you wish to go and then give it to the cops when they pass out trays in the evening. There is no guarantee they will say yes and no guarantee you'll go at the time you requested. Nothing is ever straightforward or easy.

If the cops decide you can go, the process is as intentionally annoying as you can imagine. The cops will show up and open your outside door. You will then "cuff up"—turn around, stick your hands through the bean slot, and be handcuffed behind your back. Whenever the cops need you to put on handcuffs, it's called "cuffing up." There will be two officers present at all times, one to maintain control of you and one to hold the steel baton. Once the door is open, the guards will pat you down, swatting your groin and groping aggressively, then hold you by the arms and walk you down the hallway to the law library cell. Once inside, you have an hour and a half to do your research. If you have to use the restroom or finish early, too bad. You cannot leave early for any reason. Sometimes I would go to the law library just to have something new to do, or just to be in a new room. I would sit in there and read old lawsuits that other ADX prisoners had filed—not the most fun way to spend an hour and a half, but it was something different. Even a room that is exactly the same as your room but in a slightly different location can still be new and exciting. Such is the exhilarating life of the supermax prisoner.

Most of the people on C-Unit were placed there for getting a "shot," which is a disciplinary write-up. Shots come in four categories: 400, 300, 200, or 100 series, with 100 series being the most serious. A 101 shot is a murder. A 401 is talking back to staff. I only ever saw three 400 series shots in my entire bid, and two of them were my own: first for my shoe touching the table during a visit, and the other for talking rudely to a guard. These are the most petty and ridiculous wastes of time and are almost always dismissed by your counselor. The people on that range with me were there for a variety of reasons, including circumventing phone protocol (three-way calls, giving orders on the phone, talking to someone not on their list of approved callers), throwing trays at the cops, refusing to leave the recreation cage, and getting caught with drugs.

Some of us are placed into C-Unit straight off the transfer bus. This is done as an attitude check for prisoners with a long history of disruption, severe violence, or multiple shots. The administration uses it as a way to show us who is really in control and also as a reminder of how bad things can get. (Things can get really bad, and things can always get worse.) South Carolina from the bus was also placed on C-Unit in C-B Upper. He was a white GD (Gangster Disciple) from South Carolina, a state prisoner who was so rambunctious, so murderous, and had so much influence that the state prison system felt it could no longer control him, so it got permission and ran him through the ADX process. There were a handful of other state transfers, and they were always very serious people. It is extremely difficult to get a state-ADX transfer.

Another state transfer I met while in C-Unit was a Puerto Rican drug dealer from Iowa. He had been on trial for a double homicide. While being transported to trial, he broke out of his handcuffs. When the transport officers came to open the bus doors in the court parking lot, he busted out, stabbed an officer to death, and went after another one just to make sure he had a clean getaway. With nothing to lose, he then stole the transport vehicle and drove that damn thing all the way to Nebraska before being caught. Murdering a cop and escaping from court are two things that can get a state prisoner sent to ADX. He was the orderly on the range for about two weeks.

The unit manager would select a prisoner to be the orderly. They would get paid around seven dollars a month but also got to come out on the range two times a week to sweep and mop. The officers would come on the range and place the cleaning supplies in the hallway, then leave. The cops would electronically open the orderly's two doors, and the orderly would get to come out and clean. They would have about an hour out of their cell, and this is when "kites" (notes) could be passed between cells. When I first arrived, this is how I received stamps. The orderly was a Black dude from California, a Black P. Stone (a Chicago gang that once ran as bodyguards for MLK and was cofounded by

ADX captive Jeff Fort), and he hollered at the two other white guys on the range to let them know that I was there and needed help. They slid magazines and stamps and envelopes under their doors to the orderly, who then slid them under my door.

Before I was later moved to K-Unit, orderlies were the only other prisoners I was ever able to speak with. In C-Unit, as in every other unit, you are isolated. Dangerously isolated. Torturously isolated. There was no knocking on the walls and seeing what your neighbor was up to. There were no daily phone calls, no conversations in the vents between cells. The walls are concrete, so you cannot hear what is going on in the cells next to you. There is no casual back and forth. For some people, this is the worst part about the unit. It is so quiet and tomb-like. In the other units, you could communicate with people at outside rec because you were in chain-link dog kennels. In C-Unit, that wasn't an option. Our rec cages were just big concrete rooms with a pull-up/dip bar inside. You could not hear anyone else doing rec. Interacting with other humans is a privilege, and it is one that can and will be taken away at the administration's discretion.

Settling In

My time on C-Unit had a rocky start. Because we are locked in our cells all day, every day, ADX prisoners are among the only in the BOP to have TVs in our cells. This isn't a gift or a reward, it's a part of the Program Statement that is signed off on by Congress. It is a means of control painted as mental stimulation. Prisoners are typically given their TV on arrival. You sign a form agreeing to pay for any damages and agreeing to the programming guidelines. After you agree to all their terms and stipulations, your unit manager is supposed to bring the TV to your cell. This should be, and usually is, a simple process. Our unit manager was rotten to the core, though. An abusive man who hid behind his good manners to go out of his way to make our lives more difficult. He had no redeeming qualities. He was the ultimate "say good, do bad" politician type.

When he finally came back to work, he proceeded to mislead me left and right, saying the prison warehouse was all out of TVs, which was an unimaginative lie. It took my unit manager five days before managing to do this basic aspect of his job. Imagine being in a concrete box with no communication whatsoever, no one to talk with, nothing to read, nothing to hear, nothing to see, for five straight days. That is a form of psychological torture, and it is a nightmare. This was intentional cruelty, and it was exactly what he was known for.

When I arrived on the range, it was quiet. Abnormally quiet. Scary quiet. Prisons are not typically quiet; they are the opposite of quiet. They can be so loud and disturbing that even forming basic thoughts is impossible. At this point, there were only six people on the range, and none of them were trying to yell through the sinks or double doors. The officers brought my laundry and linens. Every prisoner is given five days' worth of clothes from the laundry department. Five pairs of socks, five pairs of boxers, five pairs of pants, and so forth. We are also given three pillowcases (you are also supposed to get a pillow, another thing my worthless unit manager delayed), two bedsheets, and two blankets. They also provided a plastic spoon, a small coffee cup, some prison-industry soap, a small toothbrush, and one gel toothpaste packet. That was the only human communication I had for those first three days until P. Stone came out as orderly.

I am generally someone who enjoys a little peace and quiet. I was driven mad at different SHUs when people would be screaming nonstop all hours of the evening, banging on shower walls, rapping, shouting conversations all day and night. At those times I would pray to Jesus, Mary, and Joseph to please offer a bit of silence. To please let those loudmouths catch a bug in their throats just to shut them up. This was completely different. I didn't know that a building housing hundreds of other humans could be this quiet. It was a living morgue.

The only people willing to talk were the officers, and I wasn't saying a single syllable to them. Not a "good morning," not one "how are ya." I was not and am not interested in how their day was going. Hopefully it was going horribly. When they would bring food, I would not stand up to grab it from their hands. Instead, I would stay seated, and they would leave the tray in the bean slot of the inside door. When I was finished eating, I would set the tray right back there for them to pick up. Not a peep between us. My cager would not be my only source of human contact. I would rather have none.

Both the cell and the mattress I was given were horrible. In the lower custody levels, you hear so much about ADX. You even meet people who have been there before, and they love to tell the tales: the cells that are spotless because everyone is on "respect time," the comfy mattresses, the gourmet-style food, how people in this prison are treated better because they earned it through violence and being so serious. I experienced none of this. Maybe I wasn't serious or violent enough. Or maybe it was because there was and always has been a long line of misconceptions about this hell.

My mattress was a potato sack filled with half-dry concrete. It was the most uncomfortable mattress I ever experienced in my entire bid. Nothing about it was redeeming in the slightest way. I have spent months on end being forcefully denied a mattress, sleeping on pure steel, and that would have been preferable to my potato sack. The previous occupant had decided it was best to rip up the sides and take out a great deal of its foam intestines. With half of its guts missing, my potato sack was lumpy and unbearable.

The room itself was an absolute disgrace. Within prisons, it is usually common courtesy when getting moved out of your cell to leave it spotless for the person coming behind you. Cleaning your cell is a normal and expected thing to do. Every now and then you move into a cell behind someone who may be a good person but, in this context, is an absolute dirtbag for leaving behind such a mess for you to have to sort out. The person who came before me here was one of those absolute dirtbags. Chunks of food and hairballs littered the floor, water stains were all over the shower, and what can only be described as massive amounts of pubic hair took up residence all throughout the entire cell. My cellmates were clumps of bread and bundles of pubes.

It's disgusting moving into a cell like this. It can sidetrack your mood for the entire day. You spend hours on a plane, then hours on a goddamn prison bus, all shackled, then hours in the concrete holding cells, before *finally* moving into *your* cell, and then you can't even rest because it's a filthy dump. I spent the first two hours in my cell not relaxing but wiping down every surface with the vile tiny bottle of half soap, half shampoo I was given. I will never forgive that bastard who came before me, or the pig bastards who didn't provide enough cleaning supplies to even give him a chance to properly clean the place. He still could've swept, though. That way I wouldn't have had such uninvited cellmates.

Day three was eventful, because it was my first ADX shakedown. I was awoken at 6 a.m., before breakfast, to the sound of an army of heavily clad men storming up and down the range. They turn off the water beforehand so you can't flush any contraband (or use the toilet). Brushing your teeth or washing your face is off the table. One by one you hear the cell doors opening and your neighbors being walked out while you wait your turn to be herded into the freezing holding cells while a group of armed men ransack your limited possessions. When they finally arrive, you are walked to an outside rec cage. While there, you wait. And wait. And wait. You walk laps. You do pull-ups, sing your favorite songs, rip out some dips. Anything to keep your focus off the fact that three to six strangers who hate your guts are going through all your belongings.

After approximately two hours, the guards come and march you back to the cell. It's a nightmare. A tornado has ripped through your little place in the world. My only benefit was that I had absolutely nothing in my cell except what they had given me on my first day: laundry and some pencils and paper. They still found a way to make their presence felt. The shower curtain was ripped down; all the freshly folded clothes were unfolded and decorating the floor around the room; towels and washcloths were tossed on the ground or in the toilet; the mattress was stripped of its thin sheet and relocated to the recently cleaned floor.

The type of person who performs a cell search is the same type of person who has a portrait of Trump in every room of their home, watching over them and keeping them safe. Imagine going into another human's living space, seeing their sparse possessions, and throwing all of them on the ground or in the toilet. It's a dark type of sickness that prompts this sort of behavior. It should probably be studied so future generations can weed out these tendencies.

I've been through hundreds of cell destructions. Some of the men in that unit had been in prison for twenty to forty years, so god only knows how many they have experienced. It never stops being a source of eternal uproar. It never stops feeling like you've been violated. It never stops feeling like a home invasion. Except in these cases, you know exactly who broke into your home and vandalized it, and that same person will bring you lunch in an hour's time and ask, "How's your day going?" You are expected to not bite this person's throat out. You are expected to smile and nod and play the role of reformed inmate. It is insulting and degrading, and that is exactly why they do it. The whole point isn't to find contraband, it is to remind all of us who is in complete control. Many cell searches are brought on by someone being extra disrespectful to some class traitor pawn of the administration. Naturally, they retaliate by destroying your neighbors' things. Group punishment is as common as it is hideous. It is a disgusting cycle of power abuse.

The one plus was that since I didn't have any personal items, they couldn't destroy anything that meant anything to me. Also, a lieutenant saw that my mattress was cut open. It is against policy to have a desecrated mattress, so he replaced it. The new one still felt like a rock, but at least it wasn't lumpy. You take your small victories when they come.

CHAPTER 3

Nothing but Neglect: Canteen and Medical

> The minds of some prisoners are collapsing in on them. I don't know what internal strife lies within them, but it isn't mitigated here. One prisoner subjected to four point restraints (chains, actually) as shock therapy, had been chewing on his own flesh. Why is a prisoner who mutilates himself kept in ADX? Is he supposed to improve his outlook on life while stripped, chained and tormented?
>
> —Ray Luc Levasseur, former political prisoner who spent years at ADX; he was released from prison in 2004

Canteen

I was on C-Unit for two months before my commissary (or canteen) restrictions finally expired. Canteen day is one of the exciting days on every prisoner's calendar. Being able to supplement the rancid half food they serve us is a must. There is a feeling of autonomy or power in being able to decide, "I'm going to order this and eat it whenever I want." We lack that power in essentially every other aspect of our lives. We crave that autonomy and the ability to make our own decisions, even in a confined capitalist way. In C-Unit, we would get canteen sheets with the list of food and supplies on Sunday afternoon, turn in our forms on Sunday evening, and hopefully get the food either Wednesday or Thursday afternoon. You can feel the vibration in the unit as everyone waits for the officer to show up with the food bags. Every time you hear the electronic doors open at the end of the range, everyone rushes to their door to try to see. Is it our guy? Will we get some coffee or headache medicine or a sweater today? The entire vibe on the range is better on canteen day. Even though you can't hear anyone, once the bags come you can feel the tension lift.

Every Sunday afternoon, the cops would give us a canteen list, with either our lunch or dinner trays. We would have an hour or two to fill out the form and give it back to the officers when they picked up the trays. We were not permitted to put our names on the forms, out of fear that the Florence Camp prisoners—who fill our canteen orders—would be biased or put extra stuff in. Instead, we would write our prison number and cell number (27090045, Cell 2, C-A Lower). Then we would wait. If you were capable, you would save enough coffee or food or medicine to last you until the next store day. I don't think most of the people I met had that sort of impulse control. In K-Unit, you'd have people screaming and pleading and buddy-hustling for coffee shots all week. "Just a spoon, man, I'll get you back on Wednesday. You know I will!" (They never would.)

On Wednesday or Thursday afternoon, when you are watching TV or working out, maybe taking a nap, all of a sudden the doors to the unit open and the canteen workers are on the range. Your heart instantly starts to race. Finally! An officer slides your receipt under your outside door, and you reach through the bars of the inside door and grab the receipt and sign it. When the officers open your outside door, they get the receipt and then dump all your purchases right outside your inside door. This is how we would receive all the overpriced, low-quality products. The most exciting day of the week also entailed a degrading moment of having to collect the items we paid for off the floor. We were forced to essentially grovel on the ground to ensure we could brush our teeth. Even in the happiest times, they still found a way to remove our dignity. I'll never forget that. There are no gains without losses.

Some of the canteen bags that people received were enormous. It was stunning how much money some folks had and how open they were to spending all of it on expensive trashy food. We were so desperate for anything different, anything that wasn't what they shoved down our gullets. If we had to pay extra for it and feed the prison-industrial complex, so be it. Whatever it took to have those moments of peace. Whatever it took to turn this migraine down or get a more peaceful sleep or marginally happier mornings.

Canteen is expensive. Wildly expensive. Disrespectfully expensive. It is exploitative and disgusting. In other words, everything you would expect from a for-profit prison industry. In theory, all the profits are supposed to go back into programming for the prisoners. In reality, this doesn't happen. Instead, the head of commissary takes home a massive bonus based on the profits they acquire for the prison. Nothing is ever for our actual benefit. They aren't selling you this waste because they want you to feel better about being away from your family. This isn't an act of kindness and humanity. It is exploitation. *We will feed you the worst food you could dream of, but don't worry, you can always spend all your loved ones' money. That way we both win!* Only they ever win.

My first full purchase felt like armed robbery. All the small creature comforts are expensive inside: coffee ($9), peanut butter ($4), toothpaste ($6), naproxen ($6), stamps ($44), a pair of tennis shoes ($75), envelopes ($2), a sweater ($22), sweatpants ($20), some deodorant ($4), and phone calls ($3.75 per every fifteen minutes). These prices may not sound out of the norm, but when you are allowed to make only seven to fifteen dollars a month, spending half of it on a bag of coffee and then the other on two phone calls feels scandalous. If you aren't one of the lucky few to have one of the prison jobs, then it is up to your family. They either let you suffer or have to find the extra funds to support you inside. Twenty dollars for the lowest-quality sweatshirt ever made, that will fall apart within two months, is a robbery. As a vegan at the time, I would have faced starvation if it weren't for supporters finding the extra money every month. I felt scammed and cheated (because I was), but then the consumerist joy took over. I hadn't had real toothpaste on a real toothbrush in over four years. If you've ever had to scrub your teeth with part shampoo, part gel toothpaste on a washcloth, you'll understand my glee. I hadn't worn tennis shoes in over four years. I hadn't worn cozy clothes in over four years. Sweaters and sweatpants feel essential. It is so icy in the ADX cells. Frigidly cold. Having sweats allowed me to function and feel safe. I felt shielded from their stares, from their hands, from their filth. They weren't just sweatpants, they were armor.

This was very conflicting for me. Prison is sad. ADX is the most extreme punishment that the Bureau can put on someone. It removes you from the entire prison population, removes you from all real human contact, and dumps you into a concrete box. Yet this was the most tangibly comfortable I had been in years. The last four years had been so traumatizing, so rattling, that they made parts of ADX feel like an upgrade. I scrubbed my teeth like they were filthy linoleum. They would finally be clean.

NUMBER: _____ **UNIT:** _____ **CELL:** _____ **DATE:** _____

UNITED STATES PENITENTIARY - ADMINISTRATIVE MAXIMUM, FLORENCE, CO ** COMMISSARY LIST **
MAXIMUM SPENDING LIMIT - $285.00 PER MONTH
G/P, K/A, K/B, B&C, J/A, J/B units

POSTAGE STAMPS (POSSESSION LIMIT $29.40)

$0.01	_____	(SINGLE)
$0.21	_____	(SINGLE)
$0.50	_____	(SINGLE)
$10.00	_____	(BOOK OF 20 $0.50 STAMPS)
$1.00	_____	(SINGLE)

TOILET PAPER – (LIMIT 3)

$0.70 _____ EARTH FIRST SINGLE ROLL TOILET PAPER

TOILETRY ITEMS –
(LIMITS: SOAP 2, SHAMPOO 2, TOOTHPASTE 2, DEODORANT 2)

$0.95	_____	DIAL ANTIBACTERIAL BAR SOAP
$1.40	_____	2/PK IRISH SPRING BAR SOAP
$1.85	_____	AMBI COMPLEXION BAR SOAP
$2.40	_____	DOVE BAR SOAP
$3.15	_____	SUAVE BODYWASH
$0.50	_____	SOAP DISH
$1.80	_____	BODY GUARD DEODORANT
$1.15	_____	DIAL ROLL-ON DEODORANT
$1.90	_____	BABY POWDER (RC)
$3.90	_____	SULFUR 8 SHAMPOO
$3.45	_____	SULFUR 8 CONDITIONER
$0.85	_____	DANDRUFF SHAMPOO
$1.45	_____	VO-5 SHAMPOO
$2.80	_____	CREST TOOTHPASTE
$0.40	_____	DENTURE BRUSH
$5.75	_____	COLGATE SENSITIVE
$4.15	_____	FIXODENT CREAM
$3.50	_____	DENTURE CLEANING PASTE
$1.90	_____	DENTAL BATH (denture tray)
$2.10	_____	AIM MOUTHWASH
$1.40	_____	TOOTH BRUSH
$0.40	_____	STIM-U-DENT TOOTH PICKS
$2.60	_____	DENTAL FLOSS LOOPS 30PK
$0.45	_____	FRESHSCENT BODY LOTION
$3.30	_____	SUAVE COCOA BUTTER LOTION
$4.20	_____	LUBRIDERM LOTION
$4.90	_____	PALMERS LOTION
$1.30	_____	STYLING GEL
$1.55	_____	CHAPSTICK
$2.15	_____	BLISTEX
$1.15	_____	COTTON SWABS
$2.90	_____	SHOWER SHOES
$7.80	_____	SEVA SHOWER SHOES
$0.15	_____	SHOWER CAP
$1.95	_____	ROYAL CROWN
$0.40	_____	DENTURE BRUSH
$6.25	_____	AFRICAN PRIDE MAGICAL GRO (limit 1)

CANDY BARS (LIMIT 10)

$0.95	_____	BUTTERFINGER (RC)
$0.95	_____	SNICKERS (RC)
$0.95	_____	M&M's (RC)
$0.95	_____	TWIX (RC)
$2.80	_____	HERSHEYS BAR 7OZ (RC)
$0.85	_____	BROWNIE

Kosher/Halal Shelf Stable Entrees(Limit 7 total) –
Submit SPO form to Unit Team

Chicken & Noodle (RC)
Beef Stew (RC)
Pasta-Garden Vegetable (RC)
Vegetarian Stew (RC)2.503.152.90

SOUPS (LIMIT 14)

$0.25	_____	RAMEN MARUCHAN HOT-N-SPICY VEGETABLE SOUP
$0.25	_____	RAMEN VEGETARIAN W/SOY SAUCE ORIENTAL
$0.25	_____	RAMEN LOW SODIUM CHILI SOUP (limit 2)
$0.25	_____	DRAGON EXPRESS SPICY CHICKEN SOUP (halal)
$0.25	_____	DRAGON EXPRESS SPICY BEEF SOUP (halal)
$1.40	_____	BROWN RICE (RC)
$1.10	_____	WHITE RICE (halal)
$1.70	_____	CHEESE RICE (RC)

CRACKERS, TORTILLAS & CEREALS (LIMIT 7)

$2.10	_____	SNACK CRACKERS (RC)
$2.40	_____	WHEAT THIN CRACKERS
$2.35	_____	SALTINES (RC)
$2.30	_____	PESOS FLOUR TORTILLAS, 12PK (LIMIT 2) (RC)
$4.60	_____	RAISIN BRAN (LIMIT 2) (RC)
$3.15	_____	CINNAMON TOASTERS (LIMIT 2) (RC)
$3.10	_____	FROSTED MINI SPOONERS (LIMIT 2)
$1.95	_____	ROLLED OATS (RC)
$3.15	_____	GRANOLA

SEASONS, SPREADS & SAUCES (LIMIT 6)

$3.60	_____	HONEY sugar free (RC)
$1.30	_____	SWEETMATE BLUE (LIMIT 1) (RC)
$1.50	_____	SWEET SPRINKLES SUCRALOSE (LIMIT 1)
$2.60	_____	PEANUT BUTTER, CRUNCHY (LIMITE 2) (RC)
$2.60	_____	PEANUT BUTTER, CREAMY (LIMIT 2) (RC)
$2.15	_____	MAYONNAISE (RC)
$0.65	_____	KETCHUP 12 PK STRIP
$0.50	_____	MUSTARD 12 PK STRIP
$3.05	_____	SQUEEZE CHEESE 14OZ BOTTLE (LIMIT 1)
$1.75	_____	SOY SAUCE 16.2 OZ (RC)
$0.50	_____	PASTA SAUCE 4OZ
$0.30	_____	BBQ SAUCE PACKETS (4 COUNT AS 1 ITEM)
$0.45	_____	RANCH PACKETS (4 COUNT AS 1 ITEM)
$1.30	_____	VEGETABLE FLAKES (RC)
$1.25	_____	ITALIAN SEASONING (RC)
$1.50	_____	GARLIC POWDER (RC)
$1.60	_____	SALT & PEPPER
$1.60	_____	SAZON W/ GOYA (LIMIT 1)
$0.90	_____	PICANTE SAUCE 10/PK STRIP (LIMIT 1)
$3.00	_____	JELLY (LIMIT 2)

BAG CANDY (LIMIT 6)

$0.70	_____	WELCH'S FRUIT SNACKS
$0.60	_____	STARLIGHT MINTS
$2.60	_____	JOLLY RANCHERS sugar free
$1.55	_____	GRACEY'S HARD CANDY sugar free

CHIPS (LIMIT 6)

$1.50	_____	DORITOS
$1.50	_____	RUFFLES SOUR CREAM N CHEDDAR
$1.20	_____	SALSITAS 3oz bag
$1.40	_____	PEPES PORK RIND
$1.20	_____	POPCORN
$1.90	_____	CHEETOS
$2.85	_____	TORTILLA CHIPS
$1.30	_____	BBQ CHIPS

PASTRIES & COOKIES (LIMIT 10)

$0.55	_____	NATURE VALLEY GRANOLA BARS
$1.75	_____	OATMEAL CRÈME COOKIES (box)
$1.65	_____	POP UP TOASTERS
$1.05	_____	BUD'S BEST COOKIES
$1.40	_____	DUPLEX COOKIES
$1.75	_____	BUDDY BARS

DRINKS (LIMIT 8)

$1.80	_____	TEA BAGS (RC)
$1.40	_____	ORANGE CRUSH SINGLES BOX (limit 2) sugar free
$1.40	_____	HAWAIIAN PUNCH SINGLES BOX (limit 2) sugar free
$6.50	_____	LIQUID COFFEE CREAMER (RC)
$3.40	_____	DECAFFEINATED COFFEE (RC)
$9.00	_____	TASTER'S CHOICE COFFEE (RC)
$7.45	_____	FOLGER'S COFFEE
$3.20	_____	KEEFE COFFEE

MEAT & CHEESE ITEMS (LIMIT 10)

$2.40	_____	CHEDDAR SQUARE
$1.75	_____	MOZZARELLA CHEESE BAR
$1.90	_____	BEEF HOT SAUSAGE
$1.95	_____	HALAL BEEF SAUSAGE (halal)
$1.45	_____	TUNA (halal)
$2.40	_____	PEPPERONI SLICES
$1.20	_____	MACKEREL (RC)
$1.60	_____	SALMON (RC)
$0.90	_____	SARDINES (RC)
$5.20	_____	FULLY COOKED BACON STRIPS
$3.40	_____	PANCHO'S SHREDDED BEEF (halal)
$3.50	_____	BRUSHY CREEK BEEF BARBACOA

BEANS & LEGUMES (LIMIT 6)

$1.70	_____	JALAPENO REFRIED BEANS (RC)
$3.75	_____	HUMMUS (RC)

FRUITS & NUTS (LIMIT 8)

$2.20	_____	RAISINS 1.0 OZ 6PACK (RC)
$2.90	_____	PITTED PRUNES (RC)
$3.05	_____	PITTED DATES (RC)
$1.40	_____	OLIVES
$0.60	_____	KOSHER PICKLE (RC)
$2.65	_____	PEANUTS (RC)
$0.95	_____	SUNFLOWER SEEDS 2.5OZ
$3.40	_____	KARS MIXED NUTS 8 OZ.
$3.00	_____	GOODY GOODY TRAIL MIX 12 OZ.

WRITING & READING MATERIALS

$0.70	ADDRESS BOOK (LIMIT 1)
$0.45	FLEX PENS (LIMIT 2)
$0.20	ENVELOPE 10" x 13" (LIMIT 20)
$1.50	NOTEBOOK 8.5" X 11" (LIMIT 2)
$2.25	LEGAL FOLDER W/VELCRO (LIMIT 2)
$1.40	ENVELOPES 50CT (LIMIT 2)
$0.90	NOTEPAD 8.5"x 11" (LIMIT 2)

PERSONAL ACCESSORIES (POSSESSION LIMIT 1 EACH)

$1.15	AIR FRESHENER (LITTLE TREE) (LIMIT 2)
$1.80	KLEENEX/8 PK
$1.50	BAND AIDS 30 PK.
$3.75	SHAKER BOTTLE/1 QT
$0.50	DRINK TUMBLER
$2.00	COFFEE MUG 22OZ
$2.60	PHOTO ALBUM
$4.50	PHOTO ALBUM INSERTS (LARGE)
$0.40	EAR PLUGS
$0.40	PALM BRUSH
$1.20	SHOELACE 54"
$3.80	EAR-BUD (STEREO HEADPHONES)
$1.30	HEADPHONE ADAPTER
$0.65	HANDKERCHIEF
$4.95	EYE GLASSES STRAP
$2.10	VELCRO WATCH BAND
$2.60	BICYCLE PLAYING CARDS
$5.60	MESH BAG
$0.40	GREETING CARDS (INDIVIDUAL) (LIMIT 10)
$4.70	2'FT HEADPHONE EXT CORD
$2.55	BOWL (3 CUPS/750ML) (LIMIT 1)

WATCH BATTERIES

$2.60	CASIO WATCH BATTERY
$2.60	GRT CLEAR WATCH BATTERY

$5.20 to $6.50 _____ FRAGRANCE OIL (LIMIT 1)

VITAMINS (POSSESSION LIMIT 1 EACH)

$4.15	ADVANCED ULTREX PLUS
$4.25	CALCIUM
$3.20	VITAMIN C
$4.20	VITAMIN D
$3.60	VITAMIN E (400 MG)

CLOTHING (POSSESSION LIMITS: SWEATS - 2 SETS; SOCKS - 6 PAIR; GYM SHORTS - 2 PAIR; T-SHIRTS - 6)

$15.50	SWEAT SHIRT RUSSELL------ L, XL, 2XL, 3XL, 4XL
$23.40	SWEAT SHIRT RUSSELL------ 5XL
$17.55	SWEAT PANTS RUSSELL----- L, XL, 2XL, 3XL, 4XL
$26.00	SWEAT PANTS RUSSELL----- 5XL
$18.00	PRO 5 GYM SHORTS------------- L, XL, 2XL
$19.00	PRO 5 GYM SHORTS------------- 3XL, 4XL
$9.10	THERMAL TOP------------------- L or XL
$10.40	THERMAL TOP------------------- 2XL, 3XL, 4XL
$9.10	THERMAL BOTTOM------------ L or XL
$10.40	THERMAL BOTTOM------------ 2XL, 3XL, 4 XL
$1.95	TUBE SOCKS (WHITE)
$11.65	CREW SOCKS 6 PR.
$5.85	ATHL. SUPPORTER------------- M
$5.85	ATHL. SUPPORTER------------- L
$5.20	ATHL. SUPPORTER------------- XL
$5.85	T-SHIRT (1 PK)-------------------- L or XL
$7.05	T-SHIRT (1PK)--------------------- 2XL, 3XL, 4XL
$8.80	T-SHIRT (1PK)--------------------- 5XL
$9.75	A-SHIRTS (3 PK)------------------ L or XL
$12.05	A-SHIRTS (3 PK)------------------ 2XL or 3XL
$1.70	COTTON GLOVES (WHITE)
$2.95	BASEBALL CAP (WHITE)
$8.45	WEIGHT LIFTING GLOVES------- M
$10.40	WEIGHT LIFTING GLOVES------- L, XL, 2XL
$18.85	HANDBALL GLOVES------------- L or XL
$1.30	SWEAT BAND (WHITE ONLY)

RELIGIOUS ITEMS

$13.65	PRAYER RUG (LIMIT 1)
$1.65	BANDANA AZTEC RED (**) (LIMIT 2)
$8.00	KUFI (WHITE)
$1.45	MISWAK STICKS

OVER THE COUNTER MEDICATIONS (LIMIT 1 EACH UNLESS DESIGNATED BELOW)

$2.00	ACETAMINOPHEN 325MG (LIKE TYLENOL)
$2.40	PINK BISMUTH (LIKE PEPTO-BISMAL)
$1.80	MUSCLE RUB (LIKE ICY HOT)
$1.45	ANESTHETIC ORAL GEL
$2.35	ROLAIDS
$1.95	ARTIFICIAL TEARS EYE DROPS
$1.40	ASPIRIN 325MG
$3.80	HEMORRHOIDAL OINTMENT
$1.80	HYDROCORTISONE CREAM
$2.75	IBUPROFEN TABLETS 200MG
$2.60	MILK OF MAGNESIA
$1.85	LORATADINE ALLERGY TABLETS
$1.30	ALLERGY RELIEF - CHLORPHENIRAMINE
$6.00	FIBER CARE PILLS
$1.80	SALINE NASAL SPRAY
$1.15	HALLS COUGH DROPS (LIMIT 2)
$2.45	FOOT POWDER (MEDICATED)
$3.75	NAPROXEN (LIKE ALEVE)
$2.10	TRIPLE ANTIBIOTIC OINTMENT (LIKE NEOSPORIN)
$3.35	ANTACID LIQUID (LIKE MYLANTA)
$10.95	OMEPRAZOLE 20MG (LIKE PRILOSEC)
$1.40	CLEAR ZIT (ACNE TREATMENT)
$1.70	TOLNAFTATE CREAM (ANTI-FUNGAL) (LIMIT 3)
$1.30	CLOTRIMAZOLE CREAM 1% (ANTI-FUNGUS)
$3.90	ACID REDUCER (RANITIDINE)
$18.25	NASACORT
$4.45	STOOL SOFTENER
$2.50	COUGH SYRUP

NEW ITEMS (WRITE IN): _____

_____
_____
_____
_____
_____
_____
_____

INMATES ARE RESPONSIBLE FOR NOT EXCEEDING POSSESSION LIMITS OF ITEMS SOLD THROUGH THE COMMISSARY.

ALL PRICES ARE SUBJECT TO CHANGE WITHOUT NOTICE. NO SUBSTITUTIONS WILL BE MADE UNLESS REQUESTED ON SLIP!

ALL SALES ARE CONSIDERED FINAL ONCE AN INMATE HAS SIGNED THE SALES RECEIPT AND THE STAFF MEMBER HAS DEPARTED THE CELL FRONT. NO EXCHANGES ARE ALLOWED. ALL PRODUCT WARRANTIES ARE THAT OF THE MANUFACTURER AND ARE NOT OFFERED THROUGH THE COMMISSARY.

INMATES MUST HAVE AVAILABLE FUNDS ON THEIR ACCOUNT PRIOR TO PLACING THEIR ORDER. IF FUNDS ARE NOT AVAILABLE ON SELLING DAY, THEN THE COMMISSARY LIST CANNOT BE FILLED.

ALL ITEMS WILL COUNT AGAINST YOUR MONTHLY SPENDING LIMITATION WITH THE EXCEPTION OF STAMPS, VITAMINS, AND OVER-THE-COUNTER MEDICATIONS.

YOU MAY SUBMIT A REQUEST TO A STAFF MEMBER (COP-OUT) ADDRESSED TO THE COMMISSARY COMMITTEE TO MAKE SUGGESTIONS OR REQUEST CHANGES IN THE COMMISSARY.

(RC) - ITEMS MARKED WITH (RC) HAVE A RELIGIOUS CERTIFICATION. PLEASE REVIEW ALL INGREDIENTS TO ENSURE THAT THEY COMPLY WITH YOUR RELIGIOUS DIETARY REQUIREMENTS.

WATCH THE CLOSED CIRCUIT NETWORK TV FOR INFORMATION ON NEW ITEMS, PRICE CHANGES AND OUT OF STOCK ITEMS.

THE COMMISSARY WILL ORDINARILY BE CLOSED FOR INVENTORY DURING THE LAST ACCOUNTING WEEK OF EACH QUARTER.

ANDRE MATEVOUSIAN, COMPLEX WARDEN
JUNE 5, 2018

The ADX canteen list. Different units are allowed different items. Note that this list is outdated and everything shown here is wildly cheap compared to now. In 2025, for example, chips cost $4.50 or more.

I was blessed to have fiscal support at this time. Not everyone was so lucky. You would hear people yelling at commissary workers, blaming them for the money not being in their account. They felt hurt and embarrassed that they didn't have the amount they thought, or sometimes any amount at all. For me, financial support ebbed and flowed over the years. If not for ABC Bloomington, Fire Ant, individual supporters, and later the Anarchist Black Cross Federation Warchest, I would have really struggled. Especially the first couple of years inside. So many days and nights eating nothing but black beans, rice, and soggy veggies. So many days spent listening to my stomach scream at me, begging for something more. Every day was essentially a minor hunger strike. Canteen is such a necessity for prisoners. It allows you to feel safe, knowing that you can afford the medicine they will not give you, decent hygiene, or backup food if you get a particularly rancid meal. For vegans and vegetarians, it is even more necessary.

In the BOP, you are not served a vegan option. Instead, you are given the "no flesh" meal plan. This is the most disgusting name for a meal plan I have ever heard in my life. This plan ensures that you will not be served actual meat, but that is all. Eggs, milk, and something almost like cheese are all still served. This is problematic. Even worse is that often the soy or tofu they serve is disgraceful: served as cold, wet chunks or bathed in a seasoning that is so salty it makes your throat clench. Or you are served beans. Beans every goddamn day. Beans for lunch, beans for dinner. Black beans in the morning, kidney beans in the evening. Your pores begin leaking legumes. You dream of beans, and it's nothing but nightmares. No matter how vegan you are, no one on earth would enjoy a meal of salty black beans, sopping wet spinach, two pieces of bread, and a putrid "salad." Being able to buy nuts of different sorts, peanut butter, and other vegan staples is a necessity. Unless, of course, you enjoy chunks of soy that are designed to look and smell like beef but taste like monkey ass. In that case, please feel free to indulge in the Bureau's fine delicacies.

One of the most expensive things for political prisoners or anyone who sends lots of letters is buying stamps. Stamps can cost thirty to forty dollars per month, depending on how many letters you're sending and what type of packages you're sending out. Stamps are sold as "flat books," which are twenty to a pack. Two flats, two bags of coffee, two containers of peanut butter, a bag of nuts, and a bag of cereal could be half of my monthly budget. With prices this high and funds so limited, it was always important to budget appropriately. I never wanted to hit up my wife or friends and say that I had blown through all the money people had saved for me. This was part of the reason I stayed away from drugs inside. Along with being an ex-addict and not wanting to spiral back, I also didn't want to hit up Rochelle and beg for drug money. I watched men do this every week. I watched them scheme and say whatever it would take to get the funds sent to them. They had to. When you're hooked, you aren't thinking right, you aren't thinking levelheadedly. You are devoted to only one thing. I didn't ever want to be that person. I didn't want to put drugs before the struggle, before my family, and before my own health. I would save my money—and possibly my life—and just focus on stamps and coffee. Not as big of a buzz but equally as rewarding. Not everyone is able to make that choice. Some get far into their addiction, then far into debt, then far into the hospital or the grave. People do not play around with drug debts. You will pay one way or another.

When people were told that they didn't have enough money in their account or that their purchase had been rejected for whatever reason, this was crushing and was never received well. I would hear other convicts screaming at the workers, telling them to come back and check again. They would yell that the workers were fucking them over, that they were bitches and punks. This rage wasn't unjustified or unfounded. Canteen workers can be the most helpful people you ever run into at this joint, but also some of the ones who can cause the most damage to you if you are unlucky enough to get on their bad side. Two things can be true at the same time.

The pigs would mock these convicts, taunting them: "Nobody loves your bitch ass," or, "You're broke as fuck and that isn't our problem." This cowardly taunting would only get the prisoner even more upset, and justifiably so. I would get pissed off just hearing it. If they treat the other prisoners like that, they will treat you like that. One wrong word and now you're the victim of their resentment. These petty cops are known to hold grudges. If they have a problem with you, it wouldn't be a surprise if the item you want most on canteen suddenly goes out of stock. Just happened to run out right when they got your sheet, and happened to get it back right in time for the next person. They deny people hygiene and medicine, coffee and stamps.

Imagine: You are at your most vulnerable and most restrained. You have letters from your family, and that is the only contact you have, because they cannot afford to fly to Florence. You are desperate to write them back, but you don't have stamps. They are waiting to hear from you, and they are just as desperate to know what you are going through and that you are safe. You put in the order for stamps, and the officers tell you they are on back order. This pisses you off, but you swallow it. Another week goes by, and they say the same thing, but this time you notice other men on the range are getting their stamps. You ask the canteen workers what's going on with this, and they say you are being paranoid, that it was just bad luck. Then it happens again, and you know absolutely that they are playing cruel games with you. You call them out, and they mock you, disrespecting you in ways that are entirely designed to provoke you. Then they cackle like a gang of hyenas as they walk away. Imagine the powerlessness and rage you would feel. Then imagine having to feel that way for years. They go home to beat their wives or attack homeless people outside of bars, while you just sit and let the rage simmer.

This is the unique power these bastards hold. They have the power to hold a grudge over a dispute you may have had two or three years ago. It isn't just denying you access to your extra food—which is insulting enough—it is also denying you access to your family, and that is totally inexcusable. There is never a reason why cops should stand between people and their family, and yet that is the expected and normal behavior of these dismal demons. I've seen people go months without being able to buy stamps. Every time, they would complain to the warden, and the warden would talk to the head of the commissary department, who would find an excuse for his workers, never once claiming responsibility or fixing the issue. Even workers who are not usually a part of this department but are just filling in walk this line. You can hear them saying, "Sorry, pal, not today," muttering fake, half-ass empathetic comments. Patronizing you as if they don't know what's happening. They all know, and they are all complicit. *ALL* cops are bastards.

This cowardly behavior is par for the course for guards at prisons like these. They know that you have no way to retaliate against them, at least not without catching new charges for assault. They use our inability to contact our families or respond on our own to gain whatever sense of self-worth they are lacking. They are true cowards. Sometimes men will scream and bang in the shower, demanding to talk to a lieutenant (who will also do nothing). Sometimes they will wait until the next time and douse the pigs with liquid fecal waste or piss (and then get beaten savagely and charged with assault). Sometimes, though, they wait. They wait quietly. These men are the most terrifying people I have ever met. They have mastered their emotions and rage and have nothing but time. Nothing but time to wait for one of these fine federal officers to slip up and let their guard down (pun intended).

These aren't acts of impulsive violence. No. This is well-calculated, thought-out, justified violence. This is a thing of beauty. A brutalist art form. A drama played out in the underground hell where these men are stored. An act of war that could only exist under the most extreme repression. This rage steams and simmers. They can't take it out too early. It must grow and develop over weeks or months. Weeks and months and years spent knowing that the person who is actively ruining their life has something coming their way. They can wait as long as it takes. The longer it goes, the more hate is poured into this vengeance brew. It is a child on Christmas morning, knowing that the gift they've been waiting on for half their life has finally arrived. Nothing will stop them from having it now.

I have spoken to men who have made these decisions and caught years' worth of extra time for it. Been beaten beyond recognition for it. Had every ounce of comfort forcefully stolen away for it. They all say it was worth it. Of course it was worth it. It's always worth it. Striking down your torturer is never an act of violence but instead an act of self-dignity and self-preservation. Radical self-love in the defense of your humanity. There has never been a single act of prison retaliation that wasn't 100 percent justified.

One of the men I spoke with said he waited six years for his chance. Six years to teach a lesson to someone who had gone out of their way to prevent this prisoner from having any piece of mind. Years of abuse dished out by someone who foolishly assumed they would never have to answer for their crimes. When Bro got his chance, he didn't hesitate, and he paid the price for it. The same price we all know will come the moment we decide to stand up for ourselves. But I know that it was the best feeling they've ever had in their lives, making that worm of an officer eat all their abuse. Or eat something. Street justice.

A lesson everyone should learn no matter your profession: Never mess with someone's family.

Medical

Collin had a bone spur. He was in the prerelease unit, K-A. This meant he had an outdate and would be going home within the next four years. Collin had been through a lot, and this goddamn bone spur was just another thorn in his side (or foot). Bone spurs cause immense pain, and after months of request for care, months of filing grievances to plead for care, months of begging the warden for care, Collin was finally given word that he would have surgery. Note: His pain and suffering were dismissed and disregarded every step of the way. Even after an X-ray showed a serious bone spur, the medical treatment was Tylenol, which he had to purchase from the canteen.

This would not be an easy surgery. It would involve breaking bones and rearranging his toes to fix the hammer toe that was causing so much pain. But Collin was excited as hell. Finally, he would be able to exist without the burden of constant and immense pain. He would be in the hospital for two or three days, and then he would be returned to the unit.

Collin was back on the unit for three days when he started to notice that his foot was still bleeding a little. He spoke to the medical department about this, and they said it was normal. Then it started to swell and throb. Dr. Oba—the rottenest bastard ever to live—said this wasn't an issue, nothing to be concerned about. When it started to ooze pus two days later, Collin was given fresh gauze and some cleaning soap that was supposed to solve the issue. His foot was a disturbing reddish pink, leaking stinky yellow liquid, and the solution of the doctor who had gone to medical school and gotten certified (allegedly) was to give him some goddamn gauze and soap. Dr. Oba was not concerned when the pain began to move from Collin's foot up to his knee and then his thigh. Collin's toes started turning a ghastly milky-white. The nurses were terrified and requested urgent care for Collin, yet Dr. Oba refused.

Ten days after returning from the hospital, Collin was finally rushed back to the same filthy, unsterilized hospital for emergency surgery. The nurses had panicked enough to force Dr. Oba to do some doctoring. Collin was in the hospital for another five days before being brought back to ADX and held in the infirmary for another week.

When he arrived at the hospital, they rushed him into surgery immediately. They had to clean out his foot and put him on IV antibiotics. His wound had turned into a blood infection and was traveling up his leg, making its way to his heart. He could have died. He had to wear an antibiotic IV bag around his neck for over two weeks. And all of this was avoidable. It is mind-boggling the level of hatred one must have for prisoners to let things like this happen—again and again.

During Collin's first surgery, he was taken to a hospital known within ADX as being notorious for botching surgeries. Before and during this surgery, the medical staff never removed his filthy khaki prison pants. These butchers parading as doctors sliced this man open and exposed him to every possible vicious germ instead of just taking the time to put Collin in surgical clothes. While he was awake, he had no recollection of them ever cleaning his foot. The two most obvious things that should have happened during a surgery—both of which are basic common-sense hygiene—never occurred. His postsurgical care consisted of the gauze they sent him home wearing and the instructions to keep the wound clean. He was not given crutches, and he was not moved to a cell on the bottom floor of the range, meaning he had to walk up and down the stairs while recovering. He was not given clean, fresh socks or anything to wrap around his foot to keep it from getting infected. Everything that would have been avoided at a real hospital was normalized and encouraged at ADX.

This is the norm at this hellhole of a prison where human life has no value. Collin's story isn't unique. In fact, later that same month the *exact same thing* happened to another prisoner, Abdul Shahid, who was even in the same unit! He was sent to the same hospital, was given no postsurgical care, was ignored entirely as his symptoms got worse, and was rushed to the hospital for emergency surgery when it was clear he had run out of time. To the men in ADX, this wasn't shocking and didn't raise any alarms—we all knew what to expect from this medical staff.

The road to medical care is windy while inside. You first turn in a "sick call" form, which is a piece of paper that states what the issue is and what help you need. This is given to the nurses or physician assistants who do daily walks around the units. They will take this with a positive attitude and assure you that you will be seen soon. A week or two later, when no one has come and spoken to you, you will attempt another sick call. You will tell the nurses that this is your second time filling out these forms and you need help. Please, for the love of god, you just need help. They will assure you that they will talk to the doctor and not to worry. If you believe this, then I truly pity you. There is nothing you won't believe. Without question, absolutely nothing will occur to aid you or heal you, and you will be forced to file a BP8, which is the first step in the prison's internal grievance process. When the warden walks by on his weekly walk-through, you will stop him outside your door, desperate, and you'll complain about your pain or illness. You will be told to fill out some sick call forms for the nurses. When you tell him you've filled out two of these and even a grievance form, he will direct the head of medical to you. Wardens do not deal with problems, but they are masters of delegating them to someone else.

The director of Health Services is not a doctor but rather a bureaucrat who is the liaison between the medical department and the prisoners. They will get you seen for the first time by an RN. The RN will take notes, nod their head, and tell you which medicine you need to buy from the canteen. If you have already bought the medicine they've requested you purchase—usually Tylenol or a cream of some sort—they will then prescribe you something unnecessary and unwanted. A steroid of some sort, always just what the doctor ordered. You could be bleeding out of your pores, with your teeth turning into moldy stumps, and you would be told to buy Tylenol and take some prednisone.

This maniacal masquerade will go on for months and months before you ever see a doctor. The seasons will change and you'll suffer all the while, never once being considered to see a doctor. By the time you ever do see one—if ever—your issue will be so advanced that immediate medical care is necessary. The administration will do everything possible to assure that you don't get the care you need, because proper care costs money. All prisoners are insured, but the Bureau pays that insurance and they don't like it and will do everything possible to avoid using it. Your death is significantly cheaper than your premiums. This is why we get the bare minimum. This is why the hospitals don't care enough to put you in a real hospital gown.

In December 2022, I tore a muscle in my neck while overdoing it with workouts while watching the Qatar World Cup. My neck and shoulders were already decimated from being four-pointed, and at this same time I had a swollen lymph node in my neck that had previously been seen and recorded after an ultrasound at a previous prison. Before I was transferred to ADX, I was even scheduled for a surgical consult (only two years after I first reported it to sick call). For months at ADX, I was gaslighted about the lymph node and ignored about the neck muscle tear. I struggled to keep my head straight. I struggled to hold it up. It caused outlandish discomfort when just resting on my bunk. Simple things like walking or sitting up were so miserable and painful that I couldn't tolerate them.

It took seven months and a lawsuit filed by my attorneys before I was seen for the muscle issues in my neck. When I was seen, it was for something I didn't need. I was prescribed steroids, then given an X-ray (for a muscle tear—imagine how stupid that is). Next, I was sent to a "neck specialist" for the swollen lymph node. This sick fraud saw me for literally thirty seconds before saying that I didn't have a swollen lymph node. When, moments later, his assistant showed him the previous scan, he relented and ordered *another* ultrasound. The officers who had driven me to the specialist said that was the longest they'd ever seen that specific doctor talk to any prisoner. He had the BOP's medical contract, and his role was to claim that no further care was needed. Chained, handcuffed at the waist, an electric band on my arm in case I tried to escape, crowded by four armed officers, just to spend thirty seconds being called a liar.

When my second ultrasound was scheduled, I was not surprised when the write-up told the medical worker to do the scan on the wrong side of my neck—the side where the swollen lymph node wasn't, and on the back of the neck instead of the side (let it sink in how insulting that is). Convicts inside would expect nothing less from these buffoons. Their goal of course being that the new ultrasound would reveal nothing and I would be shown to be a malingerer. By the grace of the goddesses, I was able to convince them to scan the correct side, asking them to please feel the lymph node. Just please treat me like a human and feel my goddamn neck. They did, thankfully, and changed the order. I was very, very fortunate. By this time, it had been another three months. Ten months total to get an ultrasound that said exactly what the previous one had already said. Instead of pushing forward with a CAT scan or MRI, I was prescribed steroids (again). My lawyers' lawsuit may have bullied the staff into action, but not quality action.

However, I had managed to get scheduled for an MRI for my neck strain, and I foolishly allowed myself to feel hope that I would actually get care. On the day of the MRI, I was told it was scheduled for hard tissue, to check out the bones in my neck instead of the muscles. When I explained the entire issue, the contracted MRI staff gave me their apologies, then did exactly what Dr. Oba told them to do. Turns out the bones in my neck are a little displaced, a little crooked, and my issues had absolutely nothing to do with a muscle strain. Cruelty is the norm inside.

I was at the ADX for sixteen months total and I saw the doctor one time, and that was immediately following the advancement of my lawsuit. By the end of my bid, I'd still never had a proper scan on my neck muscles and never had a biopsy of the lymph node. Enragingly, there is nothing unique about my experience, nor about Collin's or Shahid's. Our lives are not valued at all in the BOP. Our quality of life is not important to the bureaucrats who decide whether we get to live or die. Just to get an MRI, your case must go before a commission of top admins within the prison and then be approved by the regional director. All these people are standing between the prisoner and any chance of decent health care.

The doctors at these prisons are exactly what you would expect. They treat us like we are dirt because that is how they see us. The doctors assume everything we say is a scheme to get some sort of narcotic or valuable medicine. I have never once felt believed by those in the medical department. Dr. Oba has a history of this as well. He was the doctor at FCI Englewood when I was held pretrial there, and he did everything to prevent my first ultrasound. This is his MO. Doctors are hired by these prisons to walk the company line, to be complicit in the avoidance of care. It can be either incompetence or cruelty, but the result is the same: a lack of care.

People who get seriously ill at the ADX have a desperate road ahead. By the time you are seen, given a blood test, and given proper scans, whatever deep illness you have will have progressed. It is only when the prisoner is close to death that they will be transferred to an actual medical prison such as FMC Butner or FMC Springfield (FMC stands for Federal Medical Center, a prison that is also a hospital or long-term care facility). This is what happened to John Gotti, Ted Kaczynski, and Dr. Mutulu Shakur; Dr. Shakur was at FMC Lexington when he was released. But it is also what happens to *every* prisoner who has the misfortune and bad luck of getting seriously ill in a prison where being swept under the rug and forgotten about is the norm.

Dental care is not any better. Why would it be? When prisoners arrive at ADX, within a month they are seen by the dental staff. They are kind, they have bright attitudes, they will make you feel safe. At this visit, you will have your cleaning and initial scan for cavities that are at the stage of needing removal immediately. After this initial meeting—which is legally mandated per the BOP Program Statement—prisoners are at the whims of the dental department. I have seen people rip out their own teeth because the pain was so torturous. I have seen men manage to somehow make a flame to melt plastic and use it as a cap over their cavernous teeth. I have also seen people slice their wrists to bring attention to their lack of care. Remember hearing about the men at Red Onion State Prison in Virginia who attempted to light themselves on fire in 2024 just to get the peace of mind of knowing that the truth would finally be heard about the conditions in that vile facility? That is not uncommon.

In November 2023, my upper jaw began to throb. At first I thought it was a slight toothache, maybe too many sweets (sarcasm—maybe too many starches and processed garbage). The next day, my whole mouth was radiating pain, shooting down through my entire body. It was maddening. It pulsed with every heartbeat. I gave the medical department seven different sick call forms, begging them to talk with the dentist. I spoke to the warden, I spoke to the head of medical, and I spoke to the head of dental. I was grinding up naproxen and Tylenol and rubbing it on my gums and under my tongue. I'm not even sure this does anything, but mentally I had to try anything and everything to ease the pain. I couldn't sleep full nights, and I couldn't eat without screaming. I didn't know how to keep experiencing pain at that level.

It took ten days before I was seen by the dentist. Ten days *after* the first sick call. They said my nerves had died and they had to pull the tooth. No matter what had happened, they were going to pull the tooth. It could have just been plaque buildup and they would have pulled the tooth. I am fairly confident they get paid per tooth. They were kind and sociable while I was there in person, but they had no problem making me wait ten days. Ten days of pain so severe I still struggle to describe it. When I asked them why it had been necessary to make me wait so long, their response was exactly what I figured: "You weren't going to die. We got to you when we got to you." Our suffering isn't real, because they do not see us as real. We are the "worst of the worst," not your neighbors, husbands, or fathers.

People suffer in ADX. Every single day, someone is going through horrible pain that will be completely ignored. Partnered with this suffering is the knowledge that there is nothing that can be done to ease it. You can scream as loud as you want, but you'll only annoy your neighbors. You can buck and try to force medical care through resistance, but you will be further brutalized and still not receive any care. That is the psychological torture perpetrated by the medical department at the world's most hidden prison. They have complete control over every aspect of your care. They decide which of the over-the-counter medicines you can purchase from the canteen. They decide what stupid, unnecessary treatment to force on you. And if you refuse that treatment, they can decide to remove you from any other medical care. Imagine going to your doctor for a sprained ankle and their first response is to check your knee. Then imagine you correcting the doctor and, instead of fixing their mistake, they accuse you of wasting their time and then remove all further care from your file. It is a miracle that medical officers aren't stabbed every single day in the BOP.

This is one of the main problems with this level (or any level) of isolation. There is no help, and there is no accountability for those who refuse to help. When you file a grievance, you are asking the prison to hold their own doctors accountable. When you file a lawsuit, you are asking the government to see that the ADX doctor was deliberately indifferent toward your suffering. The ADX doctor will show the judge all the treatments they provided you, all the unneeded procedures and medicines you never asked for, and will claim that you've been given not just legit care but quality care—better than most on the streets. The judge will dismiss your case, and you will still have absolutely no quality care. When you are not seen as a human, you will not be treated as a human. See how the Zionists treat the Palestinians. See how the US military treated Iraqi and Afghani prisoners. We do not have families in their eyes. We do not have hopes, futures, or emotions. We are nothing but prisoners, and prisoners are bad. Prisoners are violent, disgusting, vile creatures, and creatures do not deserve, and will not receive, quality health care.

Collin could have died. It was an easily preventable situation, and it was clear to every medical professional except the actual doctor assigned to him that his situation was dire. Shahid could have died for the exact same reasons. It is nothing to offer someone clean gauze, disinfectant, and bandages after a serious surgery, but it was too much for the staff at ADX. To Dr. Oba, our lives are worth less than the goddamn gauze. Hundreds of men are still faced with this lack of care right now—faced with the fear of knowing that they may die, faced with the mental torture of knowing that their illness or wound will only get worse and may cross the line of no return. How do you maintain any sense of self or hope with that terror bearing down on you, while you are left to suffer, left to wither away, with no one to witness your agony or cares?

||| CHAPTER 4

A New Type of Institutionalization

> I was at war physically and mentally. I survived but now I suffer from PTSD so it's hard for me to talk about some of the things I've been through. I've tried to block a lot of it out by escaping through writing. Every day in here is like a landmine field, one wrong step and I may snap back to that nightmare, something I don't want to do.
>
> —Harold Cunningham, former ADX prisoner

For me, it usually takes about a week to begin to settle into a new location. When you've been transferred so damn much, it's normal to develop a routine with it and learn how to adapt to new spots. ADX is no different. If you can't adapt, then you can't survive. One thing most prisoners learn early on is that the days go by faster and feel better if you have a solid routine. This doesn't change in the supermax. The only thing that changes is who you are accountable to.

At ADX, you are on your own. You answer only to yourself. No one will make you get up for breakfast, no one will make you go to bed at a reasonable hour, no one will check to see if you're doing your burpees or push-ups. No one is going to find out or care if you are sitting in front of the TV staring like a zombie all day. The TV can be another chain if you aren't careful.

Not everyone can handle this self-accountability. There are people who lose hope inside and stop caring about their bodies or their minds. They sit in front of the TV all day and night, their lives revolving around what programs are on. This is exactly what the administration wants. They want to see the "worst of the worst" become tamed puppies. Once you become obsessed with that screen, they own you. Any threat to take the TV will bring unquestioned compliance. You become submissive and they achieve a victory: breaking another one of us.

This was taught to me by older prisoners who had been at ADX well before I ever got there, and I kept this in mind daily. I never wanted to be one of their victories. My routine was solid, and it was the same one I used at other institutions and one that was shared by many others. Here is the routine I used:

1. Wake up either a little before or at breakfast. Clean the cell. Set the precedent for the entire day: clean and productive.
2. Workout time: burpees, calisthenics, whatever you've got going on, just get an hour or two of good fitness in to keep your body and mind sharp.
3. Shower and then lunch.
4. Free time. Between noon and 4 p.m. is time to write letters, read books, watch *First Things First* or soccer. Just time to unwind.
5. "Count" at 4 p.m., where the guards walk by to make sure you are still alive, and then dinner immediately after.
6. Letters and a light workout. If I got mail, this is when I would read it, and reread it just to feel the happiness of it all. Then I would do a light workout, jogging around the cell or walking for an hour or two.
7. TV time/unwind/bedtime. This is when I would sit down and focus solely on whatever shows were on. If nothing good was on, then it would be reading time. Usually, it would be reading time with the TV on in the background.

This routine was a lifesaver. I have seen thousands of variants of this system. Having routines like this gives your entire day structure. It provides a purpose that otherwise would not exist. The prisoner creates the value of each object and the value of each day. We get to determine what means something to our day and how much it means. Cleaning your cell may not sound like fun, but having it as a task and then accomplishing it feels soothingly satisfying. It means that before 7 a.m., I've already accomplished something. Anything. When the workout is complete, you can say to yourself, "Despite all their attempts to lobotomize us, I chose to do something positive for myself. I chose me over apathy or sadness." It can be so hard to choose yourself, to choose productivity over apathy. It isn't just a push-up. It isn't just a clean toilet.

It is a conscious decision and an act of control. I am making this choice, and they can't stop me. They can't take this decision away from me.

The administration runs on a routine too. Laundry goes and comes back on the same days every single week. Every Friday we got fish for lunch, and every Wednesday we got hamburgers (plant patty for me). The administration walked through at the exact same time every week. Cleaning supplies (bristle pad and some pink liquid soap) always came on Sunday at approximately 2:30 p.m. Canteen same time, rec same time, psych same goddamn time. Prison is a very regimented place, and if nothing else it can provide structure. It can also supply absolute boredom. You are living a continuous *Groundhog Day*. You know that you may change your workouts or your habits, but everything else will run exactly the same as the day before it. That is one of the problems with having a routine. If the administration switches things up or disrupts it, you can feel really out of whack. After a shakedown, when you have to spend an hour cleaning up your trashed home, it can throw off your entire day, because it sets everything else back. I have seen otherwise put-together, great people ruin their lives because of discombobulation and rage. The routine can become a mental boon, a crutch, and a tool to beat us with all at the same time. Prison contains multitudes.

After about a week, I finally received the TV from the unit manager, got my first commissary bag—I was still on canteen restrictions, meaning I could only spend thirty dollars, so it was only toothpaste, coffee, and a jar of peanut butter—and, most importantly, got my first batch of mail.

History's greatest poets would struggle to describe how good it feels to receive mail inside prison. That is especially true when you aren't allowed any other forms of contact. At this point, I was still restricted from receiving email (no computer), making phone calls, or having visits. Mail was my only communication with the world, and I was thirsty for it. I would fantasize about letters, trying to will them into existence. I'd do mail mantras: "I'm getting mail today. I am definitely getting mail today. Without a doubt mail is coming today." If I wanted it badly enough, there would be letters sitting on top of my dinner tray. We all want mail. Every prisoner inside is desperate to receive letters showing that their people (or any people) remember them, that people still care. No TV channel or program can replace the joy of family or friends (or strangers) reaching out to you.

My first mail day was joyful, then enraging. There were seven letters stacked on top of my tray. Joy! But all seven were two to four months old. Enraging! Previous institutions had sat on letters or just refused to give them to me, and they were now being passed along. Damn you, prison mail rooms around the country!

At ADX, everyone is assigned to a specific Special Investigative Services tech. This tech is responsible for reading all your mail, listening to all your phone calls, and reviewing all your visits. They decide who you can talk to, how often you can talk with them, and when you are allowed to do so. They can decide on a whim to block anyone from communicating with you, and if that happens, you are out of luck. They have full discretion to block any letters from coming in if they deem them inappropriate (and they are not hesitant about using that discretion). Getting mail means that one of these cynical sociopaths finally sat down, read through your family and friends' personal thoughts and feelings, and decided they were safe enough for you to receive. More than that, though, it means that someone took the time and cared enough to write to you. They bought an envelope and stamp, typed or wrote a letter, and put it in the mailbox for the postal worker to bring into your life. I cannot count the times when the only bit of joy I experienced all day was from mail call. I also cannot count the times when there wasn't a single second of happiness in an entire day.

My unit manager couldn't stop being a miserable troll. He was addicted to the rush of being horrible to people who couldn't retaliate (legally) in any way. These vampires lurk among us, bouncing from person to person, sucking all the joy they can out of someone's life until all that is left is a miserable, vengeance-starved shell. Our unit manager, who was doing double duty as the unit counselor as well, was also responsible for arranging legal calls and picking up legal mail. His failure at both was almost inspiring. It takes more effort to *not* do your job than to just actually do it. Every person on the range had the same view of him: human scum.

The unit manager would come to work but not bother to come onto the range, ignoring all the people who feverishly needed him to actually do his job. He would refuse to pick up our grievance forms (BP8s) and would refuse to hand out grievance forms despite being the only person who could hand them out. He would delay picking up time-sensitive legal mail. This was, I believe, his entire motivation in life. He had been in the BOP for twenty years and was trained by some of the laziest, most worthless, and successful BOP operatives around.

My first legal call was with a group of people who were no longer my lawyers, who hadn't been my lawyers for several months, and who had no business calling me. They had let my unit manager believe that they were my legal team and that no other lawyers should be allowed to get calls, thus preventing my legitimate legal team from getting a hold of me for over a month. I still harbor a resentment about this situation deep within my core. I ended up having to file three different forms declaring that the old team was not involved in my case and that I did not want to speak with them. I should have only had to file one form, but my unit manager lived up to his reputation and lost the first two. He had a refined system of ensuring that what you needed to get done would never get done.

While waiting to have legal calls with my actual lawyers, I had absolutely no one to speak with except for the orderlies, and P. Stone was my favorite of the orderlies, mostly because we could talk about things I was into. He had radical Black politics and had been in ADX with revolutionary Black elders. We read the same books, which may sound artificial, but having *anything* in common is a big thing, and I loved our conversations. Also, his story was wild and he loved talking about it, which was a fun way to pass some time.

P. Stone had been in the ADX for ten years. He had stabbed someone so badly that their arm had to be amputated. Also, this wasn't his first stabbing. Or his second. Or his third. He was a very active guy. After the de-arming, he was sent to the federal death row in Terre Haute, Indiana. He wasn't on death row, but they placed him there until they figured out what they wanted to do with him. This is called "holdover status," and it can last six to twelve months. I did six months of holdover status at the USP Leavenworth SHU after the assault by Lieutenant Wilcox.

There was a white fellow on our range from Boston who had also been on death row in Terre Haute. He murdered his mom and then drove across state lines to murder another person and get rid of the bodies. When his death sentence was reduced to life in prison, he was sent to USP Lee, where I completed my ADX referral. Within a month, he had strangled his cellie, who he'd thought was in for child molestation. Was it true? Doesn't really matter, because he felt it was true.

Now he and P. Stone were on the same range and could share death row tales. Fascinating perspectives.

P. Stone would roam the range while out on orderly duty, passing messages and notes and just enjoying being out of his cell. During my first week, Boston sent me a magazine via P. Stone. Inside the magazine (which was some weird metal music magazine that I didn't enjoy in the slightest and wished I hadn't received) was a kite. The handwriting on this kite was almost indecipherable, but the gist was, "Hey, if you need anything, don't be afraid to ask." I sent a kite back saying, "Thanks, yada yada," and forgot all about it. A week later, I got another kite, this one from another white guy who was from Indiana and had attacked a lieutenant. This little note asked me why I had disrespected Boston, that it was rude and dangerous to not respond when someone was reaching out to you. Immediately, I got on the door and screamed at the top of my lungs, "I did! It's in the damn magazine!" A minute later, a muted voice from the end of the hallway yelled back, "Got it, sorry!" Disrespect is a very big thing in prison, and even in a place like ADX, where you will have no physical contact with other people, you don't want to be known as a disrespectful jerk. You want your time to be as easy as possible. You want it smooth and drama free. Sometimes to maintain that smoothness you need to placate overbearing creeps.

Indiana later sent me a kite asking to go out to rec to have a conversation with him. He wanted to get to know me better, he said. This is always a trap. People will try to get to know you so that they can then use that intel against you with other prisoners or guards, stacking up social cred along the way. I sent word back saying, "No thanks," I was good. I watched early-morning soccer and didn't want to stand in a freezing-cold concrete box to yell back and forth for all the world to hear. He wasn't happy about this, but because I had come straight out and said no and given a legit reason, he couldn't say anything about it. Social dynamics were very weird in there.

So were some of the people. There are fragile egos among some of the men. Everyone wants to feel like they are interesting and important, that they know something everyone else doesn't. That their opinion really needs to be heard. A lot of this is because they don't have anything else. The prison has taken everything, and now they've got to build themselves up by being aggressive or needy. I wasn't a stranger to this attitude from others, but I didn't have any problems dealing with it. I'm not a social person, and I don't want to discuss politics through the bathroom sink drain. So just like in any other prison, I learned to delicately set my boundaries. To let them know that from one to three o'clock I had either *First Things First* or soccer on and I wouldn't be talking. That I wasn't going out to rec while we were in the concrete boxes. That I would always bet on the Chiefs to win.

After a week or so, things settled into a normality. I knew who the abnormally rancid guards were, I knew who the most obnoxious people on the range were, I knew which administrators might be helpful and which deserved a stomp on the neck. Having my routine, having my mail, and having the TV and some canteen allowed me to feel significantly more comfortable. I had everything I needed or could ask for (until visits were eventually allowed).

Being in possession of the prison basics can do a lot for your mental health. I could fully dive into my routine, dive into my books and letters, and start being a convict. Now I was ready to just do my goddamn little bit of time and make my way out of there. I didn't want to learn about how hard ADX could be; I didn't want to buck or get into unnecessary hardships like I had at other institutions. I would talk with the orderly twice a week, watch my little shows, do my little workouts, eat my almost edible food, complain about the letters being suspiciously delayed, and just go about my day. That is what you are supposed to do; that is what you are taught. Do your time. Just do your time and get home.

III CHAPTER 5

How Did I Get Here?

I have been in administrative detention and faced brutal and systematic mental, spiritual, and psychological cruelty. I never believed that such an unusual punishment would be extended up until today, where I have lived in a prison cell for the last ten years that is the size of a closet.
—Mahmud Abouhalima, convicted for involvement in the 1993 World Trade Center bombing and held under SAMs (Special Administrative Measures) in H-Unit at ADX since 2005; he is still there as of 2025

Note: Trigger warning for sexual assault and violence.

In early August 2023, I was pulled from my cell in the USP Lee SHU and taken to a holding cell. After an hour of waiting in confusion, seven guards descended on the holding cell. The lieutenant leading this gang of fascists walked to the door and told me to strip. He wanted me to strip off all my clothing. I knew what was coming, but I couldn't do anything about it. I asked him what was going on, why I needed to take off my clothing. There was nothing I had done that should have led to this. The lieutenant told me they had found a torn bedsheet on my floor, that I was being given a write-up for "destroying government property."

This was a wicked lie from a wicked person. Me and my cellie both made sure not to have a goddamn thing in our cell. We had seen what these cowards did to every prisoner they had it in for. We didn't want that attention or that retribution. The pigs knew they weren't being truthful. They knew that I knew that they were lying, and that it didn't matter. I hated this. I hated this powerlessness. They didn't have morals; they didn't have decency. The truth was worthless in these moments. All that mattered was that they had control, and if you resisted, they would unleash hell on you.

I said, "No. No, I'm not doing it. Fuck you." The lieutenant held a pair of see-through, stretchy, orange lace bikini bottoms. This is called being "put on papers." They give you one paper shirt, one paper sheet, and one pair of bikini bottoms. They remove every other item from your cell, including stamps and any books you might have. You'll do this for five to ten days, depending on how much humiliation they want you to feel.

The six other guards started unstrapping their weapons. They all had large pepper-spray containers and steel batons. Each one had gloves with metal plates over the knuckles. I didn't have any weapons or any way to block the spray or the assault I was about to suffer. The lieutenant told me again to get naked or they were coming in. I'd seen it before. I'd seen these same burly Virginia officers rip out men's beards, stomp on testicles, slam faces into walls and onto the concrete floor. This was their game. They wanted you to refuse so they could come in and get their jollies gang-beating a defenseless person.

I had to turn off my brain. Everything inside me was saying to spit in their faces and go to war. Your ego will get you hurt inside prison. I stripped, handed them all my clothes, and stood there naked with as much defiance as I could muster. The men were jeering, making childlike comments about my body. "This is what antifa looks like?"

It wasn't over. "All right, n****r lover, turn around, squat, and cough."

I turned around and went through the procedure. I turned my back to them, squatted down, and coughed—the basic humiliations every prisoner is forced to go through. It wasn't enough, though, not for these vile perverts.

"Straighten your legs, bend at the waist, spread 'em!"

"Yeah, n****r, let's see your insides!"

Their glares were as abusive as their words and actions. They wanted me to spread my anus, to use my hands to open my body.

And I did. I was sweating in terror. I had seen what they are capable of. They have stuck those batons inside people. They have destroyed men's bodies and minds. They are rapists in every sense of the word. I needed to do whatever it took to prevent this from going to a realm I couldn't return from. I had a family desperate for me to make it home.

They needed Eric, the real Eric. But I hated myself. I hated myself for being so pathetic and weak and having to forfeit power *again*! How could this abuse keep happening? But I felt so much empathy for myself too. I didn't deserve this. No one deserves this. I was not the issue here; their unrelenting sickness was the problem. I spoke to my soul, pleading with it to not self-condemn. I tried to show myself the same empathy I would for anyone else in this unthinkable situation: *I am so sorry. I am so sorry this is happening to you. You don't deserve this. They are doing this to you, and you are not culpable. You did not do this to yourself. I am so sorry. It will be over soon. Please hang in there, don't lose it, don't give them what they want. It will be over soon. I am so sorry. Please, Eric, you didn't do this. This is why we fight. This is what we fight against. I love you, Eric, you are not bad, you are not trash. You do not deserve this.*

Your choices are to either swallow your rage and humiliation and get it over with, or to resist, in which case it gets much, much worse. I convinced my brain to be safe and do what they asked. It is degrading, it is sexual assault, and it is an everyday occurrence in the BOP. They crave humiliation; it's opium in their veins.

"All right, let's see that n****r-loving dick, f****t!"

I turned around and they told me to lift my scrotum, to see if I was hiding weapons underneath my body. We all know this is an impossibility, but they get off on the charade. I did what they asked, trying desperately to suppress the shame and disassociate enough to remove my brain from the situation. It didn't work.

"Pull it out."

"What? What the fuck did you just ask me?"

"Pull it as far as you can, n****r!"

I grabbed my penis, pulled it as far away from my body as possible, and pleaded with my ears to block out their verbal grenades. I begged my tears to stay hidden. *Not now, friends, we will sob later. Not now.* They wanted to dehumanize me, and I could not give them that power.

"Lift it up! To the right! Pull it farther!"

I stared at the wall. *Please don't cry, Eric. Please don't sob. They can steal this moment, but don't give them everything.* I had already been hospitalized by guards, I had already been tortured by guards, and I didn't want to put myself or my family through more of the same. It can always get worse, and they want you to discover the depths of their violence. They were calling me every homophobic and racist term you can imagine. Tobacco spit dripped from their mouths while they laughed in unison at my physical defeat. A group of Confederate Civil War reenactors. Their great-grandfathers and heroes were defeated in the 1860s, so this was their revenge. They had absolutely no power or control over their actual lives, so this was their time to shine. Their time to feel like badasses, like real men.

How the fuck did this happen? How did I end up in a holding cell being forced to open my rectum for seven gawking Confederates?

In September 2014, on the anniversary of 9/11, in solidarity with the uprising in Ferguson, Missouri, I threw multiple Molotov cocktails at the office of Congressman Emanuel Cleaver. I am an anarchist, and solidarity is a part of my ethics. Seeing the murder of eighteen-year-old Michael Brown by the racist police was too much for me. I had spent the last fifteen years trying to live *my* anarchism. At times this was mutual aid built around supporting vulnerable communities, and at other times it was fighting back against our attackers.

The police were, and are, the enemy of the people. Every single congressperson is a creator and benefactor of the laws the police enforce. There cannot be a separation between the two, and at that time I felt that direct action was the only appropriate response. I wasn't seeing the mass protests that were later held globally after the murder of George Floyd. I didn't feel the rage radiating from my peers, but I felt it. I couldn't shake it.

My actions escalated and escalated until they culminated in the congressional office attack. Things started with a visit to Ferguson that should have been much longer but ended up having a lasting impact. When I returned home to KC, I started casual street actions against the banks that financed the KC and Ferguson police. Small actions against KCPD vehicles and property. Things that felt good but weren't bringing any attention to the issue of police brutality or solidarity with the people of Ferguson. I wanted those people to know that I saw their rage, that it was valid, and I wanted to stand with them in tangible ways.

My anarchism to that point was centered on insurrectionism and a bit of individualism/illegalism. I wanted to wage a thousand mini revolutions. The goal was to live outside of capitalism and government interference. It wasn't my job to force my revolution on others, but I wanted to exist in a way that I could feel proud of. I wanted to be able to look at myself in the mirror and not spit at the fraud looking back at me. It was an immature anarchism, and it was rooted in class solidarity and anger. Anger that I wasn't doing enough, that I wasn't achieving the goals from my thousand revolutions. If I was losing my own revolution, there was no expectation that the world would join me.

When the pigs killed young Michael Brown, it shook me. He was a child. The media portrayed him as a monster, doubling down on all the hateful copaganda. It was sickening, and to do nothing felt like a betrayal of my entire being. He deserved more, his family deserved more, and his community deserved more. When I threw those two Molotovs, it wasn't out of pure anger, it was out of sadness. I was so sad that there would be no community justice for Michael Brown's family, and I knew that the vilification of both him and Ferguson as a whole would continue to let the police off the hook. And it tore my soul to pieces. My heart was so clear that serious action was necessary and was the only appropriate action.

I lasted a week while on the run after the act. It was stunning how stupidly some of the people who knew me acted. I was getting text messages multiple times a day with people laughing about it, sending me links to articles, all the dumbass things you want to avoid, everything you aren't supposed to do to keep yourself or your comrades safe. There was absolutely zero security culture. People in my affinity group were posting on my Facebook, bragging about it in my voice. That I lasted even a week is a minor miracle.

When, five days later, the police rolled up on me with guns drawn, I knew it was over. Mentally, I was prepared for whatever was going to happen. I had hardly taken any precautions to avoid being caught. At that point, I didn't care. There was a battle to be had, and whether it was in the free world or in prison, it didn't matter to me. I had no idea how bad prison could be. I had been to county jails, and I knew how to fight. I knew what I was doing, I thought. I had no clue what I was doing.

One and a half years later, I pleaded guilty and received 120 months in federal prison. My first plea offer was sixty years, then forty-five years, before finally settling on a realistic plea of ten years. The prosecution always presents wild numbers early in cases to ensure you'll be scared into eventually taking a plea. I had absolutely no idea how sickening prison could get. I expected a revolutionary university. I expected class solidarity and anti-police unity. I thought I could exist outside of the racism and horridness of it all. I was naive, cocky, and stupid. You have to exist in the world you inhabit, and thinking I wouldn't have to was me asking to get hurt.

"You Like Pulling It, Don't You, N****r!"

Now I was here. Taking a pitstop at USP Lee on the way to ADX. I was sliding on the bikini bottoms and fantasizing about the guards' horrible, painful deaths, yet also understanding at this stage in my prison life that you cannot fight every battle. At some point, you have to fight to win, and you will not win against seven armed men. None of this was shocking to me, not in the slightest. My entire bid up to that point had been marked with racist cops, sexual assault, violence, and repression. I'd been called a race traitor for seven straight years by hundreds of different cops. I had seen things become exponentially worse once Trump came to power, but it had always been bad. I'd been put through "diesel therapy" (constant prison transportation), I'd been hospitalized, I'd been through all of this, over and over, on repeat.

"F****t on the range! Look at the f*g!" The officers were yelling on the range to make sure other inmates could come to their doors and gawk or shout along with the pigs. Only a few bootlickers play along with this. Most people understand what is happening and know that it could be them next. One slip-up with guards like these and then you're the one set up and placed in bikini bottoms, forced to expose and manipulate your body. Forced to endure a different type of prison rape. I was grateful it hadn't gone further. It can always go further. I would take their abuse and not give them an excuse to make me a victim. The only victory that matters in prison is getting out alive, and I would get this win.

III CHAPTER 6

Stolen Moments of Freedom

> Sitting in a small box in a walking distance of eight feet, this little hole becomes my world, my dining room, reading and writing area, sleeping, walking, urinating, and defecating. I am virtually living in a bathroom, and this concept has never left my mind in ten years.
> —Mahmud Abouhalima

> It is 09:33 and I look out my window on a sunny day. Not a cloud. Guess what? The huge security lights are on again!
> —Richard McNair, former ADX prisoner

About six months into my stay on C-Unit, a miraculous event occurred. Sometime between nine and ten at night, all the power in the entire facility turned off. The TVs, the cell lights, the hallway lights, and, most importantly, the outside spotlights. (Maybe something to keep in mind that the most secure prison in the United States can be shut down with a flip of the switch.)

Every cell on the lower ranges inside ADX has the same view. All the cells face in the same direction. We all see a wall and a spotlight, and that's it. The spotlight is a ghoulish bastard that haunts the cells. They are called floodlights because they flood our cells with blinding light. Prisoners use paper or extra clothing to block the light, but it's always there. It is your most annoying cellmate, preventing you from ever enjoying the night sky.

On this night of miracles, we were finally freed of the spotlights and reintroduced to the natural world, the real world, the free world. Without all the blinding technology, we were able to see countless stars, stars I had longed for and missed deeply. With the two or three inches of sky that was visible above the wall, the universe revealed itself to all of us. The universe didn't care that we were the worst of the worst. It didn't care what you had done or who you had hurt or what title the government used to justify your torture. Its only goal was to reunite with us, to give us a brief chance to feel whole again.

The lights only stayed off for about twenty or thirty minutes. When I heard the electricity start to buzz again, I felt tears come to my eyes. The celebration of life was coming to an end. It felt like I had been robbed, like I had been given the most wonderful gift and then had it snatched away. My spirit longed for the stars, the trees, the bugs, the fresh air. Having had the brief thirty-minute respite from our normal prison view, it felt especially cruel and painful when normal procedure returned and the blinding bastards came back to ruin everyone's night.

I could count on one hand the times in the last five years that I had seen stars. They were a myth. Sometimes you wondered if you'd ever seen them at all, or if maybe you were imagining them. Experiencing the night sky was a gift I longed for desperately. To share the sky with my family, the same sky they were seeing, the same burning balls of gas and fire. Some of the men I spoke with had not seen the night sky in decades. It was an illusion that no longer existed, was no longer even a possibility. Stars were for TV shows or movies, fiction used for dramatic effect on the big screen. They weren't for us. Stars were for free people. Stars were out of our reach.

Being this removed from the natural world affects your psyche. It hurts in a deep way. There are times you no longer feel real. Real people walk on trails or smell flowers. Real people take in vitamin D and take baths or go swimming. Real people can pet their cats or hear dogs barking. This is an aspect of psychological torture that the BOP has mastered. ADX didn't come out of nowhere; the practice of this hellhole is an amalgamation of decades of research and development on how to break people. They studied how to hurt people most efficiently, which tactics worked the most effectively.

When you are removed from the real world, you begin to only exist in *their* world. The prison takes on the role of home instead of a human rights violation. You no longer look to the outside world for inspiration or hope; instead, you turn completely inward. This empowers the BOP, because they know exactly how to handle prisoners. They desire nothing more than the institutionalization of the convict population.

I'll know I am free

when I am stretching out

feeling the wind on my face

doing all sorts of weird yoga poses

and I when I turn my head

to the left or the right

I wont see

a single god damn fence

with a single god damn piece

of razor wire that a worker in some factory

helped make to keep other people

locked in cages

Stop making the fucking tools

to oppress other people

Remember what color shirt you're wearing

I'll know I'm free

when the color of shirt someone is wearing

will mean less to me

than the color of their shoe laces

A poem Eric wrote while locked inside.

It is when you seek more than the walls of your mind that the admins have the biggest problem. It is the prisoners who thrive on tearing down the prison, instead of being an aspect of it, that cause the most headaches for our captors. One of the tools they use to promote the institutionalization of the most troublesome prisoners is removing us completely from the real world, isolating our brains from the things that provide the most stimulation.

You will not feel the summer breeze and be reminded of going to ball games with your pals. You will not hear children laughing and be reminded of those who are longing for you to return home. Instead, you will hear electronic doors, the sound of chains, the sounds of unwell people screaming and banging on their walls. You will smell only recycled air and sometimes another human's feces, but never the smell of your favorite treat in the oven. They want you to forget any of those things existed. You will not feel your partner's hand when visiting, because they want you to forget the promises you made, the letters waiting for your response. This isn't an accident. It's calculated. You are forced into a situation where you must rely on them for everything. They become your guide, your father, your mother, your provider. You don't want to make them mad, because then they will "punish" you. This is a tactic, and too often this tactic works.

When you have forgotten the beauty of freedom, you fall easily into the patterns they desire. Kuwasi Balagoon tells us that "freedom is a habit." You have to actively work on your mental freedom. You have to constantly reinforce in your daily life that they are not the providers, that they are not just "doing their jobs," that they are not "good cops." Since they succeed so well in removing the outside world, you have to find hope in other ways. This is why I created a system that worked for me.

Five-Star Days

While in the SHU for the previous four and a half years, I learned what many before had already gathered: If you don't provide meaning to your day, no one else will. The cops will not care if you are depressed and miserable. They will not be bothered in any way or try to cheer you up if they see you are having a hard time. They want to see you fold; they want to know that the punishments they implement actually work.

Those who survive the SHU and ADX with their hearts intact all have their own methods, whether it be a militant workout routine, cleaning routine, reading, or whatever works for them. I wanted something more than just a workout and cleaning routine. I needed my day to have more value than how shiny my toilet was. I didn't want happiness on their terms; I needed it on my terms.

The ADX is a deeply psychologically horrendous experience. The food is indescribably bad, the cells are rancid, and the staff are all devils and deserve any horrible things that happen to them. If you want joy, you must seek it out. You must dig within yourself and find whatever motivates you and cling to it. Hold it close to your chest and never let them get a sniff of it, because as soon as they do, they will try to spoil it (much like the milk you get for breakfast). This is a gift to yourself.

Mine started with finding every tiny little thing and magnifying it. Giving the little things massive importance tricked my brain that I was having really good days instead of nothing but horrifically bad days. I would add up everything I hoped to happen at the start of the day: The guards won't bother me; I will get mail; food will be tolerable; I will get a workout done; I will get toilet paper. Then at the end of the day I would go over *everything* that could be interpreted as positive: I cleaned the floor; my neighbors took a nap so there was some quiet time on the range; the rapping on the range was better than usual; the guards didn't shake down my cage; I got to see a couple of bugs; I remembered some song lyrics; my headache wasn't too bad; the shower went well; I'm still alive; I still have family; I am loved.

Going over these things helped immensely with my mental health. I had been feeling the rage build in me over the injustice of being held in lockdown for so many years. I was tired of it, and I was angry. With that anger comes stupid decisions that would only hurt me and my family. I needed to completely adjust how I handled my situation, and this method was the first step. I started feeling so much better regarding my day-to-day life. I felt totally in control of my emotions, which is a huge victory. No longer submitting to their emotional manipulation or bullying was a huge victory. These bastards thrive on being able to control us and be our puppet masters. They know exactly what will get a reaction, and they know exactly what will cause someone to lose control. They get off on being able to trigger violent reactions and get under people's skin. They used to play me like a fiddle. They would intentionally disrespect my wife, my food, my politics, and I would play into it exactly how they hoped. When you react, it allows them to punish you. They can laugh at you, and they can feel big knowing that they ruined your day. I would no longer be their ventriloquist dummy. I stole that sick joy away from my captors. They would have to get their jollies somewhere else.

At ADX, I updated my system. I started a star system. This almost certainly sounds ridiculous, but it helped me in a huge way. I got to decide not only what the best day possible would be for me but also what I could tolerate while still having a good day. Five-star days were very rare, but when they lined up it was the greatest feeling. Five-star days had to meet specific standards, including:

1. Either Manchester United or the Kansas City Chiefs played, were on TV, and *won*.
2. I had to have some sort of contact with Rochelle. Either a call (as of the last two months inside the prison I had two monthly calls), a visit, or up-to-date letters.
3. Good mail day. Cool books, neat magazines, letters from friends, anything that could lift me up out of that dungeon.
4. No problems with staff.
5. Edible food.

I think I only had two or three five-star days, but they were amazing, and I felt so alive afterward. I was finding ways to snatch joy from the jaws of misery, being able to reflect on all the blessings I had received that day. Intentional, constructive thinking was often the only positive thing I had all day, and a lot of times that was enough.

One-star days were a little more common. Everything had to go badly, with all the annoying or brutal aspects happening in the same day. The main thing, though, was that there were no zero-star days. Every day had something beautiful in it, some sort of joy to be found if I only looked hard enough. Some days it was harder than others, but I always found something. My toilet worked and didn't overflow. The shower worked. Even if the food was horrible, it was still food, and I was capable of eating it. I had an outdate, I had my health, and I had my family. I would not go to bed without going over every remotely positive thing, ensuring I went to bed with a grateful heart and looking forward to whatever the next day had in store. Another day is never guaranteed, so finding the light in each and every one was a must. Life is sacred. Finding joy is honoring the sacredness and gratefulness of getting to experience life.

This wasn't just a cute way to pass the time and be all fake bubbly happy. This was an effort to save my life. I had seen so many people fall into a cycle of despair, rage, and sorrow. The consequences of forfeiting control of your psyche are dire and not to be taken lightly. At that point, the prison not only gets to control your body and your living situation, they also get to control your thoughts. They get to fester inside your brain and rot your spirit. I've seen people lose all the joy in their lives and begin obsessing over every infraction. They couldn't find a single good thing in their lives, and having to exist within that suffering is painful and hard. Sometimes it's too hard. I didn't want to have that be my life. Maybe if I had been there for fifteen years or knew I would never see the free world again, I would have viewed my situation differently. As it was, I refused to give them more of me. They don't get everything.

Segregation can suck the life right out of you. I had family who wanted me home, and they were fighting for me to return as "me," not a nightmarish, destroyed version of me. I had supporters doing everything possible to make sure I could see the light at the end of the tunnel. I owed it to myself and my family and comrades to come out of prison better than I had gone in, in spite of the BOP. The BOP intentionally did everything they could to destroy me and keep me in that hell longer. So many people in ADX lost their minds, hurt themselves, or took their own lives. I don't blame those people; I don't judge them in any way. But I couldn't let that be me, and thankfully I had enough people pulling for me that I was able to stay afloat and never sink into those depths of sorrow.

CHAPTER 7

Who's in Here? A Breakdown of Demographics

> Though I know that I want to live and have always been a survivor, I have often wished for death. I know, though, that I don't want to die. What I want is a life in prison that I can fill with some meaning.
> —Thomas Silverstein, confined for over thirty years in isolation, nine of which were spent in ADX

When you hear about prisoners at ADX, what you mostly hear about are the infamous people—huge cartel bosses or those who participated in well-publicized "terrorist" activities. What you don't hear about are the other 350 prisoners within those walls, silenced by double doors and whatever restrictions the Bureau has slapped on them. Their cases didn't make world news, or maybe even local news. They didn't have publicity following them into the dungeon. These men were already within the federal hell when they were slotted into the dungeon. They earned it. One way or another, they earned their way here. They were quietly and painfully dispatched through the Bureau's referral process, then hidden away without any notice. No one protested to ensure their safety and mental health. There were no international campaigns for these men's well-being or humane treatment. They faced prison on their own and faced down ADX on their own. I am always fascinated to find out the reasons for referrals and the type of people who are placed inside. What does the BOP consider the worst of the worst? Every type of prisoner group or sect on a normal yard will still be present at ADX. The only difference is that those inside ADX are the most extreme versions of those groups.

Sex Offenders

Sex offenders are very much present within the federal Bureau of Prisons. You would be stunned at the number of men out there who would do these things. There are so many within the Bureau that they had to designate specific yards as sex offender yards. These yards contain other prisoners as well but are filled to the brim with sex offenders. Their large presence on these yards is what keeps them safe. In prison, except at lower custody levels or on those specific yards, sex offenders are not safe.

If you have touched children, or if you have downloaded, sold, or *made* pictures or videos of children, you will have a very hard time inside prison. The safest place for these creeps is within designated SOMP (Sex Offender Management Program) yards. These yards exist to allow offenders to have a safe place to do their programming, which is supposed to cure them of their "sexual illness."

Sometimes, though, the Bureau doesn't even half care about them and sends them to normal active yards. This puts the offenders in a delicate situation. If they attempt to walk those yards and are discovered, they will be in trouble. Best-case scenario, they will be badly beaten. At worst, they will take a Life Flight out of the prison. I have seen it go both ways.

At the penitentiaries, they will be killed, or as close to it as possible. You will not make it out of a penitentiary safely if you have a sex charge of any type. Not a single race or gang within the BOP will tolerate these charges. There is no safety on these yards. There is no negotiating, no buying safety, no explaining your situation. As soon as someone finds out your charges or even suspects that you are a sex offender, your life is on the line. It doesn't even have to be your most recent charges. It can be something from twenty or thirty years ago. It doesn't matter. Someone will gain their stripes or status within the walls by smashing your head to a pulp. In the penitentiaries it is extra dangerous, because the officers will often tell folks about any sex offenders of their specific race transferring to the prison. The convicts will know everything about you before your boots even hit the ground. Then their boots will hit your skull.

At FCIs (Federal Correctional Institutions), the medium-security prisons, offenders will still have an exceptionally bad time, but the chance of it ending in murder is much less (though not totally absent). There is a distinct difference in the level of violence between an FCI and a USP. What isn't different is that if you are found out, you will be severely hurt. Sex offenders essentially have two options once they arrive at a prison, and they both suck. The first is to attempt to walk the yard and try to fool people. This is difficult, because prisoners who are new to a yard are required to prove what got them placed inside prison. The burden is on you to prove that you are not a rat, that you did not cooperate, that you did not snitch, and that you do not have a sex crime.

All yards and regions are different, but usually you will have approximately fifteen to thirty days to get your paperwork into the prison. Your paperwork can include your docket sheet or your Judgment and Commitment (a court form that shows what you were charged with and what your sentence is), anything that unequivocally proves your charges aren't unacceptable. Sometimes offenders will try to delay this, saying they can't get the paperwork in for whatever reason. No one is fooled by this charade. In those cases, the offender will either get fucked off the yard (attacked) or someone inside will have their own family or friends research the offender's case—and *then* they will get fucked off the yard. Either way, the outcome is often the same.

The other option on the table for sex offenders is to immediately go into protective custody. The term *protective custody* makes it sound safe, comforting, like a place to receive help and care. But going PC is anything but safe or protective, and the process is humiliating and degrading for anyone involved. The guards and administration hate the offenders almost as badly as the prisoners do. They are never safe. Being PC and at the mercy of the guards is a dangerous situation. They can place someone in your cell who will certainly attack you. They can place you with someone who is just waiting to smash someone. They will air all your business out onto the range for everyone to hear, thus ensuring that when you transfer, everyone will know your story, and that can follow you to the next institution.

When prisoners arrive at a new yard, they will sit in R&D and go through a classification process of sorts. You will talk with psych, your unit managers, medical, and SIS (Special Investigative Services). SIS are the only people who can place you in protective custody. They will sit you down to conduct an interview and ask, "Is there any reason you can't walk this yard?" These pukes know without a doubt that the offender cannot in any world walk the yard, but they make them say it. SIS knows with absolute certainty that if the offender sets foot on that yard they will be decimated. SIS knows this because they are usually the ones passing on the information to prisoners on the yard. Once the

Abdulrahman El Bahnasawy (right), a Canadian entrapped by the FBI as a child. He was placed into a dangerous USP without medication and was later transferred to ADX. See his story and how to support him at bringabdulhome.ca.

offender directly asks for PC and explains why they aren't safe, SIS will place them in the SHU. If the offender is lucky, SIS will place them in a cell with another offender or someone else who is seeking PC. If they are unlucky, SIS will place them with a normal person from the yard and the offender will get destroyed.

Over the next couple of weeks, a member of the administration will come to the SHU and ask the offender if they will leave the SHU and come to the yard. When the offender says "hell no," they will be given a disciplinary write-up for "refusing to program." The admin will then take away good time, phone privileges, and canteen privileges. This will happen three times over the next six months. The offender will have to suffer through the SHU and staff abuse for a minimum of six months before they are transferred to another yard, although this is not guaranteed to be an actual safe yard for them.

The sex offenders at ADX usually had chosen a different approach. When they were placed at a new yard, instead of seeking PC, they went out onto the yard and attacked the first person they saw. This would repeat at every transport center, every yard. They would get transferred over and over, and every time they would attack the first person they saw. After *years* of an offender doing this, eventually the BOP has no choice. The offender has shown themselves to be unmanageable and unwilling to participate in their facade and to have taken their safety in their own hands.

I hear there are a handful of offenders at ADX, but I only saw one. He was an older, small man. He had long hair and was treated exactly how you would expect an offender to be treated: disrespected in every way possible, including by staff. He did everything he could to convince people he wasn't an offender, swearing he was Muslim and had a terrorism case, talking about all the fighting write-ups he had. But word spread and everyone knew what he was about. This offender refused to leave his cell and refused to program. He refused to pay restitution and refused to talk with psych. Because of this, the administrators took away the one thing the offender had left: his TV. He was placed on TV restriction until he participated in some sort of programming.

This is how the administrators try to bully people into behaving how they want. If they think you are just hiding out there or think you are trying to not ever step down, they will make your life even more difficult than it already is. They will give you disciplinary write-ups, once again accusing you of not programming, they will take away good time, they will threaten you, they will try to bribe you. Once everything else has failed, they will resort to the final ace up their sleeve: snatching your TV. This offender didn't seem bothered in the slightest. He had been conditioned to doing hard time and would not bow to their pressure.

What he would do, however, is piss off everyone on the range. All the men trying to do their own time would now have to deal with this clown. He would be loud. He would bang on the stainless steel shower all throughout the night, trying to keep people awake and furious. He would wait until two folks were trying to yell to each other and then start yelling over them, shaking his inside cell bars and kicking the walls as hard as he could. Anything to make others feel the same indignity and anger that he was feeling. There were hundreds of people in that institution who would have paid money to murder him. Prison is not a fun place for sex offenders, and ADX is no different.

Dropouts
KC had been in ADX as long as my entire bid—ten years of total isolation. He was a bigger guy with a Nazi insignia tattooed on his bald head. He was in ADX after "accidentally" murdering someone at USP Coleman II. They had gotten into a fight in the SHU rec cage after guards placed two people together that had no business being in the same area. They do this shit on purpose. They wanted someone hurt, and they got it.

KC had severe trauma from being placed in these situations so many times. He wasn't going to wait and be a victim. There is nothing gained by waiting for someone to act first. You get punished by the cops whether it's self-defense or sadistic barbarity. It's all the same. By waiting, you place your life on the line, and that's nothing to be proud of or feel morally superior about.

KC had savagely stomped this other man out, and then, as the fight was ending, he elbowed the man's liver and it ruptured. Unlucky as fuck, for both of them. A casual fight had turned into an unintentional murder.

That's the thing in prison that many may not realize: Fights are not taken lightly, because every fight could end someone's life. You never know what's going to happen, how far someone is going to take it. You must understand that every person you come in contact with may become someone you go to war with. This reality creates a constant tension within the walls, and you're forced to always be "on." You must also be willing to accept that if things get to that physical level, you *must* be willing to go as far as needed to either win or stop the fight. There is no time to worry about the disciplinary process. No amount of lost good time or canteen privileges is worth your life.

KC eventually signed a plea deal. He was sentenced to an additional eight years due to the unintentional nature of the killing and was

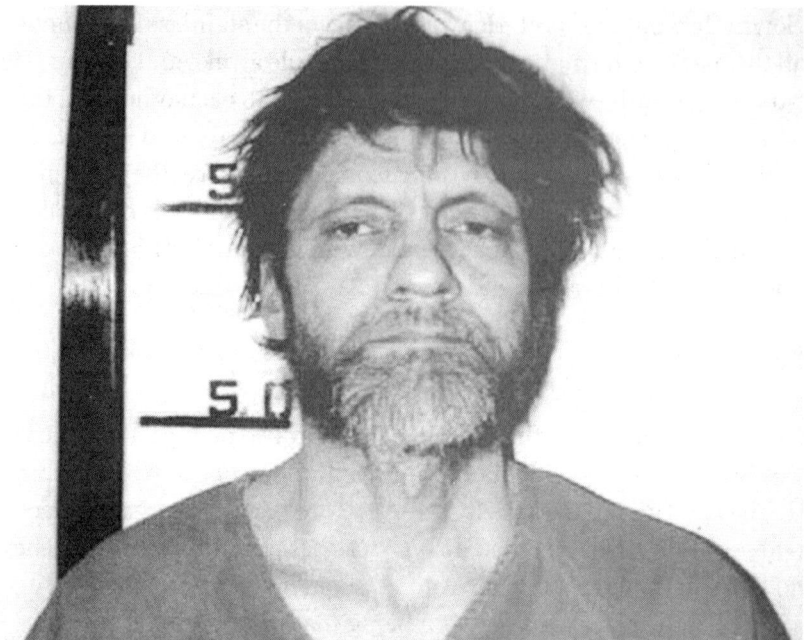

Ted Kaczynski, known as the Unabomber, did over twenty years at ADX. He passed away at FMC Butner in 2023.

immediately placed in ADX. KC had issues. He had anger issues, family issues, mental health issues, and physical health issues. ADX is not the safest place for a person like this, a person who needed social interaction but also had so much trauma that he never felt safe, anywhere. The isolation caused his paranoia to expand, and all the paranoia caused his rowdy behavior to extend, thus exposing the main tactic of the ADX: the use of torture to cause symptoms, and the presence of the symptoms to justify the existence of ADX. The perfect scheme.

Getting out was his only priority at this point. When you are desperate to get out of ADX, the only options you have are attempting to program your way out (sometimes doing enough psychology programs convinces the administration you no longer need to be there) or filing lawsuits and keeping your fingers crossed. Without access to a lawyer, he chose programming. He took every psych program available, every rec program, every ACE (Adult Continuing Education) program. His entire schedule was working out, prison programming, and making art. These programs were mostly over the TV, watching some nonsense and then filling out a packet about it. Some were held in the gym, where prisoners would be shackled inside little caged phone booths to listen to psych and participate in group discussions.

KC was a gang dropout, which is one of the absolute worst things you can be inside prison. No matter the custody level, dropouts are given zero respect, and at some custody levels it can and will get you killed. People view gang dropouts the same way they view sex offenders: the lowest of the low, bottom-of-the-barrel trash. They are viewed as cowards, backstabbers, snitches, people you cannot trust. Dropouts dedicated their life to the gang, put in all the work to join and become official members, and then sold the gang out, whether out of fear or to avoid getting in trouble themselves.

Sometimes gang members would get deep into debt due to drugs or gambling and not have anywhere near the funds to pay it back. The gangs would try to work with them, allowing them to pay a bit at a time. But if you don't have ten dollars, then fifty dollars may as well be a million. To avoid the consequences of not paying their debts and making the gang look bad—the consequences are always violence, sometimes murder but always severe—they "check in" (seek protective custody to get off the yard and be placed in the SHU). To check in, you go to staff, usually a lieutenant or an SIS officer, and tell them you are no longer safe on the yard. They will then place you in the SHU. This is the same process as with the sex offenders, and you are viewed the same way.

After two or three days in the SHU, an SIS officer will come and pull you out of the cell to have a normal, casual conversation between two men just trying to figure things out. This will usually occur after hours so that everyone on the range will know exactly why they are pulling you out. SIS never works after 5 p.m., so it is well known that if they are there to speak with you, it can only mean one thing. This is a social isolation tactic. By isolating you from the other men in the SHU, you'll start to feel that you have no other option, and therefore you'll be more likely to help those who you think can keep you safe, foolishly believing the cops care what happens to you. They cannot, do not want to, and will not keep you safe. They do not give a shit about you. Never forget: These people are not your friends or your helpers. As soon as you are not an asset, you are back to the trash heap.

The SIS officer will interview you because they want information. They will tell you straight up, "Give us what we can use or get your ass back in that SHU for the next six months." You have an option now as a check-in. You either give these pigs information about the people you considered "brothers"—information that could get them more time inside prison, get them transferred, get them sent to ADX—or you sit in the SHU for the next six bleak months, knowing that either way you are dead to your previous friends. Everyone from every race and organization will see you as no good. They may be social with you in the SHU, but you are now a pariah.

Checking in is serious business in the BOP. Once you do it, you cannot undo it. You will never be able to safely walk an active yard again. You cannot redeem yourself from it, and you cannot justify it to anyone. No one cares. You have given yourself the mark of Cain. No one likes someone who ran to the cops for safety. No one likes a snitch. For some folks, this can cause a serious existential crisis.

There were gang members who had crafted their entire self on being a "stand-up guy," on being "solid." They'd spent years or decades bemoaning check-ins. They attacked them, talked shit about them, bashed them. Now they *were* them. I've seen people dive off the deep end mentally or change personalities entirely from how they once were. Maybe the "gang self" was just a mask for them, used to create an identity they felt safe within. Or maybe the "check-in self" was the mask, used to shield its wearer from the shame and disgrace of their new status.

If the check-in ends up giving the SIS department information that it finds valuable and officially drops out of the gang, they are then transferred to a PC yard. These are select yards set up around the country by the Bureau specifically for official snitches, sex offenders, ex-cops, and official gang dropouts. These exist at every custody level, but I will focus on the USP dropout yards, which are USP Coleman II, USP Tucson, and USP Terre Haute. These are the strangest yards in the entire BOP. They are still violent, and they are still run by prison politics, but they ignore the fact that every one of the inhabitants willingly decided they needed the protection of the prison system. The prisoners will still push steel if necessary. People still get murdered and stabbed on dropout yards just like they do on active yards. Derek Chauvin was stabbed at a nonactive yard. Doctor and serial sexual abuser Larry Nassar was stabbed to hell on a PC yard. Even Elizabeth Smart's kidnapper was butchered while at a nonactive yard. Just because the BOP prisoner population no longer takes you seriously doesn't mean

Ramzi Yousef, plotter of the 1993 World Trade Center bombing and cousin of Khalid Sheikh Mohammed. He was one of the first people placed on SAMs (Special Administrative Measures) and has done over twenty years on those restrictions.

you stop seeing yourself that way. You don't just shed five, ten, twenty years of prison skin. These are switches you can't turn off.

KC was at a PC yard, USP Coleman II, in Florida. A disproportionate amount of people I met in ADX either came from dropout yards or had decided to drop out to secure their exit out of ADX. This is a sneaky, vicious move that the ADX admins pull. It is strategic and intentional. The admins place high-level gang or cartel leaders in ADX for five, ten, fifteen years with absolutely no chance of getting out. The admins tell them every week that there is no chance of ever being released, that they had better get comfortable. They do this for years, intentionally, to mentally take hold over the gang member or leader.

After several years, however, SIS will begin to drop hints. They will come by the door and ask, "You still wanting to get out?" Or little cryptic messages like, "Hey, there's something in the pipeline about you..." The SIS or admins will drop these little nuggets for months, or even a year. Then the day will finally come, and the admins will pull the gang member out of their cell and take them to an interview room. This will be a very solemn occasion. Everyone involved will have their serious faces on. All business. The scum will have their folders and files in front of them to make it seem like they've been really digging into the issue. The SIS lieutenant will be there, the captain will be there, and different SIS officers will be there.

The prisoner will be seated, and the scum will begin their routine, all well rehearsed:

"We've been talking about you a lot."

"We all feel that you deserve to get out of here."

"You've been respectful and well behaved. We know you don't belong here anymore."

"Regional is still worried. You know it's Regional that makes the calls on these sorts of things."

Then they will edge toward the issue at hand: "You know, we've reached out to Regional. We've told them what we think, and they have some concerns, but I think we can work around that. They want to make sure that you've fallen back, that you aren't going to be running things anymore. They need some assurances."

The prisoner will try to interject: "I told you I was falling back! I wasn't active, I've been here ten years and haven't spoken to anyone!"

SIS is ready for this, as they've played this game countless times. "I know, I know," they'll say. "We know that, but Regional has been fooled before, ya know. If you fuck up again, it's on them for letting you out, so they have to play it safe. We spoke with them, though, and they think there is a solution. They say that if you commit to not being active, if you give us some info, if you show Regional that you're serious, they will work with you."

Maybe the prisoner is prepared for this and has wanted to drop out this entire time. Maybe they really thought they could talk SIS into letting them out without giving up any information. Either way, this is the moment of truth: Give them information, potentially getting your friends and comrades arrested or put in ADX themselves, or stay put in your isolated hell. Walk out of here without a shred of dignity, or stay put and keep your head held high.

I don't know how many prisoners tell the SIS to get fucked. But many take the offer and make the unthinkable choice. Many of these prisoners have either attacked or ordered attacks on other dropouts. Then they shake the devil's hand. Some of these flips are stunning. Hitmen who have literally killed for their gang and gotten life sentences from within prison for their gang who are now willing to flip. Every act of commitment is now deemed meaningless.

There is a deep, smutty aspect to all of this. Gangs almost exclusively recruit young men. They are looking for people who will put in good work, make them money, be loyal, and truly buy into the program. These young men usually do not have stable families or home lives. Their community is their family. Gangs make people feel like they've found a community, a place to be accepted and valued. Feelings these young men have most likely never felt before in their lives.

The problem with all of this is that what you believe when you are eighteen or twenty years old may not always be what you believe when you are forty or fifty, but the consequences stick with you. The validation you felt from your brothers when you were a young man may have completely vanished after decades of seeing their ugliness and hypocrisy, seeing how the love and support you thought you'd gained is performative at best, a complete lie at worst.

I can't imagine being a twenty-year-old kid, killing for my gang and then landing in ADX all by myself for the next decade. You have the respect of the men around you, but they aren't putting money on your books. Maybe you get a little support from outside representatives for a while, but that will fade. Your time is your time, and only you can face those years inside.

This doesn't happen to everyone. Many stay solid, and most will stay in ADX or some sort of twenty-four-hour lockdown for decades. They will be prison legends. People will talk about them with awe, until they don't. I was in federal prison for eight years before I was placed in ADX. I was at every custody level and in different regions of the country. I still hadn't heard about most of the people I met. They were strangers, once legends but now forgotten soldiers.

This is the potential sadness of gang life: the realization that it might have been all for nothing. How are you supposed to survive when the entire meaning of your life has vaporized?

I don't give a shit about dropouts, honestly. I don't necessarily bother about gangs, and therefore when people want to leave them, it doesn't really concern me. What bothers me is the hypocrisy. Some of these people have hurt so many others who made similar choices, all because the BOP holds people hostage and doesn't give gang members a feasible way out of the gangs besides potentially putting their lives on the line by debriefing. The BOP does nothing to allow gang members to safely leave their organizations. This is on purpose. They want you isolated. They want you to have to rely on the Bureau for safety. This is setting people up to get killed.

I may not hate dropouts, but I do hate the snitching involved. There is no other way to describe what debriefing is. It is someone making a conscious decision to give information to the police, to the BOP, to help them identify and target other prisoners. Prison life is hard as shit on its own without one of the people you trust telling all your secrets to the investigators. I do not believe in ever assisting your enemies. The prison guards and SIS are 100 percent our enemy inside. They are legalized gang members who swear an oath to uphold the law and then break the law in every way possible. They are everything disgusting and wrong with the world.

They will abuse your family members to get information; they will plant evidence to scare you into giving information; they will set you up to be hurt or killed. They will convince you that your friends are going to kill you, and then after you have given them information, they will threaten to tell those same friends if you ever decide to quit working with SIS. They are so coercive, and it is sickening. The lies, the manipulation, the carrot dangling from the snitch stick, all the while knowing they will not care if a knife lands in your throat. Their job is to collect information to use against you, not to keep you safe. If you expect them to do anything noble, you are playing with your life.

And it isn't just gang members who drop out. Solid prisoners can throw away their active status and drop out as well. They do this for the same reasons gang members would: debts, drugs, "dry snitching" (not actually going to the authorities but saying things that could get someone in trouble out loud, such as on the phone, knowing that cops will listen), and just not wanting to be on active yards. It happens. People who have been on active yards too long have grown tired of all the drama and all the violence. Prison is exhausting. It is exhausting to constantly be on your toes and have to keep your guard up. Some people just want to make it home without losing more good time and risking getting new charges. They have seen what happens when you have to put in work over and over, and they are done with it.

You can't just leave a yard, though. The prison staff must benefit from your stepping down. They will only allow you to leave the yard and go to a safer location if you give them what they want. These men are expected to do the same thing the gang members are: snitch on people. Someone on the yard will face serious consequences because of your actions. When you drop out as a non-gang member, you face the same risk to your life that gang members who've dropped out face. You can never walk a non-PC yard again. If anyone ever finds out that you dropped off a yard, they will attack you.

There is nothing that will keep you safe; there will be no compassion. And maybe there shouldn't be. If you decide to turn your back on the prison class and work with our enemies, you are making a well-informed decision. Every person in prison knows that if you get caught working with the authorities, there will be violence inflicted on you. You shouldn't need threats to know that you should not work with the government. This should be common sense. The people who lock your cages are not your friends. They will never do what's best for you. So many lives could be saved if the BOP allowed people to step down without snitching. So much violence could be prevented. But they don't want that. They want you to snitch, your life be damned.

KC had seen enough of that life. He was tired. He wanted to breathe fresh air again, and he wanted to feel at ease on a yard. He didn't want to live in fear, and he didn't want to constantly be in fight-or-flight mode. He made a choice and seemed fine with it. It doesn't define him, and maybe it shouldn't. He is out of ADX now. He is on a dropout yard and hopefully doing as well as possible. Despite dropping out, he is still a human. He is a human with a family, and he deserves to return to them. He should have never had to play by the admins' rules to gain his safety. He should never have had to put his life on the line to stay away from violence.

This is what they want. They do not care if you die. They are not our friends.

Elders

The BOP is filled with aging and elderly prisoners, and at times it felt like ADX was an old folks' home. These are also some of the most vulnerable people within ADX, both having poor health as well as having been forgotten by the public or their families. I was stunned by the amount of older prisoners I saw or came across. Most of these elders had been at the ADX for decades and would stay there until their health gave out on them.

I met men who had been in prison since the 1970s, others who had been in isolation since the 1980s. Men you've never heard of who have

> March 10, 1999
>
> Cop-out to Mr. Irvin, Unit Manager
>
> from Theodore John Kaczynski 04475-046
>
> Some time ago I sent you a cop-out about the fact that the officers who sit outside my window to watch me at night often have their radios turned up loud. After that there was a great improvement. However, the problem has recently begun to come back. For example, on the night of March 8-9 the officer had his radio turned up loud.
>
> Ramzi Yousef also has complained to me about being awakened at night by the officer's radio.
>
> *Your concern is again noted and we will take steps to address the noise level.*
>
> *[signature] 3/15/99*

Ted Kaczynski's "cop-out" (written complaint) to an ADX officer, which references Ramzi. The administration's response is at the bottom of the page.

been in twenty-four-hour lockdowns for thirty to forty years. Many of the most infamous gang leaders from the wars of the 1980s were still there. Folks who had used violence against staff fifteen or twenty years ago, powerful "gang" leaders, infamous prisoners. Larry Hoover was still there and in his eighties, until his federal sentence was commuted in 2025. Jeff Fort is still there. I am disgusted at both the fear and vengeance the Bureau holds for certain men. The BOP never forgets, so those who did serious harm decades ago will never be forgiven or forgotten. And those who are admired and respected scare the BOP to hell and will never be allowed out to be with their comrades or families.

One of the sickest things about the ADX is the reluctance to let elders step down out of the prison. Even when they are seriously ill, the administrators will not place them at a medical facility until they are terminally ill. You must be close to death for them to consider letting you go to a facility built for medical care (not *good* health care, but still, it's something). The Bureau will often justify keeping elders at ADX by claiming that after thirty or forty years the prisoners won't be able to adapt to normal yard life, thus using their own torturous behavior to justify continued torturous behavior.

Some people argue that the "worst of the worst" deserve to spend their entire lives in the ADX, that they are getting exactly what is just. I find that argument to be disingenuous. Those bitter, hating bastards have never met someone who has spent twenty or thirty years in serious isolation, nor given thought to the human experiences that these men have had to miss out on. Can they remember what a hug feels like? What a kiss is like? What it feels like to be held (without the threat of violent gang assault by staff)? Do they remember what holding hands is like, what sitting next to another person is like? Simple things like sharing the TV, drinking out of the same glass, opening a window, closing a door?

Every day these prisoners must strive to give life some sort of meaning, to *feel* something within a world that is built to exhaust all feelings. ADX is a slow termination of the human spirit, and if you are okay with that, then I think you are disgusting. There is nothing decent, nothing "just" about twenty years of complete and total isolation, complete and total discomfort. Twenty years of sleeping on rock-hard mattresses, eating garbage food, never having any control of their own lives. When we say men belong in isolation for years upon years, we are saying they no longer deserve to feel human. I can't think of a more inhumane thing to say.

Gang Members

Full disclosure: Before coming to prison, I was not some expert about gangs, especially not prison gangs. I'm still not. I knew gang members and lived in neighborhoods with gangs, but that wasn't my life. I didn't exist within that world. I had no idea how they were connected, their views, the *why* in their existence. You hear about gangs like the Brand (Aryan Brotherhood), but what you hear isn't describing their reality, it's describing the media's interpretation of them.

What I learned in prison is that many gang leaders see themselves as revolutionaries, not as the common street gangs the media would have you believe. They see themselves as uniters of their communities, protectors from outside forces (including other gangs). Many of them seek financial independence in their communities, and because they are not accepted into the folds of capitalism, they exist outside of it. When you aren't invited to the cool kids' party, you can always throw your own. For their communities and comrades, they are the party. They can be disgustingly cruel or honorably noble. They can be the most respectful people you've ever met or the most scheming, bastardly creeps you can imagine. They can be both controlling and at the same time the best practitioners of mutual aid within prison (they'd never call it that, though). Everyone contains dualities, and trying to pigeonhole an entire group of people as "thugs" or whatever veiled racist or classist term the media wants to use is lazy and intellectually dishonest.

As you go up in custody levels, the type of gang members you meet are very different. At lower custody levels, you are more likely to meet either (1) dropouts, those who quit the gang and are now trying to hide away from them to avoid violent retribution, or (2) low-level members, people on the fringes with no real power or abilities. This isn't always the case, but in my brief experiences this is what I saw. In medium custody levels, you can begin to meet people with more rank. They will know how to run a "car." (A car is the group that you roll with in prison. It can be as broad as just "whites" or as detailed as "Kansas City, Missouri, whites." Your race is your car. Your gang is your car.) They know how to handle themselves with respect and how to demand respect from their people.

You will meet people who have such high standards of living that they could be military commanders. They will ensure their people are awake at a certain time, ready for war the moment the cell doors are open. Their people will have their cells cleaned to a compulsive degree and will practice fitness at a high level every single day. These leaders also handle discipline very seriously. If a member of their group acts out of line or disrespects someone else in an unprovoked way, these serious members will take care of it (meaning bash them up). They run a tight ship. This isn't true for every gang of every race, but I am talking about the big ones, the most powerful groups. I am generalizing, but these people are not to be taken lightly.

At the penitentiary level, you will begin meeting people who either run the gangs currently or hold high levels of power. You meet the killers, the shot callers, the hitmen, those who are willing to put in serious work. You meet people who can pull off things you have never even imagined (smuggling and controlling the officers, mostly). There are people who will kill someone for the most minor infraction, who will not question an order to take someone's life. There are extremely serious people at this level, and they aren't to be dismissed. They will be respected. Everyone at this level demands respect at all costs, and they will either get it or take it.

There are also members who will demand respect but not have a clue how to give it. They will operate through brute force only. Gangs need infantry just like the military does. In a world where those who are capable of the most violence gain the most respect, you are likely to meet people who will make your skin crawl. They will do whatever is asked of them, good or bad. They can produce high levels of violence. That is critical to remember at this level of captivity. You need to assume every single person you meet can and will do serious damage. When you assume everyone you meet may potentially try to kill you, you are much more likely to behave properly.

You can't just join a gang. It isn't a simple process for even the smallest of gangs. There is a feeling-out process where they watch you and observe how you move to see if you show the qualities they are looking for. What type of routine do you have, how do you handle yourself, what do you value the most? Then there is an initiation period. They won't call it this, but that's what it is. You will be asked to do certain tasks and to stay in constant good standing. You'll need to keep your room looking sharp, your hygiene on point, your fitness game tight. You'll need to show that you don't go into debt or, if you do, that you pay your debts off. In some gangs you'll be required to share part of your hustled earnings. In all of them you'll be required to show that you aren't afraid of "action" (violence). You will have to "put in work" (jump someone or worse), and you may be required to do this countless times, over years, to show how serious you are. You may be required to stab someone. You may be recruited by gangs because they've seen how willingly violent you already are.

They want people who will hold the line. They want people who are in high standing on the yard and who garner respect for their actions. Not all gangs are like this, as I said. With some, whatever gang you were in on the streets is what gang you are in within prison. For some, if you were in a neighborhood street gang, you may fall under the control of a larger prison gang, especially for Mexican gangs like the Sureños or Norteños. That doesn't always mean you will have to kill for those gangs, but it does mean you will be expected to walk the line and hold yourself accordingly.

It is mind-boggling to think of how many gangs there are inside. Just off the top of my head, without doing any research, breaking them down into race, there are:

- White gangs: Brand (Aryan Brotherhood, or AB); state ABs (very different from the Brand—for example, the Missouri Aryan Brotherhood is not the same as or recognized by the Brand); ABT (Aryan Brotherhood Texas); AC (Aryan Circle); WAR (White Aryan Resistance); ARM (Aryan Resistance Movement); SAC (Soldiers of Aryan Culture); SAW (Soldiers of Aryan World); Valhalla Bound Skins; Aryan Nation (Tennessee state gang); Aryan Warriors (Nevada state gang); Dirty White Boys; and Nazi Low Riders.
- Black gangs: Gangster Disciples (GDs, the largest); Bloods (and countless different Blood sects); Crips (and countless Crip sects, all depending on what region of the country you are from); Vice Lords; Black Guerrilla Family (BGF); and the Black P. Stone Nation. The Blood sects are often unified under the Blood Nation. There are also the alliances for all the Chicago gangs. Then there are the DC Blacks. I'm not sure if the DC group counts as an actual gang, but they have a huge population within the federal prison system. Washington, DC, does not have a state prison, so every person sent to prison in that area is sent to the BOP. There are thousands of them, and they stick together and will not be told how to behave or what to do.
- Mexican/Hispanic gangs: Mexican Mafia; Sureños (the soldiers for the Mexican Mafia); Nuestra Familia; Norteños (the soldiers

for Nuestra Familia); Ñetas (Puerto Rican); Texas Mexican Mafia; Texas Syndicate; and countless other street gangs that all fall under one of the larger groups or MS-13. (MS doesn't seem to fall under any gang, at least not anymore. In 2022, in the most audacious move I saw during my ten years inside, multiple MS members attacked members of the Mexican Mafia and Sureños. This resulted in the entire federal prison system being placed on lockdown, entirely shaking up the BOP.) Because of the size of the big groups, they absorb all the street gangs under their wing based on what city or region they are from. If you are from a Los Angeles street gang, you will most likely fall under the Sureños. If you are from a Denver street gang affiliated with the number 13, you will most likely fall under the Sureños. If you are from a Denver northern-affiliated gang, you could fall under the Norteños. This is all generalized. Every yard can have variations, but generally this is the structure.

There are so many tangled webs within these gangs, and sometimes it was hard for me to keep track of what was going on between them—who was rivals with who, who had what treaty with what group. They are also almost always kept on separate yards. Within the Bureau, there are yards known as West Coast yards and others known as Texas yards. West Coast yards will have California gangs that are affiliated with each other, such as the Mexican Mafia, Sureños, the Brand, NLR, Dirty White Boys, and other gangs that aren't involved in West Coast politics, such as SAC. Texas yards have the Nuestra, Norteños, ABT, AC, Texas Syndicate, and Texas Mexican Mafia, as well as other gangs that aren't beefing with anyone.

The rivalries between the gangs are not simple. Some of them go back decades and revolve around mountains of bodies and unspeakable violence and betrayals. It isn't a basic thing of "claiming their turf." It runs so much deeper than that. There is truly generational trauma involved with these historic organizations. There are peace treaties that have been broken with savage murder. There are backstabbings and betrayals that most free-world people could never imagine. Decades of trust being broken. Decades of watching the people you love get hurt or get set up or get removed from this earth, which builds a hatred that is difficult to describe. In the federal system, there is no talking between some of these gangs. It is "go on sight," no talking, no negotiating. If there are weapons around when they meet, they will be used. This isn't new or secret information. As soon as you land on a yard, you will know what type of yard it is and where you align.

The prison administrators are terrified of these men. The admins understand that at the drop of a dime the leaders could shut down every single prison in the nation (as seen with the MS-13 lockdown). If more people had taken Dr. Mutulu Shakur up on his Thug Life code, the Bureau would lose all control. These are the leaders of thousands of men, and they take this life goddamn seriously. The tragedy, of course, is that too often there is absolutely no unity against the administration, at least not in any lasting way. The prison system needs separation and division to control the prisoner population, and it is easy to use the gangs to enforce this. When humans who are powerless in every aspect of their lives are given just a sniff of power or control, it can be addictive and hard to say no to.

The gangs, if they chose, could call work strikes that would immediately shut down the prisons. The leaders could call on all BOP prisoners to lie down and resist acts of violence, and it would work (for a while at least). They could organize for the better, to force better conditions for all the prisoners. But that would get in the way of their business, their hustles, their one feeling of control. Those who do wield that influence, men with righteous hearts and power, always end up buried. ADX is where they bury any chance of unity or resistance.

What makes ADX's gang population so unique is its amalgamation of leaders and founders. The concentration of big-name gang members is almost unbelievable. Scattered throughout every range you will find groups of people who at any other facility would run the yard and demand the respect of everyone around them. Some of the people I met were so infamous there were documentaries made about them. Some of them I had heard legendary tales about ever since my first day inside. Most of them were so respectful and humble it was almost surreal, yet others were egotistical psychopaths and every word I heard from them was terrifying. They flaunted their victories and brutalities, and in a way that's understandable. If you were spending your entire life in prison, if your entire identity was built around prison, then your ability to survive and thrive within prison would be something to be proud of.

Anyone who can control the situation around them while inside is winning completely. They have mastered the environment they occupy.

It isn't institutionalization for everyone; to some it is just surviving within a brutal world that you didn't create, that you are forced to live in and may never leave. It is their eternity. It is ingrained in every molecule of their being. I don't really justify or condemn anything they have done or will do. I am not their judge, and how they live is their business. I am not the morality police.

Interesting Leaders I Met

C: C is a high-ranking general or counsel member of the Nuestra Familia. He was born into the gang life and has been in California state prison and then ADX since the late 1970s. He has seen everything and met everyone. He has participated in riots and assassinations. He has kept his people safe, and he has been a leader and an inspiration for his people. C was one of the first people ever placed at Pelican Bay. He was placed there with essentially all the real-deal leadership of every California-based gang. He would not debrief (give the cops intel), so he was kept in the SHU there for approximately ten years. The repression at Pelican Bay was the predecessor for ADX: twenty-four-hour lockdown, single cells, and the occasional gladiator fight. (A gladiator fight is where guards intentionally place rival gangs in common areas to provoke bloody battles. The guards bet on these battles and often use live ammunition to break them up. Our lives, routinely sacrificed and diminished all for the guards' amusement.)

It was at Pelican Bay that C, along with several other high-ranking Nuestra members, was federally indicted on a RICO conspiracy. They were accused of ordering murders, attacks, and money-making operations from within the prison. C and the others were found guilty and sentenced to life inside the BOP. Once found guilty, they were all placed directly in the ADX. C is a very big name inside prison. He is old school and as serious as it gets. C did fifteen years in ADX and was in his seventies when I was there. He had been on the ranges with all the big names: Ted K., Terry Nichols, and even the largest prison celebrity, Thomas Silverstein. C knew everyone and had a story about them all. He told me that Ted Kaczynski was considered a weird guy.

By the time I met C, he was on his second ADX bid. He had been out for less than six months at USP McCreary before he was accused of murdering someone on the yard. C, a person with multiple life sentences, a person who has committed himself to his cause that strongly, is not worried about *more* life sentences. He will never leave ADX. Even if he is found not guilty, he will be stuck in that hell for being too influential, for having too much power. He is one of the many elders within those walls. Seventy-year-old hips and knees were not built to be surrounded by steel and concrete.

With all of that, he told really great stories. He had an amazing memory that was bursting to be shared with anyone who would listen. Most prisoners don't want to hear someone else's prison history. Having a listener clearly made him happy, and that felt nice. There aren't many people alive who don't deserve at least a little kindness throughout their day. Even if it is just an open ear for a moment, it's something. He was respectful in every sense of the word, and that showed a lot about his character. I am nobody within the BOP, especially within ADX. But he never spoke down to me, and it was always positive when he was on the range. When he eventually passes away, there will be no stories about him on CNN, but it will be a huge event in the prison world.

Larry Hoover: Larry Hoover is the leader and maybe the founder of the Gangster Disciples, arguably the largest Black organization in prison, with thousands of members. Larry is revered: He is a legend among prisoners and is not in any way seen as a gang leader. I cannot speak for him, but my understanding from meeting many higher-up GDs is that Larry Hoover is a revolutionary community leader. He found a way to unify the city of Chicago and to bring people together in ways that didn't seem possible.

Larry isn't a saint regarding white capitalist views of society and what is considered acceptable. However, he is a CEO in an amazing way that bypasses legal capitalism, viewing it as racist and benefiting only one class of people. Larry created an organization that is unmatched in the gang world. He brought financial stability to countless people and provided a roadmap to success and leadership positions in a community where many people are overlooked or thrown away. He is an elder statesman that I have never heard a single soul—no matter their race or affiliation—say a bad word about.

When I spoke with Larry, I was almost in awe. You hear about someone for decades, and then you finally run into them in a place you never expected to experience. One thing I wasn't prepared for, stupidly, is that Larry is old. I don't know his exact age, but he is an elder who has been in captivity for fifty years. For fifty years he has had to eat prison food, sleep on a prison mattress, and deal with prison gang politics, riots, and brutal, cowardly guards. For fifty years he has navigated a world meant to break people and has not bent the knee once. But time stops for no one, and I was not expecting it. I had just watched a documentary featuring him the week prior; he was still young in that documentary, and that is how I viewed him.

Despite his age and half a century within prison walls, he was vibrant and upbeat. Our conversations were incredibly brief, and he had no idea who I was, only that his family had often spoken with my wife after visits. They would have conversations about how horrible the justice system is, how cruel this bastard of a prison is. There was another time when he was walking to medical, surrounded by more cops than was necessary, and I was able to give him the power fist. He shouted back, "Always!" He looked so small surrounded by that horde of pigs. But his age and health are not relevant to his status and power. Those badged bastards understood who they were surrounding; they understood that he may be the most powerful person in the prison system. Fifty years of captivity, countless years in constant isolation, and he wasn't hobbled one bit.

In May 2025, following a commutation of his federal sentence by President Trump, Larry Hoover was transferred out of ADX to a prison in Illinois to continue serving his two-hundred-year state sentence.

King Blood: On a random Thursday while living in K-A Unit (the pre-release unit), I was watching Court TV. This network is very popular in ADX, because often you end up seeing someone you either know, know of, or are neighbors with. It is the wildest sensation. On this Thursday, I watched a documentary about Luis Felipe, the founder of the Latin Kings in New York City. This man had immense love and respect from his community and was honored as a true leader.

About ten minutes into the documentary, I realized the young man they were talking about was King Blood, the elder I had just spoken with two days prior while he was heading to medical.

King Blood is infamous in ADX. He was in a state prison in New York when he was accused of ordering the murders of several people on the streets. When King Blood was convicted, something unprecedented occurred: The judge didn't just order him to life in prison, he ordered that King Blood must do forty-five years in solitary confinement with the harshest communication restrictions possible. This is unthinkable. I cannot recall a single other time a judge has ordered someone to ADX with court-ordered restrictions. It is typically the BOP or attorney general who makes these decisions, but for a federal judge to do it is wild. The courts ended up ruling that the attorney general is the only person who can order that sort of sentence, but until then the BOP was happy to oblige. They placed King Blood in ADX, and it is only in the last few years that he has been able to communicate with his family or any remaining friends.

Many people argue that he deserves what is happening to him, that he made choices and that there are consequences to those choices. Those people harp on the same dull tropes, like "Don't do the crime if you can't do the time." My problem with that ignorant blathering is that "the time" isn't a real thing, it's a concept that the cruelest people in our country have determined is justified. There have been countless Italian mob bosses, captains, and hitmen locked up in this country. Only a small handful have ever been placed in a supermax prison. And only one that I am aware of (Vinny Basciano) had to experience restrictions even close to those King Blood experienced. Are those men not as violent? Are they not as much a "danger to their communities"? If the law-and-order hypocrites are going to preach the "do the time" rhetoric, why doesn't it apply to all people who are a threat to the community (in their eyes)?

King Blood ended up doing twenty years of total restrictions. Twenty years during which he could only talk to his lawyers. He was also allowed to speak with blood-family members, but they either weren't alive or weren't always around. All the friends he had grown up with were now ghosts. All the people he had considered his family his entire life were now memories. Not only was he not allowed outside contact, he also wasn't allowed inside contact. Twenty years in ADX is vicious on its own; they don't need to pile more on top of it to add to your torture. But they gleefully do, and they did so with King Blood. Imagine being cut off from everyone you have ever loved and then not being allowed to develop new friendships or bonds, not being allowed to experience any emotional connections? What crime justifies that?

I think there is a clear difference in how the criminal legal system views leaders and members of Black and Brown organizations versus how they view leaders of white street organizations. I think leaders of Black and Brown organizations are seen as more of a threat, especially within prison, where they can educate and radicalize those around them. This scares the BOP deeply, and you see this fear in how they treat these elders. King Blood is an old man. He is small and quiet. He is currently in K-B Unit, the lifer unit, and he will probably be there until the day he dies or is transferred to a medical facility. People look at him and understand that he is someone who has suffered and been through more than was ever necessary.

Queer and Trans Prisoners
Being queer or trans in the federal prison system can be terribly dangerous. At the higher custody levels, being queer can be a death sentence. In the hypermasculine world of prison, being anything other than a macho cis-hetero man is seen as a sign of weakness. All "others" are looked at and spoken about with disgust. Some people I have met seem to spend every single moment of the day discussing how much they hate gay and trans people. It can become an obsession of theirs. Queer prisoners become the outlet for all the anger and powerlessness some prisoners have.

In the rare instances when queer prisoners are allowed to stay on a yard, it can be a horrible existence. They are often treated as property, kept as sex slaves, kept addicted to drugs, kept to be pimped out. They can be stolen, fought over, raped, beaten, traded, sold. It is as nightmarish as it sounds.

When Trump became president for a second term, he managed to make life even worse for queer and trans prisoners. Everything is magnified when the hatred comes from the top. Trump's hateful rhetoric seemed to fire up those who didn't need any further inspiration to be cruel. These prisoners needed someone to feel better than or feel stronger than. I cannot think of many other reasons for the incessant need to attack and belittle other prisoners.

Something I have seen on more than a few occasions is that those who cannot stop talking about queer prisoners are often projecting. They are practicing self-hate, trying to put the attention on anyone but themselves: *I can't be gay, look at how much I hate them!* It's sad, but it is a serious thing that can get people hurt. I have seen the loudest homophobes get drunk and admit to having gay sex or even try to pursue someone to engage in sex with. Sometimes that person will be attacked and taken off the yard. Other times they will get violent and force their victim to either unwillingly participate or face the knife.

I never met anyone who was openly gay or trans within the ADX. I know these individuals have been through that prison, I know they exist, but it wasn't something I ever encountered. There was a trans prisoner I heard of through lawsuits and word of mouth. They were once a Sureño and then became a prison rat. While being shuffled around the Bureau from yard to yard, they transitioned and came out as female. Around this same time, they filed *hundreds* of lawsuits against the Bureau. They called out what was an open policy within the federal system: that protective custody prisoners were often intentionally set up by guards and administrators to be hurt. This included people who proffered (snitched), people who checked in for their own safety, and especially those who identified as queer.

What they discussed was everyday knowledge to those inside. Of course the guards helped coordinate attacks on prisoners they did not like or those they found distasteful. Often guards will take on the biases of the prisoners they watch over. If the yard hates check-ins, so do the guards. If gay or trans prisoners are targets of fellow prisoners, they are also targets of the staff. This unity between certain prisoners and certain staff in coordinating attacks on vulnerable prisoners makes me nauseous, but it is a reality we need to deal with.

Guards would regularly let different prison reps or shot callers—those who have a lot of respect and leadership roles within the units or gangs—know who was being transferred into the prison. If the person was openly a snitch, gay, or known to have checked in from a previous institution, the prisoners knew about it. This inside information would be used to justify attacking the prisoner as soon as they walked onto the compound. Whitey Bulger, the infamous Boston gang leader and known FBI informant, was murdered at USP Hazelton within hours of his arrival there. The prisoners on that yard knew he was going to be there before Whitey himself knew. The guards let all the prisoners know what was going on, and they were ready. What happened to Whitey is totally justified within the realms of the prison universe, but taking info from staff should never be.

Queer prisoners are among the most vulnerable, because the guards are happy to display their hatred to get these men and women hurt. Guards will intentionally put a queer prisoner into a cell where they are clearly not safe. Guards will march queer prisoners down the SHU walkway, announcing to the entire SHU that a gay or trans prisoner is on the range, inciting jeers and catcalls along with serious threats. Guards watch as queer prisoners are beaten or raped, refusing to break it up, enjoying the spectacle of unprovoked violence.

The trans prisoner at ADX who filed these lawsuits was not rewarded for spilling the beans about prisoner abuse. Whistleblowing in the BOP is not a safe option. This prisoner was given SAMs (Special Administrative Measures; more on these in chapter 13) and placed in H-Unit. Instead of acknowledging or working on the real issues they were bringing up, the BOP silenced them completely. Now, not only could they not write articles and lawsuits habitually, but they couldn't write much of anything. They were on SAMs and in ADX for approximately one and a half to two years. Once the SAMs were stopped, they were transferred to USP Tucson, which is a protective custody yard. If the BOP had sent them there to begin with, instead of continuously putting them in situations to be killed, there would never have been any lawsuits. Just as Margaret Thatcher conceded once the IRA hunger strikes were over and ten men were dead, the BOP conceded once the lawsuits were over. They are treacherous.

ADX, much like any other federal prison, has both supportive and incredibly bigoted staff. The psychology department would do everything they could to protect the dignity and mental health of trans prisoners. I had through-the-door discussions with the head of psychology about the pathological obsession some of her colleagues seemed to have with trans people, and she agreed. There was absolutely no reason for it, and the bigotry had a disproportionate effect on trans prisoners because they were at the absolute mercy of these same guards. Prisoners had to rely on Dr. Oba, the same doctor who allowed KC and Shahid to almost die because he did not want to help them clean their surgical wounds. He was the one in control of distributing all gender-affirming care. If it is a war just to get gauze to clean up an infected wound, you can imagine how difficult it can be to get estrogen.

In his second term, Trump has made it a priority to attack trans prisoners. All over the BOP, these prisoners have had all medication and mental health care paused. There have been attempts to place trans women back in men's prisons and trans men back in women's prisons. This is not only an attack on their dignity and right to exist but also an attempt to get these people hurt. Trump wants to eradicate this deeply marginalized community, knowing that placing trans women in a men's prison can get them killed. Not hypothetically, but literally. I believe this is his intent. Removing medication trans folks have been on for years can cause unthinkable pain, yet he does not care. And the BOP does not care. They want trans people to suffer even worse than they want the cis prisoners to suffer. This is the agenda.

I cannot imagine what it is like to be a trans or gay prisoner at ADX. I cannot imagine the amount of verbal and psychological abuse they face every single day. I have heard how other prisoners and staff talk about them. I have felt the pain that comes with solitary. But that is not the same. It is not even close to the same. In other institutions, I saw how queer prisoners were treated, and it was horrible enough to make me weep. It is the worst schoolyard bullying you have ever seen, with the addition of deadly violence. In ADX, where staff is already empowered by the ability to harass prisoners behind double doors, the verbal abuse is diabolical.

To my trans friends and the trans community around the world and within the prison system, I see you. I see you and I see the abuse. You do not deserve it. You do not deserve to be abused and harassed and diminished. This should not be how you are forced to live, and it is not fair. I will speak out for you, and I will stand with you, but you will always deserve more. Your humanity should never be under attack, and I curse the BOP for every action that causes you any more unnecessary pain or suffering. Trans lives are sacred. You are loved.

CHAPTER 8

When the Fascists Hold the Keys: A Look at the Guards

> It's a struggle to simply reach out to one's family and friends from this slave plantation, Neo Nazi camp (ADX). These racist crackers that run ADX are so foul they tear up, if not all, most of my outgoing mail, so it's difficult for me to reach anyone, and these crackers also tear up my incoming mail and lie to justify rejecting most of my mail.
>
> —Wayne "Silk" Perry, ADX prisoner as of 2025

The guards at ADX see themselves as a militarized force. They are not interesting or important in any way. Many of them are ex-soldiers and enjoy treating the prisoners as enemy combatants. The level of extreme pettiness dished out by these officers is mind-boggling. They withhold mail and delay passing out food trays until the food—already the worst in the Bureau—is freezing cold. These officers will disrupt the prayer of Muslim prisoners, mock their faith, and ridicule their beliefs openly and without fear of consequence. There are no consequences because the administration agrees with everything the guards are doing.

There are different types of guards, and all of them are bastards. Some of the guards have been in the Bureau for twenty to thirty years. They pretend to be respectful. They call you "Mr. So-and-So" and say thank you when you do as they ask. They aren't as quick to resort to violence, but they have a long history of abuse to fall back on. No matter how respectful these guards pretend to be, they are not your friends. Never think that they will have your back or keep you safe. You are your only protector. These "respectful" old-school guards will kick your face in if given the opportunity. They will watch their coworkers stomp your groin, throw away your mail, trash your cell, and not bat an eye. They will never step in to do the right thing.

These creeps are also significantly more rigid. They see the prison as theirs and want things to run exactly according to their whims. There is no working with them. They are just as institutionalized as the prisoners, but in a different way. They have internalized all the ugliness of the prison industry. They are abusive and see themselves as gods and the prisoners as petty humans who must bend the knee and carry out their will. Some of these long-term guards seem bored with prison life. These tired guards will give you what you have coming, they will give you mail or recreation, but that's it. They will give you exactly what you are supposed to have and not a single thing else. They are prison constitutionalists. They see themselves as pure; they know the score.

Then there are the troops. The officers who wear the Punisher badges on their stab vests. The guards who wear Oakley shades while walking the halls. These guards can be ultrapathetic and ultraviolent. Say the wrong thing and these are the brutes who will slam you, spit on you, trip you, kick you, trash your cell, throw away your possessions. These are the guards filled with racist venom. If you search their social media accounts, you will see countless posts bashing Muslims, gays, African Americans, immigrants. They are prison Proud Boys. The guards meant to serve food and mail and handle prisoners instead spend all their time online ranting about how much they hate those inside.

When these guards work the visiting room, you are in trouble. One visiting officer covered in Nordic runes and white power symbols made visiting a nightmare. This wannabe Thor would have you brought down to the visiting room and then delay an hour or more before having your family brought up, leaving you and them to anxiously wait, not understanding what was happening. This guard once sat me and my wife in different booths. There are cameras in all the prisoner booths and all the visitor booths. This guard monitors all these cameras, and it is their sole discretion where prisoners are placed. He watched me and my wife sit in different booths for over thirty minutes. If she hadn't gotten up to use the bathroom and walked past my booth, I would not have seen her. Another time, he removed all the visitor chairs. The elderly mothers and fathers of prisoners had to stand until they got the courage to ask him for a chair. My mother, recently recovered from breast cancer, stood for over forty-five minutes. (Full disclosure: There were a few ultrakind visiting guards who went out

The ADX visiting room. All visits are noncontact. The phone on the right is used to call the visitor.

of their way to be kind and helpful to my family. These were few and far between, but they existed.)

There are many people like this, who go out of their way to make things more difficult. The men in ADX have no control over their lives. We do not get to decide when we eat, where we live, what we do, who we speak to, when we speak to them, when we go outside, and so forth. There are men working in ADX who take full advantage of this power dynamic. They do everything possible to make our days worse. They will prevent us from going to recreation, robbing us of the one measly hour a day we may get outside of our cells. They will do unnecessary room searches just to disrupt our days and our living spaces. They are the officers who have diarrhea of the mouth, bashing prisoners from the safety of the hall. Feeling macho and superior with two doors between them and the prisoner. These cowards will also suck up to certain prisoners. They will try to gain favor with big-name prisoners, feeling badass milking the status of the men behind the bars. They are pathetic.

Worse than these types of guards are the apathetic ones. These officers are robots, walking the halls, doing the bare minimum in every regard. They will be too lazy to bring the phone on the range, too lazy to do recreation time, too lazy to bring mail to the cells or call the mailroom to ask where it is. They will participate in abuse, standing straight-faced as other guards watch you get abused. They will never speak up, never step in. They do nothing. They are a waste of space. They are the officers watching Chauvin put his knee on all our throats. They will never call medical to assist someone in trouble. They will never call a lieutenant to solve an issue. They are nothingness personified.

Then there is the Special Investigative Services. SIS has too much power and will take every opportunity to abuse it. As mentioned earlier, they are the ones who will set up everyone who doesn't assist them. They have the power to move prisoners to different ranges, to place people around their enemies, to plant lies about prisoners in order to get them assaulted or killed. SIS controls all communication. They decide who you can send mail to, who you can receive mail from, and how long it will take to reach you. My mail would often take at least a month but regularly two to four months to reach me. SIS will do everything possible to disrupt our connections with the outside world.

A social media post by an ADX officer.

These men, with the most power in the prison to ruin our lives, are among the most bigoted in the prison industry. They post the most racist, horrendously vile propaganda on their Facebook pages. They mock those inside on a regular basis and then return to prison and pretend to be our helpers. They pretend they want the best for us, if only we help them. They promise to make our lives easier if only we provide them a little assistance. Then they return home and post about how we deserve to die. These men are trusted to monitor the communication of the same prisoners they see as human dirt.

No one checks them. No one in the administration cares. There will never be a consequence for an SIS officer who abuses prisoners. They will never have to answer for their crimes against those inside. Why would they? They act out the wishes of the BOP. They do all the horrible things those in charge want carried out. They are the ones who placed me on a mail ban for two and a half years. They are the ones who took away my phone calls for five and a half years. No lawsuit can affect them. No amount of grievance forms will affect them. They are unchecked monsters.

I will never understand what type of human would want to take this job. All the talk about it being the only work in town falls on deaf ears. These men and women take a paycheck to lock other humans in cages.

Ira Akens updated his status.
March 31, 2017

It was brought to my attention that I should be more careful how I represent the uniform that I wear. For the record I wear the uniform of the US Navy and of the Bureau of Prisons. I have always been a man of higher moral value respecting others and the law. I am charged with upholding the law of the land while in uniform. I was brought up this way by a loving family who taught me the value of honesty, standing up for those that cannot and having a solid moral foundation. The law is the law regardless of what I think about it! I uphold it faithfully though I disagree with some of it. I am a good sailor defending our country, obeying the orders of those appointed over me! I believe in order and the chain of command adhering to it regardless of personal feeling! I however have personal feelings that some find offensive. As a man, I am entitled to my moral value, thoughts and opinions with free speech of it!! I wear the uniform of our nations Navy, finest in the world because I believe in the concept penned down by our founding fathers! With that said I need to make something clear. I cannot under any circumstances acknowledge Islam as a religion, I rather view it as a Cult and security threat group!! Islam's treatment of women and of other religions is beyond horrible! Islam is nothing more than a sanctioned hate group protected by the ignorant and foolish! I say this because it is the truth and needs said even though some find it offensive. Does this make me a bad person or representative? No, it makes me a patriotic American!! Does any of this effect how I discharge my duties..... NO!!! I will discharge my duties in accordance with the law regardless of personal feeling!! Why, because that is how I was brought up and that is what's expected of me! Blessed be and God bless

22   10 Comments

👍 Like   💬 Comment   ➡ Share

View 3 more comments

Dan Clark Very well said!!!!!! To bad so many people in the US would think what you said is inappropriate, because you hit the bullseye!!!!!!
Like Reply 2y   2

Another post by the same officer, whose job it was to monitor and police Muslim prisoners.

They have no qualms cracking our heads open, disrespecting our families, sexually abusing our bodies. They are a gang, and a pathetic one at that. Nothing is more pathetic than seeing seven heavily armed and armored guards attacking a single prisoner trapped in their cell. Even the best of guards is a horrible person. They may treat you well, they may not antagonize you or file false write-ups against you, but they will for someone else, and they won't stop their coworkers from doing it to you.

All it takes is one guard to dislike you and your entire life and future can be ruined. The shots they write can keep you away from your family for years. They can fabricate any story and keep you in prison. They can get new federal charges pressed against you. They can prevent you from hearing the voices of your partner or children. There is no check on federal officers. When Lieutenant Wilcox attacked me in the closet, it was SIS who filed the report with the FBI. When the USP Lee guards sexually assaulted me, it was SIS who wrote me a disciplinary report for having an imaginary rope in my cell. They are vindictive; they are worthless.

I have a tattoo on my back that reads "Every Cop Is My Enemy." This tattoo isn't an accident. These officers have made it clear that they are the enemies of the prisoner class. They will ruin your life and then go home to their families without a care in the world. They will lie, scam, manipulate, and attack, and no one will lift a finger to stop them. I have seen guards strangle prisoners, beat them black and blue, set them up to be attacked, rob them of all communication with their family, and place them in outrageous situations—and these were just things that happened to me.

There are more than a million prisoners who face these subterranean urchins every day. We exist within their brutality because otherwise our worlds can be turned upside down. One wrong word or move and you can have an enemy who has complete control over every meaningful part of your life. They are the worst people the world has to offer, with no redeeming qualities. I do not know what has happened in their lives to lead them to this point. I do not know what abuses they might have faced or what joy they got from bullying. I don't know and I don't care. I care that they let T. Smith have his shoulder ripped out of its socket while four-pointed and didn't think to stop. I care about the officers who stomped Randy Platt's head so savagely that medical thought he might die.

This is my reality. I see them for what they are. Every single officer had a choice and decided it was in their best interests to take this job. To carry on this tradition of abuse. They all had a probationary period, saw what was happening, and still moved forward. There is no forgiveness for this sort of behavior. When we say All Cops Are Bastards, this is what we mean. Every single officer participates in and preserves a racist and horrific profession. They are not our friends.

CHAPTER 9

Support Saves Lives

> We know that the fight against control units or the punishment industry is not an attractive and glamorous one. To wage it and achieve a modicum of success is almost an impossible task. But such a reality should not discourage you and those of us in the gulags, who love freedom and justice, to continue struggling against control units. The moment might require more creativity and to look for ways to reach more people.
> —Oscar López Rivera, former Puerto Rican political prisoner who spent years at ADX; he was released from prison in 2017

In the radical and abolitionist movements, prison support is a necessity. Politicals face a unique type of repression, and if we aren't supported on the outside, we have no leverage on the inside. You cannot have a revolutionary movement without a robust prison support movement alongside it. They go hand in hand. If a movement abandons its fighters once they are put behind the walls, then that movement will fizzle out quickly.

During my bid, support for me came in waves. At times I felt like I couldn't be more supported. Thirty books a week, fifty letters a week, money coming in, feeling on top of the world. Other times I had to beg people for stamp money so I could respond to the few letters I was receiving. Amazingly, once the mail bans finally ended, there were still people who looked out for me. Honestly, still having any support at all after that stunned me. I had gone two years without social mail by the time I went to ADX and had my mail ban revoked. Thankfully, I didn't have to wait long for people to show up for me when I needed it most.

Supporting someone in a lockdown prison is a unique experience. I didn't need money for phone calls or email because I wasn't allowed to call or email people. I couldn't get messages out as easily as before because everything was so delayed and so heavily censored. Mail takes forever in prisons like this, and more than a couple times I would respond and the letter either never reached its target or I never got a response.

There were times I would get incredibly frustrated because it didn't seem like many folks understood what was actually happening. Kindhearted people would ask me if they could mail me stamps or food, ask me to look up their websites, ask if I could eat with my friends or what the yard was like. It really shocked me that so many people had no idea what ADX was or what the experience was like. That is part of what led me to write this book. I was never mad when this happened, but I definitely used it to help people learn about the brutality of the BOP and what they are capable of.

The most important aspect of my support was getting word out so that people understood my situation and could keep eyes on me. I was terrified of these pigs getting their revenge for Wilcox. It wasn't a hypothetical threat; I'd seen what they were capable of, and I didn't take it lightly at all. I needed my writings about the prison to get posted as quickly as possible, and I needed my team to spread the word and post as many things about ADX as they could find. I needed people to care. I was so afraid that people would get tired of hearing about all the over-the-top repression I was going through and just walk away from me. I always had that fear. I still have that fear, honestly. That I am not good enough, that I do not deserve support. I needed people to understand that I wasn't faking, that I wasn't just trying to get attention—that this was real and it was hurtful and dangerous. Imposter syndrome can show up anywhere, and I experienced it at a high level. I was terrified that because *so much* horror had happened, people would either stop believing it or stop caring. It is a scarcity mindset, where you feel you only deserve so much, or only have access to so much. That people will reach their limit with you.

This scared me every day of my imprisonment. It was compounded by the fact that many people on the outside do vanish. You will have great conversations and biweekly letters for a year or two and then all of a sudden you'll never hear from them again. This does something to your psyche. Being ghosted in the free world sucks badly, but being ghosted in prison is a nightmare. Did my pen pal die? Did I do something wrong? Were they tired of me like everyone else? When people are up front about their capabilities, it is so much better. When folks let you know, "Hey, I may not be able to keep writing," it helps a lot. It's not knowing that can kill you, along with the expectation that they will be there.

This fear started my first day inside. I expected people in Kansas City to rally behind me and show up, and I was severely disappointed. My closest friend, Dev, is the only person from KC who wrote to me and visited and did all they could to maintain our friendship and relationship. Other people would send word through Dev, but nothing consistent. This hurt badly. There were people who would claim they wrote me and their letters had vanished. Maybe? But more likely, it just never happened. Dev was in communication with Rochelle and my mom. Dev would send me books and magazines. They would send my family gifts and love notes on holidays. Dev spent countless dollars and hours making sure I felt loved and connected, and that is what I expected from my city as a whole. I had horrible security culture when I was free, because I didn't care about the consequences. Maybe that is why people initially didn't want to step into the support realm. But once you've been in for months and years, going through hell, you really expect the comrades in your backyard to at least write a couple of letters or come and visit. It's the expectation that gets you.

Almost all my support came from complete strangers. People who had never met me or spoken with me were sending me the kindest letters, books, and magazines. At one point M had four or five expensive magazine subscriptions for me, just because they knew I was suffering. Thankfully, Bloomington ABC did fundraisers. Denver ABC started a support team for me, and they came to my trial all the way in KC. I met Rochelle through Denver ABC. Unicorn Riot showed up at my first trial, which stunned me. Then they continued to show up through my entire bid, which stunned me even more! They are even working on a documentary about my life postrelease. They are unreal. It felt amazing making all these new friends. I felt seen and validated; I felt that I wasn't alone. Josh Davidson started writing to me before I was sent to ADX, and we became deep friends, which led to our book *Rattling the Cages* (as well as this one—Josh is amazing) and to a continued friendship to this day. Prison support can reap long-lasting fruit, and I've been prancing through the orchard ever since.

Every mail call when I didn't see a familiar name on an envelope would hurt badly. I've reconnected with a few of those KC friends, and we've had heart-to-heart discussions about what happened, about where they were when I needed them. It was fear. They were afraid the government would go after them if they showed up for me, which is exactly what the feds want people to think, so that they can kill off support through terror. (Thankfully, those friends and I have reconnected, and I feel close to them today.) My anarchist comrades, though, I never heard from. I still haven't heard from most of them. I hope they're still doing something, even if they vanished off the face of the earth when I needed them. No one owes you their time, however, and that includes supporters. I understand that I am not entitled to love or support or friendship, but I do wish I had been the recipient of them from my local radicals.

While at ADX, though, people did show up, and in massive ways. Thank the goddesses that people did care. It's the strangest thing in the world going from a two-year mail ban to receiving letters by the bundle. I never felt like I deserved it, and I was stunned when people wrote back over and over. Friends I thought I had lost during the mail bans returned in abundance, and it was so surreal. With all the scary happenings in my life and in the world, people still found time to write or type a letter. Each letter was a visit from a new or older friend. It touched my heart deeply. That was my strength and power, knowing that I wasn't alone. That even if they took my voice again and again, others would keep me in their hearts, and the prison couldn't touch that. Once every week or two, I would get a stack of mail from the prior two months. I would also get a stack of rejection letters of mail I wasn't allowed to receive. Rejection letters are forms from SIS stating why a letter was rejected and what specific rule it had broken. This was usually for an envelope that wasn't white or someone allegedly writing something that encouraged some sort of radical behavior. (Shockingly, people would send me zines or letters encouraging escapes or how to make weapons. These people did not seem to care about me as a person, or at the least had horrible situational awareness.) I would get my books and magazines. I was sorted, and I felt so goddamn loved it would make me emotional. I fucking love prisoner support.

What I didn't love seeing was how few of the men inside got any support whatsoever. They had either been forgotten, were being purposely ignored, or were never known about to begin with. Some of these men had been in here for a decade or more and hadn't gotten a piece of mail in years. The problem for them was that ADX worked. It worked in cutting them off from the free world, in burying them and any chance they had of developing relationships with those outside. I would write friends about folks who had been in this prison for ages, and my comrades would have no idea who I was talking about. But how would they? This broke my heart, because if my *abolitionist anarchist* comrades didn't have a clue who these people were, then what chance did others have?

Part of the support I began asking for was support for other prisoners. This is a common theme with politicals inside. I've never met a former political prisoner who didn't try to help as many people as they could inside. Some are really gross about it and abuse and manipulate friends into supporting others. Some, like Jake Conroy, try to build up libraries and stores to help people who aren't receiving anything. When you have something and someone else has nothing, it isn't a difficult idea to grasp that you should look out for them. It felt important for me to remember that although I was experiencing this prison *now*, they had been experiencing it for *decades*. I needed these people to know that their stories would get outside the ADX walls and that I would do what I could to get them letters and books.

It is depressing thinking about the mail situation in that hell and how few letters made it inside. I had a wife who loved me, comrades who cared, strangers who hated the prison system or wanted to stand beside me. I was unbelievably lucky. If outside communication had been our currency, then I would've been in the 1 percent, and I felt guilty for that. It was survivor's guilt, that my relationships were still surviving while many other prisoners were on their own. I felt guilty that some people seemed so genuine and had been through endless years of isolation, yet they received absolutely zero love or support. No one was calling the prison on their behalf. No one was calling their senator for them. They were the "worst of the worst," and that stigma prevented a lot of people from getting any sort of love. It still rips my heart out today.

Every letter I received was a warm hug and a message of hope. Hope that I would get out soon and could then support my forgotten pals inside. This is the entire goal of ADX: to separate people from the world and crush whatever hope they still have. They want your families to forget about you, they want your friends to abandon you, they want your kids to see you as a villain. They do not hold much care or concern about rehabilitation or family connections. The game plan is destruction, and it always has been. Your relationships are contraband, and they will take them away without a second's hesitation. In their eyes, only if you are good and well behaved do you deserve any decency or support.

One of the main things that I had, which was extra rare, was legal support. My trial lawyer S had stuck around and built a support team around me. Z Williams and Erika Unger from Bread and Roses Legal Center joined the team, and thank the goddesses they did. Neither of them liked having to deal with the federal government, but both showed up for me in ways I cannot ever properly express. I had legal calls every week. Every week, the cops would have to come and get me. They would take me to a small cell and wheel a tray with a dial phone up to the bars. The counselor would call the lawyers, confirm it was them, and then hand me the phone. These calls are literal lifesavers. When I was terrified about medical issues, my lawyers would look up symptoms or try to harass the prison officials on my behalf. When I needed information about sports, song lyrics, or current events, these are the people who would provide it to me.

Every week some combination of S, Z, and Erika would be on the phone. I would get family news from them, and I could communicate with my wife through them. This legal team joined up with my family to throw me fundraisers, put out statements, and communicate what I needed and how I needed it. Sometimes they were just there. Nothing important to talk about or go over. Just there, letting the prison admin know that I wasn't forgotten and that they would continue to keep an eye on me. Sometimes it feels good just to know that someone is giving their time for you, that with all the things happening in the world, speaking to you is still valuable. A prisoner with that type of support is an empowered prisoner.

I truly feel the prisoner should always have a say in what they need and how they want it to happen. We know what risks we are willing to take and what issues are important to us. In ADX, where you cannot communicate openly in any way, sometimes your team has to make decisions for you, and I am grateful that my team always worked with my family to make sure each choice was something beneficial and in line with my wishes. This hasn't always been the case. I've had people who supported me but openly didn't trust my judgment and didn't listen to a single thing I said. They didn't respect my opinion and thought they always knew what was best for me. They would disrespect me by ignoring me and disrespect my wife by shutting her down when she spoke out on my behalf. As good as legit support feels, this type feels equally horrible. Prisoners do not need to be parented or handled or patronized. Being infantilized by people who are supposed to care about you is troubling and feels really uncomfortable. It made me feel undeserving. It made me feel like I just had to shut up and be grateful and accept whatever I was offered. Like I wasn't good enough to have a voice.

There is too much of this, and there are not enough Joshes and Brians and Badgers. However, I was fortunate that by the time I reached ADX I had both a great support team and a great legal team. I can't imagine how beneficial it would have been to have these people in my corner my entire bid. To have Josh, Brian, and Badger helping my wife and supporting her just like they supported me. I never felt safer than when I was listened to and spoken with as an equal. When people would treat me like a human and actually have discussions or dialogue about what was best and how to push it forward. That is support. Talking to those inside like real people. We can disagree, we can argue, we can bump heads, but it should always be from a place of love and solidarity, not ownership or control.

A hard fact is that without proper support we are forfeiting prisoners to the government. We are telling the feds that these people do not hold any meaning to the community and that their captors can do whatever they like to them. Without support, the word never gets out about the abuses people are facing, the medical issues they are suffering through, and the daily laws the staff at ADX are breaking. Without support, the horrifying secrets of actual prison life stay unspoken. People had eyes on me, and there is no doubting that this kept me safe.

Legal calls tell the administration that they are being watched and that they had better act right. Support teams tell the staff that people care about this person and will not sit quietly and let them be abused. The USP Marion supermax was shut down in part because enough people had eyes on the prison and never stopped sharing the brutalities of it with the world. Inside/outside activism helped close the ADX of that time. The Thomson SMU (Special Management Unit) in Illinois was shut down because word finally got out about the staff initiating violence that was poisoning that facility. People listened to and believed the prisoners when they spoke about the forced gladiator fights and intentional instigating of violence by staff. It is only through outside support that we can even attempt to keep prisoners safe.

For whatever reason, the ADX does not always garner the sort of attention that places like Marion and Thomson received. It seems that the radical movement doesn't give much thought to it, probably because there aren't many leftists there anymore. It is a prison that once held Ray Luc Levasseur, Dr. Mutulu Shakur, Thomas Manning, Oscar López Rivera, Kojo Bomani Sababu, and many others. There doesn't seem to be any radical pressure to force the BOP or the federal government to end the twenty-four-hour lockdowns, to let civilian observers enter the prison, or to give people a chance to work their way out. ADX has done an amazing job of convincing the public that the people who are in there deserve to be there and deserve the treatment they're receiving. That we really are the "worst of the worst" and that therefore the only option is around-the-clock lockdown. One week in that prison would teach every person alive how urgently they should be fighting to get it shut down.

The men inside that dungeon need support desperately. You cannot spend five years or a decade inside a box and have your only communication come from other people in your exact situation. Those inside need letters, they need visits, they need books. Some people wrote to me asking if I still wanted books, considering I had a TV. The answer is always yes. People need to know that they are not forgotten, that they are alive in someone's heart.

I have no idea how to build this support. I have no idea how to convince people to write a mass murderer or a stabbing racist. I truly believe we shouldn't abandon anyone to the state. We don't have to like anything about the prisoner, but if we stay silent about their situation then we are telling the state that what it is doing is okay. We are stating with our silence that we agree with the government's abuse of some people, just not *our* people. I cannot swallow that at all. I've tried to do my part, having letter-writing nights for Smiles, KC, Shahid, RH, and other people I was able to meet. But there are hundreds more for whom just one letter could change their entire lives. Sadly, they will probably never get that letter.

||| CHAPTER 10

Antifascists and Political Prisoners

> The role of control units to contain the most politically aware, as well as the political prisoners and prisoners of war of National Liberation Movements and the seasoned veterans against prison repression, serves as a reminder of the true intent which accounts for the vast amount of time given for non-violent offenses with no anticipation of release.
> —Dr. Mutulu Shakur, former Black Liberation Army political prisoner who spent years at ADX; he was released from prison in 2022 and died the following year

I am proudly, openly, and visibly antifascist. This was a bone of contention throughout my entire prison bid. Many people I met inside had absolutely no opinion about antifascism. They didn't understand antifa or care to learn about it. They would say things like, "We ain't asking who you voted for, this isn't an election party." But some did care, and they cared deeply. They cared enough to act on their anger with serious violence. Predictably, most of the people I met who had a passionate hatred of antifascism were also the people perpetuating fascism: the BOP guards. They are wildly ignorant about our beliefs and more than happy to live within that ignorance if it gives them an excuse to feel morally or physically superior. The reality of the situation isn't nearly as important as the false sense of grandeur.

At the ADX, I was the only open leftist, and the guards didn't really know what to make of it. Most of their information on antifa came from Trump or his minions, but they'd never met someone who stood on antifa values and ethics. They knew they hated us, though. Trump and the media had taught them that we were the biggest bunch of dirt-eating lowlifes to ever set foot in this country. They would not tolerate us!

The guards look at you with spite and talk to you with venom; they see you as their enemy, and you are. You are the enemy of fascists, and that isn't going to change just because you are inside. You see their tattoos, their dog-whistle patches that are worn on their stab vests. They are not hiding what they believe, and neither will you, even if that comes at a cost. The guards expect obedience and conformity, and when you challenge either of those things, it is a challenge to their entire identity.

Interactions with staff and prisoners regarding antifa varied and were almost always exhausting. On more than one occasion when I was being walked to visiting or medical, one or both guards would ask me what it was like "being the leader of antifa." When I tried to calmly explain that there is no leader and there is no organization, they refused to believe it and would often get offended. They felt I was trying to get over on them and would get legitimately upset; no one likes being lied to. Some would ask if I was still trying to call the shots from ADX, ordering hits. When I asked them how I would do this without email, phone calls, or uncensored mail, they would reply, "You'll find a way." I had no idea how to respond to comments like that, and they were not uncommon. At least two to three times a week they would allude to my masterminding antifa, and no amount of confusion on my part would change their minds.

A few times, I was asked about funding: "How do you all afford to travel all over the country?" This always confused me to death. I would ask them what they meant by "travel all over the country." "You know, there are all these protests in different places. Who pays to move y'all from state to state?" When I would inform them that no one travels, that those are local fighters standing up against fascism, they would once again cast doubt on my story.

They could not fathom that there are antifascists all over the country who are willing to show up and stand against racism and bigotry. They really thought that there were forty or fifty paid antifa getting shuttled around the country just to fight and force wokeism onto good, hardworking "patriots." I would try to flip the logic on them: Who was busing around all these Proud Boy scumbags? How were they getting to Seattle and Nashville and NYC? The guards didn't see the connection I was trying to get at and would reply, "We are everywhere. The entire country is against antifa terrorists."

They would ask me strange things too: "Why do you hate white people?" "Why are you a race traitor?" "Are there antifa groupies?" They would tell other prisoners on the range that I was the antifa leader and that my whole agenda was killing superior white Christian men. Attacking Christians! I would hear them shouting this madness on the range, trying to instigate other prisoners into wanting to attack me. No amount of conversation or reasoning could get through this perception, with the cops or with some of the more clownish prisoners. I would tell the pigs briefly, "I am white. My wife is white. We stand against white supremacy in all forms, not against all white people." They couldn't separate the two, because to them there was no separation. Whiteness was white supremacy, so if you despised one, you despised the other. This is the level of idiocy I was dealing with.

Some white prisoners would yell down to me, asking what my problem was. Some would threaten me, making sure I knew that they had a knife waiting for me. No one respects a prisoner who yells through the doors, but they may be serious, so you would be wise to take the threats seriously. Others wanted to have conversations. They would come to the door during their orderly time, or in K-B during their rec time. They wanted to learn what we stood for and *why* we stood for it.

Oftentimes, serious prisoners can understand any idea that someone is willing to fight for. If you are willing to throw hands or weapons for this movement, then they can at least relate to that. Mexican Mafia members wanted to know why we cared about Blacks. Black prisoners wanted to know why we cared about trans people. There were conversations to be had, though, and I hope I represented antifascism in a decent enough way. From a prisoner perspective, being in ADX validated the movement as something real and serious; otherwise we wouldn't have been in there. After all, you weren't in ADX by accident.

Guards would ask me about recruiting. They wanted to know if I was recruiting people within the BOP, if I was trying to start a gang, if I was going to have my friends attack the ADX. They would play out these violent fantasies. "If y'all come here, we've got so many guns, we would love to mow down all of you pussies." They would be laughing to themselves until I'd mutter, "You think you're the only ones with guns?" Then they would get annoyed at my even implying that we were fighters.

The far right thought that we were trying to let kids identify as animals and use kitty litter in the classroom, that we were not fighters with a plethora of tactics and ideas to be waged against the nazis in our midst. They want us to be creeps. They want us to be the embodiment of these horrible images they've been fed by their leader. If they see us as fighters, then it doesn't fit, because *they* are fighters, they *respect* fighters, and they can't respect us. On more than one occasion, I had to tell them to maybe find something else to do other than speaking to me. I would remind them that we weren't friends. Why are you talking to me? Who are you trying to impress? Do you feel big rambling on and on about how tough you are while cowardly walking a handcuffed man two-on-one while heavily armed? This never went over well.

The weirdest thing I ever got asked about was George Soros. On at least three occasions, I was asked about how antifa was funded. The guards wanted to know if I was in touch with Soros or if there was an intermediary to keep his dirty, Jewish hands clean. Did we get paid per protest, or was it monthly? Did he pay us to have our boys get their penises cut off? Was he putting money on my books? Did he cover our insurance when the "patriots" put us in the hospital? At first I assumed they were joking, being intentionally idiotic. Then I would feel their hands squeeze a little tighter on my arm and realize that they were deadly serious about this, that it wasn't a game to them at all. They really believed that George Soros was not only funding but controlling and dictating antifa behavior.

When I was feeling more patient, I would try explaining to them that I had never met Soros, that no one I know had ever met Soros, that we would never take a penny from some liberal donor, and that we were not mercenaries. That while they would dive on their knees for a chance to lap up some Republican donors, we weren't about hero worship or receiving blood money. I would remind them that their questions seemed to come from their own identities, that since they were Koch whores they assumed we must be the equivalent.

Their accusations were always confessions, and my responses never went well. One time I barked back at a guard, "Look at my books, dude. I've got a hundred and fifty dollars, I'm sitting in a supermax, and I can't hear my wife's voice. How is Soros helping me? Where is Soros's influence? Look around you, look at my life. How is Soros helping?"

Forgetting where I was and who I was speaking with, I had turned my head slightly to speak and ended up getting my face slammed against a wall. *"Keep your fucking head straight!"*

White prisoners often had the same thoughts as the guards, mostly because they shared the same ideology and listened to the same news sources. The only difference between a nazi prisoner and a nazi guard is the badge, and sometimes not even that. Some would try to argue with me that they "saw it on the news." I would explain to them, "Listen, dude, if your enemy had a news channel, would they share true stories about you, or stories that would make your listening audience feel a certain way?" I tried putting it this way: If the prison administration were to talk about prisoners, would they be forthcoming and paint an honest portrait, or would they try to make the public terrified that we were all rapists and murderers? I implored them to think logically. The fascists are cops, these right-wing politicians and fascist groups in the streets are all supporters of cops or actual cops themselves, and we are against cops and all authoritarianism. Maybe this wasn't the most helpful approach, but it got the point across.

Proud Boys are street cops and narcs. Full-fledged, bottom-shelf tattletales. They are the quickest to call and support the police. They are frontline snitches to the highest degree. The Patriot Front are cops or wannabe cops. These groups aren't revolutionaries defending freedom, they are bootlickers for billionaires and the police state. If these white prisoners wanted to bend the knee to the same people who would eventually come for them, that was their choice, but it went against everything a convict is supposed to stand for. These fascists hate us. They are not friends of the prisoner class.

Clinging to the one thing that you feel gives you power—race—doesn't mean that those in power would give a second of their time to help you in any way. The smartest thing the billionaire class ever did was convincing the poor and marginalized to hate each other instead of them. Outside of the violence that street fascists commit to promote their cause, they have absolutely no value. They will never know that in the eyes of their masters they are not white power. They are white trash, and when not needed, they will be thrown away as such.

The most tangible effect of being labeled antifa in ADX was found in the mail room. Because the BOP considered antifa to be a domestic terrorist group, mail had to be treated accordingly. Sometimes mail would take months. Sometimes SIS would ask me specific questions about things I was receiving or sending out, and I would tell them to mind their own punk-ass business. Either approve the mail or don't. We don't need to have a goddamn conversation about it.

They would try to downplay things. "Ya know, I don't care at all, but are y'all planning an attack this weekend?" The stupidest and most unbelievable ideas were commonplace. When I'd point out it was their homies shooting up Walmarts and Black churches, they would laugh it off: "Oh, those are just lone wolves, not my homies." SIS officers are seemingly all nazis. The guards meant to regulate all the mail of the Muslims and antifa were also posting Islamophobic, racist, transphobic memes all over their social media. They would make posts about how all Muslims deserve to be killed and then lie to a Muslim prisoner's face that they weren't holding their mail or delaying their visits at all.

Never underestimate how much cowardice exists within the hearts of those with physical power. All the bravado hides the sad children deep within them. These are not honorable people; these are mental shrimps whose lack of backbone would make a jellyfish jealous.

My SIS officer was as nice as a peach to my face, but his social media posts showed exactly who he really was, and I never had any doubts about this. I'd have to get on him about my mail being delayed, and he would apologize and be really genial and say, "Oh, it just got delayed a little bit, nothing to worry about." I had a Domestic Terrorist Security Threat Group (STG) listing, so my phone calls had to be listened to live by the day officers, the guard towers, and my SIS officer. When, after a year in ADX, I was allowed to call my wife, I would only be allowed to do so on days and during times when my SIS handler could sit and listen in.

This was so creepy and invasive. Imagine a stranger listening to your most intimate moments, totally willing and ready to disconnect your call if what you say isn't up to their standards or approval. The administration claims the purpose of this is to make sure you don't pass any messages or plan any attacks. No one is buying that line; we are not naive children. The real reason is to make sure you never feel comfortable or safe with your family. It is to ensure that there is at least one more wall between you and those you love. Your connection undermines their attempts to rip your family to shreds. Assata Shakur wasn't wrong: "Love is a contraband."

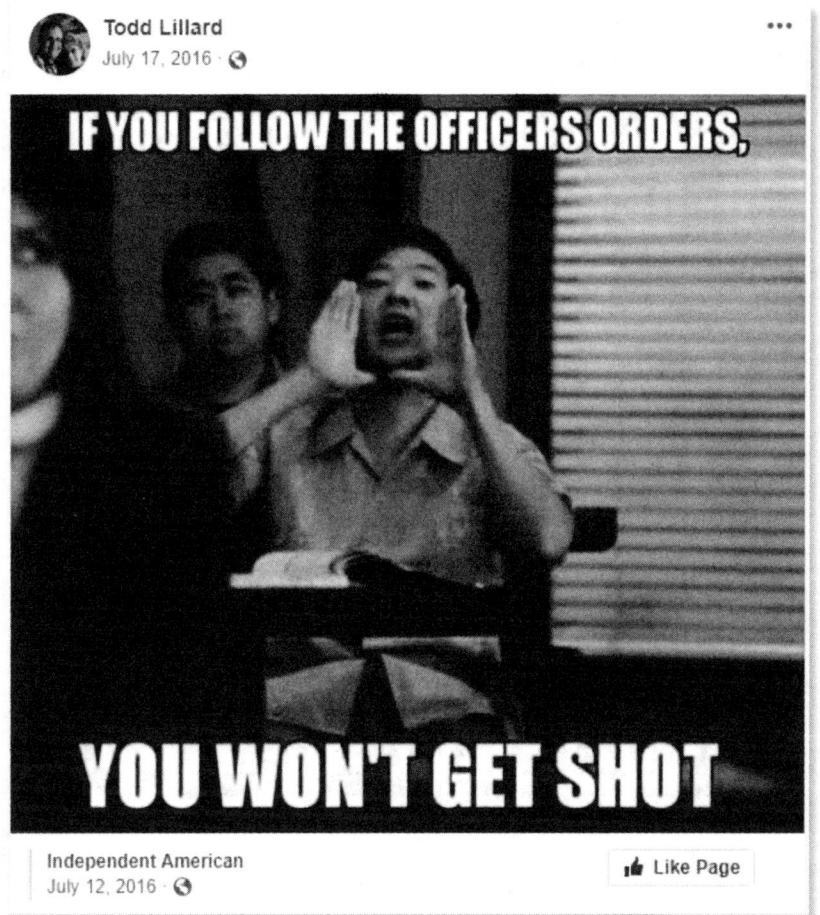

A post on Facebook by an SIS officer. Their job is to monitor the communication and movement of select prisoners, including Black and Muslim prisoners.

All these questions from guards and all the mail delays and monitoring aren't by accident. They ask these questions and hope to get answers that they can report back to the FBI or the head of SIS. They are taught to do this, to honeypot and fish for answers. They will act nice, chill, just wanting to talk off the record, just a couple of guys having a respectful conversation. All the information they gather, whether true or imagined, is given to the feds.

Sometimes prisoners will come and do SIS's job for them, asking you detailed questions, knowing that staff is listening in on the conversation via the intercom in our rooms. The BOP wants to build profiles of

Another Facebook post by this SIS officer in charge of monitoring the communication of Black prisoners. There is no check on officer racism within the BOP.

every single person and organization. They want to know the structure, the leadership, the funding, the plans, the members, the tactics, and so on. They use this information to plan how they will treat prisoners in the future. It will help determine the level of restrictions, sanctions, and security. They pass this information on to police departments and FBI agents all around the country. It is used to profile activists, gang members, or whoever they are working on.

Never think that what you are doing is not "important enough" to be noticed by the agencies that exist solely to try to find a crime within every personal interaction. What happens in prison is not much different from what happens in the streets. Never think you aren't valuable to them either as a quota filler or as a snitch. If you are a leftist activist in any way, they want to arrest you. They want to prosecute you. They want to flip you and turn you into an informant. The more they know about you, the more they can use this information against you. They can use your family against you, your children's health, your job, your mental health. Every piece of knowledge they have is leverage in potentially prosecuting or flipping you. This is why security culture is so important both inside prison and on the streets. We cannot afford to do their jobs for them. They already have every advantage imaginable. They don't need our assistance. So let's not give it to them.

It is critical to remember that our enemies do not live by *our* ethics, or even their own. There is no depth they won't sink to. Every rotten, disgusting thing you can imagine a cop doing on the streets to set someone up, they will do in prison. They will use every power imaginable to abuse the most vulnerable people and to ensure that whatever agenda they have is being enforced. They will get you killed. They will get you seriously assaulted. Your blood being spilled isn't their concern. They will intentionally lose crucial letters that can affect the well-being or future of your family. During COVID, it was SIS who would not let me contact my wife, not even once. It was SIS who gave Randy Platt a disciplinary write-up when he attempted to call my mother, who was recovering from breast cancer, to ensure that she was okay. There does not exist a "good" SIS officer, nor one who cares and just wants to keep everyone safe. You cannot exist in that world as a decent person, and anyone who tries will get flushed out quickly. Every cop is our enemy.

Politicals

I was the only antifascist prisoner at ADX at that time, but I wasn't the only political prisoner to be stuffed into the dungeon. There is a long history of the BOP placing leftist radicals or revolutionary prisoners inside supermax facilities.

Before there was ADX, there were the Marion and Lexington Control Units, which were experiments in punishment at the time. The BOP was terrified of the radical movement of the 1970s, '80s, and '90s and filled Marion to the brim with our elders, like Leonard Peltier, Oscar López Rivera, Bill Dunne, Kojo Bomani Sababu, Ray Luc Levasseur, Sundiata Acoli, and countless Puerto Rican *independentistas*. These units existed to quell the rebellious spirit, and those radicals radiated it.

Many of our elders and leaders were among the first people to fill the ADX hallways. Oscar López Rivera was one of the first to be placed in Florence and one of the first to be transferred out. At that time, in the mid-1990s, ADX, at least in theory, had set programming guidelines that allowed you to work your way out to a less restrictive prison. Oscar worked his way straight back to Marion, which was still a lockdown facility but not "as restrictive."

Ray Luc and Thomas Manning, two anti-imperialist prisoners and members of the United Freedom Front, were among the first to experience the new hell that the BOP had in store for those who wouldn't bow down. Ray Luc transferred from Marion and was held in ADX for five years. I believe Manning was there for a similar amount of time. Kojo was also at Marion before being transferred to ADX. Dr. Mutulu Shakur was at USP Atlanta, where he was radicalizing young Black prisoners, pulling them away from prison politics and into righteous thinking. This is a big no-no within the Bureau. You can drug up your homies, you can attack them, but if you think about educating them, you will face serious problems. Dr. Shakur was sent to ADX for several years, including time spent on Range 13 (more on that later), for his educational endeavors.

Susan Rosenberg was one of the first people placed inside the experimental and now-closed Lexington Control Unit, along with Silvia Baraldini and Alejandrina Torres. This was a control unit for radical female prisoners. The expressly stated purpose of this unit was to break the spirits of women combatants. Susan withstood unbearable psychological torture, all meant to erode her mind and steal away whatever fight she kept within her heart. Over time, the brutal nature of this unit was made public, and the outcry was strong enough that it was shut down in 1988 after just two years of operation. This is similar to what happened at Marion. You cannot place that many radical humans in one place and expect it to stay quiet. Their voices were heard, people in the free world were motivated, and with millions of eyes on the Bureau, the Marion Control Unit was finally shuttered.

This has not been the case with ADX. Over the years, as our elders worked their way through the program and on to less restrictive penitentiaries, the spotlight on ADX dimmed greatly. The Bureau's propaganda machine worked overtime to ensure that there was no doubt about who was within those walls: the worst of the worst. Cop killers, bombers, murderous thugs. People who deserved to die but instead would face something worse: a spiritual evisceration. They expected to stomp out the fire within our elders, and they failed. ADX housed infamous gang leaders and terrorists, and people did not want to attach their names to the fight to shut down a prison holding prisoners considered to be monsters.

The last radical held there before I arrived was Jamil Al-Amin, formerly known as H. Rap Brown. After his arrest on bogus charges in 2000, he was held in ADX for seven consecutive years, as he was considered too influential to be placed on a normal custody yard. This was the situation with many of our elder comrades. They were charismatic, dynamic, ready to both teach and revolutionize the prison population. Prison was a place not to quietly rest their heads, but to learn and grow. To strengthen their bodies and minds, and to help bring up others as well.

As these men phased out, the number of radicals in ADX diminished greatly. I suspect there are a few reasons for this. One is that the public support for militant action was on the wane. There weren't new groups taking up the mantle where the others had left off. A hole was left in the radical movement, and it wasn't being filled. Further, the Bureau set up new institutions to handle future radical prisoners. Instead of just having five to ten prisons to split up fifty political prisoners, through the 1990s and 2000s, there were now over a hundred federal prisons, and the number of political prisoners was diminishing due to medical neglect or successful freedom campaigns. The Bureau could thus spread radicals all around the country, preventing them from congregating and generating massive support.

There was also the creation of the Communications Management Units (CMU). These two special units within USP Marion and USP Terre Haute were built to house influential Muslim inmates, along with a quota of other radicals. White supremacist leaders were sent here, and animal rights prisoners who were gathering too much support or influence were sent here. The CMU became both a precursor to ADX and a stepping stone out of it. Prisoners would step down out of ADX into the CMU or step up from the CMU into ADX. There were now multiple prisons that could house, restrict, separate, and quiet the voices of radicals. ADX wasn't as necessary anymore.

I was a quota fill. The BOP has quotas for prisoners. Each prison has to have a certain number of specific groups of prisoners. This is why animal rights prisoners were sent to the CMU: to show that they weren't just housing Muslims, that they had all sorts of violent offenders there. It is similar in ADX. They need to show a certain number of leaders from different groups in order to highlight that they aren't specifically targeting any one group. I was placed there because the Bureau was incensed that their imaginary "antifa" had made them look ridiculous. Trump had made it clear that antifa was the enemy, a terrorist group, and would be handled accordingly. I had a lot of mail. I had a lot of support. I had violence on my record. I had just successfully beaten the BOP in their own court of law. I was the prime candidate to show how seriously the BOP was taking Trump's words.

I made it easy for the BOP to justify my placement. I had an extreme disciplinary write-up history. I had multiple institutional assaults on staff, even if I had been cleared by the courts. Most importantly, though, I had outside support. This is what they fear the most. When the outside world listens to you, speaks for you, and fights for you, they are threatened. By ourselves we are a stone, but with our comrades we are a mountain. I was also actively trying to "recruit" other antifascists. I was sharing books and letters, getting other prisoners more support, and challenging the prison norms of just accepting white versus Black versus Mexican. If you are recruiting for a terrorist group within the BOP, you will have problems.

I have no idea how the next crop of leftists within the federal prison system will behave. I do not know if they will buck and rise up against the prison system. I do not know if they will fight and do all they can to disrupt this machine or if they will chill out and relax, realizing that their fight is in the streets and that the goal of prison is to make it out, not make it more dangerous. What I do know is that eventually there will be another leftist within the ADX. I don't know what ideology they will come from, but I know their time will be very difficult. The staff will isolate them and ridicule them. Their communications will be halted, and they will be all alone. It will be on the radical community to not let them be forgotten. It will be on all of us to ensure that the Bureau has the spotlight directly on their hidden prison. We stood with our elders, and we will stand with the next generation as well.

III CHAPTER 11

Resistance and Consequences: Standing Up to Repression

> The greatest falsehood established by the Bureau of Prisons is the notion that rehabilitative programming exists at Marion to alter particular behavior patterns nonproductive to society and the prison system. Marion is simply a "warehouse" for human beings, used as an experiment to deny human rights under the guise of modifying behavior defects in alleged criminals.
>
> —Kojo Bomani Sababu

Imagine you are in a cell all by yourself, surrounded by concrete, and every bit of access you have to the free world is controlled by your enemy. You want something, anything, and they are the ones joyfully denying it. It could be your mail, access to your twice-a-month phone call, your ability to go out to recreation, or even just being spoken to with respect. It could be anything. But now you've grown tired of them, and you're done waiting around and hoping indecent people will develop any level of character. You know who and how they are, and you're done playing the victim. You know that resisting will go poorly for you. You've seen other people face up to them and pay the price for it. You know that you will end up hurt and in a less favorable situation than you are currently in, but you need some sort of justice. Something has to be done, and you're the only person who can do it. You either step up or keep enduring their perpetual destruction of your absolute essence.

Never underestimate the bravery and commitment of someone willing to buck inside ADX or any SHU. You are all alone. None of your homies are there to back you up—although many will shout encouragement, more than happy to watch the spectacle. You cannot run, you cannot back up, you cannot do anything except face your enemy head-on. They have all the weapons. They have the sprays, as hot as the devil's spit. They have the explosives, the shields, the batons. The odds could not be *less* in your favor. You have your body, your mattress, and your spirit. The same spirit that ADX aims to break and weaken until it is as soft as baby food. It isn't soft, though. You've hardened it, you've sharpened it, you've forged it in self-determination and grit. You've seen into the soul of your enemy, and you know they are pitiable. Throughout your entire bid, you've seen their cowardly underbelly, and you know they only have any fortitude when surrounded by their coworkers and covered in protective gear and weapons.

These jellyfish deserve no respect, and you won't give them any. You know they will hold you down seven-on-one and have a party while they beat you. You know that your possessions will be destroyed. That your skin will be burned, that your body will be broken. It doesn't matter at that moment. All that matters is that you've had enough. They've crossed too many lines, and the days of them acting invincible have run their course. It's time. Let's go, you scumbags. Suit up, you punks. ("Suiting up" is when the guards get all their safety gear on.) Go get the team. It's time. You desperately need them to know that you will stand up for yourself, even at your own peril. How do you do it? Let me tell ya.

Food/Fecal Attack

The guards come in pairs to bring us our food. They open the outside door, step into the vestibule, hand us our trays, and then walk out together. This is one of the few opportunities to get at them if you want to take a swing at it. Some people will plan this for days or weeks. They will save the morning milk cartons, or anything dairy that can become wicked. When the milk is as spoiled as the devil's underwear, you can then mix it with all the human waste at your disposal. The only limits are what you can create. Let it fester; let it turn into a physical manifestation of the souls of your captors. Rotten, putrid, unfit for human consumption. Every hour it becomes more and more wretched. This is an act of ultimate desperation. Nothing in their day has prepared them for this level of retaliation. Although they should always expect it, they never seem to see it coming.

You'll wait patiently until the glorious moment when the guards open the door to gather up the used food trays. Then, while their defenses are down and their focus is occupied by the trays, the guards are introduced to the most wretched vengeance you can imagine. It is hilarious. Gut busting. One of the funniest things you'll ever hear is the shrieking when the fecal milk showers their mouths and faces, when they are covered in the devil's soup. You will never get away with doing this without catching a large dose of pepper spray and a severe beating. You may end up in the hospital. You may also catch new charges, as this form of attack is considered an assault with a weapon. I've seen men get dinged with two more years inside prison because they stopped caring about consequences and only cared about their own form of justice.

I still get the giggles imagining some bully cop screaming in absolute terror. That's the whole point. Human waste won't do much physical damage, but we don't always need to hurt them physically. Sometimes it's about stealing their dignity, just like they do to us every day. Bringing them down to our level for just one sweet moment. It's about taking some sort of control. It infuriates them on a thousand different levels, but it also humiliates them. All their macho, tough-guy behavior is infantilized as they become crying little children stumbling to the shower. It is quite a personal thing to have another man's unmentionables nonconsensually sprayed in your mouth. It is (or should be) a stark reminder to them that they can be touched, that they can be victims too. They can be dehumanized and demoralized and humiliated and disgraced. Wearing a badge doesn't place you above it all. They can feel the same shame and powerlessness we feel. They can be made to suffer on our terms. It's a reminder that they are lower to us than the thin paper swirling around the toilet. They are the spoiled milk of our lives. Many prisoners frown on this tactic; they see themselves as above it. Not me, not at all. I don't care what anyone thinks about any act of resistance. There is no moral high ground in this battle. It works. I've done it. It's a blast.

Running the Team

This isn't a term that most people in the free world are familiar with, but those inside know it all too well. It is a long, scary process to "run the team," and you must be highly motivated to see it through. Most people aren't. Most people lose their nerve before it's time for action. But when it happens, it's fantastic.

To "run the team" is to make the cops try to extract you from your cell using force and intimidation. It is them at their most macho and pathetic. For this to happen, you must refuse to be removed from your cell, refuse to take down a visual blockade in your cell preventing them from seeing in, or refuse to "cuff up" (to place your hands behind your back and let the officers handcuff you through the bean slot, so that you can be removed from the cell). The cop bastards will come to your cell and tell you to take down the barricade. They will say, "This is a direct order, cuff up!" You don't owe them an answer; they've taken enough. They aren't saying anything new, and you wouldn't be listening even if they were. So maybe you don't say anything at all. You let your silence speak for itself. You are ready. The time for talking has long since passed.

Minutes or hours will go by before a lieutenant comes to your cell. This vermin will slither up to your cell and try playing the good cop. They will be calm and talk reasonably with you. "Come on, man, this isn't what you want. We can figure this all out, but we can't do it if you're acting this way. This isn't how to get what you want." Patronizing talk, as if you aren't 100 percent aware that every word they say is a lie. Once they know you aren't interested in listening to their foolery, the aggro comes out. This is how they really feel. This is what they've wanted to say all along. "Look, dude, we know you're a pussy, we know you're going to cuff up, let's not waste any time here."

A lot of times they are right. Sometimes a prisoner is just really upset, and they stay upset until they see the seven men with full body armor and weapons standing at their door, salivating at the prospect of a gang beating. At that moment, some will decide to protect themselves instead of fulfilling their rageful desires. For you, that moment has passed. You tell him, "We'll see," or, "How about you come in here yourself? Why do you need all your bitch friends? Why do you need weapons?" You taunt them, pointing out how spineless it is to attack someone with six of your friends. There is a better chance of winning the lottery than one of these weasels opening an ADX door on their own. If only we were that lucky.

An hour or two will go by. The tension on the range is palpable. If you have comrades, they may be hollering at you, offering support and indignation, telling you that your cause is just. If you don't have any pals, there will be silence. Everyone knows what's about to occur, because it is always the same. The only variables are how you'll respond when the door opens and how severe their attack will be. Everyone on the range has most likely either run the team or seen it done multiple times. They know the pain you are about to endure, and they know how solid someone has to be to face off with these snakes. The guards may try to negotiate one or two more times, but at that point they are already getting suited up. The lieutenant is filling out all the necessary paperwork to get approval and document that they tried everything possible to prevent this from happening. They are contacting the warden at home to let him know and get the verbal okay.

Then it's time. You'll hear them gathered at the end of the range, all their shields and armor making a terrifying ruckus. The noises test your irrepressible nerves. This is when many will bow out. The guards want to terrify you. They want you to fear the absolute worst. The psych department will show up at your door and plead with you to call it off. They will inform you that "this isn't the way to achieve your goals," rehashing the same bunk that the lieutenant just said. You will remind them, with defiant clarity, that you have done literally everything else to try to prevent this. That you have spoken to staff, filled out forms, spoken to higher-up staff, reached out to psychology, and were completely ignored. Not only have you been ignored, but some of the issues have even gotten worse in retaliation for your constant self-advocating.

You are out of options. They know it, and no one will help you. So now it's time to take matters into your own hands. They will bring out all their silly blabbery. They will pretend that if you just talk and are very nice, they will help you. But we are not brainless. We've all been through this. There is no help. There is no "nice." Sometimes they will just sulk, knowing it's going to escalate. Sometimes they will dig in and mock you. "You're going to cuff up either way. What's the point?" Or, "Well, when they beat your ass, don't come crying to me." I've heard both of those and everything in between. I've seen psych cry because they know how brutal their coworkers are about to be. I've heard psych start laughing and yelling to the goons to shut our bitch asses up. Psych is not there to protect you. They are there to fill out the facade, to project the illusion. *We* are the unreasonable ones, and they only want to assist us.

Are you ready? Are you built for this? Are you prepared for the barrage of brutality that has arrived at your cell door? It's time. The lieutenant shows up at your door. There is one guard in the back videotaping the things they need to show to avoid a lawsuit and prove how compassionate they are, how they had no other options. The lieutenant halfheartedly asks you to cuff up three times. These will be muttered orders: "Will you cuff up?" "Are you going to cuff up?" "Are you refusing to cuff up?" He will state for all to hear (especially the cameraman), "Inmate has refused three direct orders, beginning extraction process," or some similar bureaucratic drivel.

You have been preparing your cell for the attack. Your face will be covered. Maybe you've covered your entire body to prevent the spray from burning as much. Some will lather their floors or bodies with soap, to make things just a little more difficult for the attackers. You will be hiding behind your mattress or towel or maybe just facing them head-on. Each prison is different regarding which weapons they'll decide to torture you with. This lieutenant has a gun, like a paintball gun that shoots hard balls filled with pepper-spray powder. When they hit you or your walls, they explode, filling the air with that poisonous gas that sucks all the air directly out of your lungs. A thousand fire ants shroud your entire body in an agonizing service to the gods of punishment and pain. The thug will fire eight to fourteen shots but only verbalize that "six shots have been fired" for the camera. They will ask you again to cuff up, and then fire eight to fourteen more pepper-ball shots, and then repeat this process one more time. At this point they have fired at least eighteen shots, although it is always more. The most I ever experienced was twenty-two. With more dangerous prisoners, I've seen them get hit as high as thirty to forty times.

Sounds bad. Feels bad. And it only gets worse. Next they will ask you if you will comply with orders, giving you the option to cuff up once more, and you will tell them to go to hell. The reward for your refusal to submit is a nasty one. The lieutenant will start painting your walls and body with pepper spray, flooding your room with it. They have fire extinguishers full of this toxin. You'll have known this was coming and will have a wet shirt over your face, maybe some milk or milk of magnesia on hand, but this part always sucks. There is no way around the suffering. They have two different types of pepper spray, both of which are built to destroy you. The first type physically burns. It burns even if it doesn't touch you. Just being around it burns your skin and your eyes and your lungs. You can have multiple layers of clothes on and it will still burn. The other type is even more diabolical.

It steals every bit of air out of the room. It collects all the air, hoards it, denies you any access. Air is a VIP club, and you are not getting past that spicy bouncer. The lieutenant will spray both. He will spray six-second bursts of these fiendish sprays. In between each burst, they will again ask you to cuff up, then return to attempting to strangle or burn you into submission.

After three rounds of chemical warfare, the staff has an option. At this stage, they can legally open the door and rush in on you. Sometimes, though, they want more. Even with six people and all the weapons in the world, they still don't feel safe. They bring out the bombs. The stun grenades. They give you a brief warning, and then they shoot a stun grenade into your cell. This bomb will rattle the walls, and it will give everyone on the range a horrible headache. It shakes you badly. Your legs become spaghetti. The percussion has nowhere to escape, so it vibrates and clatters inside your brain. You will have known this was coming also. You squat down, cover your ears as much as possible, and always keep your mouth open. I don't know why it helps to open your mouth, but it does. It makes it so you won't bite your tongue off or clench your teeth so hard that they shatter. It lets the explosion out of your head. It hurts badly, but you will survive. Most likely. They sometimes do this multiple times. They can throw in rubber BB explosives, or they can spray pepper foam. I've seen all these things. But usually at this point you've shown them that you will not cuff up for them, you will not bend the knee for them. So it's time. The guards have been waiting for this, waiting for their chance to take out all their frustration on your body. To punish you for all their failures.

They will scream one last time for you to submit, and when you don't, they will open the door. These ultimate cowards will come in with shields first. Sometimes they are electrical, but not always. The cowards will be covered head to toe in protective hardware and gas masks. God forbid they should breathe in their own torture. Although things look bleak, you also have options now. You can rush them, charge at them as hard as you can. This is a symbolic gesture, but it does set the tone. You can also wait for them to get close and then start swinging, trying to knock their helmets off and get a clean shot. If you have a knife, you can attempt to pull their shields down and their mask up to try to get a clean shot. You may have smeared liquid body wash on the ground in an attempt to make them slip and fall. You can also just lie down.

Whatever happens at this stage, you have faced down your abusers and shown them that you will not be complicit in your own suffering. You will not win against seven of the largest officers available, but you'll have won the mental battle. They couldn't scare you. They couldn't break you. You have nothing left to prove.

No matter what you choose next, they *will* absolutely get you on the ground. The team will consist of one officer per every body part. They will attempt to hyperextend your arms and legs. They will rub pepper-spray residue in your ears and eyes and up your nose. They will gouge at your eyes and they will knee your head, neck, and body. They will call you every degrading name in the book, as if you're the one committing the human rights violations. After they are done relentlessly assaulting you, they will stand you up (and often slam you right back down), take you out of the cell, and parade you (naked, as they will cut all of your clothes off) on the way to your actual punishment, which I will discuss later. You will be in immense pain, terrible agony, but you will have never felt such satisfaction and self-worth. You have faced the most terrifying thing you can face in prison, and you did it with gusto. You have stood up to your abusers on your own terms and not bent the knee. No matter how much your body burns and aches, they can never take that victory away from you.

Miscellaneous

While there are other ways to resist in ADX, they are rare. All of these are quick statements of autonomy, and all will lead to massive beatings. The mental victory, though, is often worth the physical defeat.

You can "hold" the rec cages, which is to refuse to leave when rec time is over and run the team that way. This goes the same as doing it in the cell, but here you're even more vulnerable. But because you are outside, the percussion bombs hurt significantly less.

You can arrange to get seen by medical or dental, or get into a program. Then, when the guards come to walk you wherever you need to go, you can try to get a quick headbutt off, or spit in their faces. Once an older Brand member faked a heart attack while walking to medical and slumped down in the hallway. When an officer bent over to check on him, he launched a head butt right into their face.

One of the finest acts of resistance I've ever heard of happened in the range next to mine. This man was an orderly on his range who got to come out and clean the range for an hour twice a week. When the cops were ready for the orderly to return to his cell, the guards in the bubble electronically opened his outside and then inside door and had him reenter the cell before electronically closing both doors. They didn't know that this orderly was pissed. He wanted some action. When they opened his two doors, he stepped inside the first one, into the small vestibule area, and waited. Over the cell intercom, the officers asked if he was inside his cell, and he said, "Yeah, sure." They closed the inside door, believing he was securely inside. After an hour or so, it was time for the guards to do their count. This is where they walk through the range and check to make sure you're alive and in your cell. They do this by pretending to look into your cell. Some take it really seriously and will ensure they see your face or see you moving, which I actually appreciate considering how many elders and sick prisoners there are in ADX.

Count time came, and when they looked inside the orderly's cell, they couldn't see him. He wasn't in the bed and he wasn't in the shower. Concerned, they called him over the intercom, asking if he was okay and to speak with the guards. He remained silent. They radioed to the bubble that something was wrong and had them open the outside door. What they hadn't prepared for, what no one would've seen coming, was that he was desperate for some action and had lured them into a trap. The orderly had scaled the inside vestibule walls like Spider-Man and had propped himself up to wait for these suckers to open the door. As soon as they stepped inside, he dropped onto them, which was the most audacious way to settle the score on his terms. It did not take long for them to beat him senseless, and for other guards to join in. I guarantee you it was worth it, though. But what I also know is that the initial beating isn't the punishment. That beating just lets you know that things are about to get much, much worse. That is something that prison can teach you if you reach those levels: that no matter how bad it seems, no matter how cruel or demoralizing it feels, it can *always* get worse.

Punishment

You do not resist at a prison like ADX and walk away without severe consequences. You do not disrupt their system of physical and mental control without paying a price for it. Much like there are different levels of resistance, there are also different levels of retaliation, which include the following.

Write-Ups

The Bureau's response to basic resistance is a basic punishment. Disciplinary write-ups, called "shots," are what the BOP—after decades of research and study—have found to be the best behavioral modification punishments. The Bureau attacks you in ways that have the potential to hurt the most. The ways that would hurt *them* the most. Shots can have serious consequences. If you can't talk to your family for years, can't have visits, can't see your kids, this can have a horrible effect on your family and their mental health. It's an attack on your family as much as it is an attack on you.

I've discussed write-ups previously, and in ADX they are a real pain. They exist to make life more difficult under the guise of "maintaining the safe and orderly function of the institution." Shots are organized based on a number system: 100 series shots are the most serious (for example, a 101 is a murder), 200 series shots are the second most serious (a 203 is a fight), and so on. If you get a serious shot, you can lose anywhere from a month to several years of the few things that you hold dear. They can and will take your phone, take your visits, take your canteen. They can jack your rec time and even take away your TV. If you are in a Step-Down Unit with access to limited TRULINCS email, they will take that away too.

These punishments hurt our families and loved ones. That's the entire game plan. In order to protect them and the bonds we have, we will be good little boys and modify all the problematic behaviors. The punishments also further take away our only contact with the outside world. I lost my phone, visits, and email for five years (without a shot). It hurts badly. Every single day it hurts. Every time you see someone getting ready for a visit or getting the chance to make a call, it reminds you that you will not be doing any of those things. It sucks any chance of experiencing joy out of your days. When the BOP says that they care about fostering community connections and building family relationships, always remember that they mean "only if." *Only if* you behave do we care about your families. *Only if* you walk our line will we show any interest or empathy toward your mental health or family connections.

We are already limited to three phone calls a month at most. Taking those calls away is not a reflection of our behavior but of how depraved they are. They always attack the most vulnerable. Removing canteen is especially hard on those with dietary restrictions or who are just bigger people. I am five foot seven, 150 pounds, a wannabe vegan, and I was constantly hungry. Those who are significantly taller and heavier will be hungry or starving 24/7. Taking away the ability to buy extra food is especially cruel. We are treated like animals. If we bark too much or pee on the rug, we get no treats, and we get swatted on the nose. Hunger becomes an act of both resistance and rebellion. The feeling of an empty stomach is a reminder of why we fight and who the goddamn enemy is. It isn't the person in the cell next door, it is the bastard starving you.

Property Removal
One of the few things that can make prison even somewhat tolerable are the limited extra possessions we are allowed to have, whether those are craft supplies, extra food, extra clothes such as sweatpants and shoes, or even books and a TV. All the *extra* stuff that we aren't "entitled" to are also the only things that can ease the sting of prison on a micro, daily level. They allow us these things as a form of social control. If you are a good little boy, you can read books and watch TV programs.

Therefore, it makes sense that when they feel you haven't behaved according to their standards, they take your things. It isn't just that, though. It isn't just that they take your crochet and you are bummed for a little bit. No. They take all the external mental stimulation that you have built your entire routine around. All the things that help you feel any sense of purpose throughout your day, along with all the dopamine dumps that have come from this stimulation. All the things that provide you with any sort of self-worth and positivity.

They steal it. It's not "confiscated," it's robbed, and there is not a single thing you can do about it. They take you out of your cell and place you outside in the recreation cages, or they pretend that you have a medical appointment, and then they go into your home like low-life home invaders. They steal all the joy you've managed to conjure up. They take the pictures of your family. They take the mail you've read and then reread. They'll take the TV. While everyone is watching the game or some beloved show to help pass the time, you will be staring at the wall. Pacing, lying down, sitting, just existing in a box. When your world is limited, your brain is limited. That is their goal.

I've had to do this for approximately thirty days at the longest, and it is a real test of your will. It is a rough trial to endure. It can break you. But it doesn't have to. You can create your own entertainment. You can be your own TV show, your own DJ. We contain all the universes and experiences ever known within us. But it is hard. It is the hardest time you can do in a place like ADX, where you cannot leave your cell. There is a chance you can use the absolute solitude to work on your traumas and develop a deep, intimate relationship with yourself, but you can also lose your mind in a psychotic rage.

Four-Point Restraints

The worst pain I have ever felt in my entire life was while being four-pointed. Four-pointing occurs when you are forcibly stripped by a gang of armed guards, are forced to lie on a bed, have your arms stretched as far as possible above your head, have your legs stretched as far down and open as possible, have all four limbs handcuffed to the corners of the bed, and are then left there. Struggling to breathe, losing all feeling in your hands and feet, losing all sense of what it was like *not* to have burning pain in every part of your body. Then you wait. And wait. And wait. Occasionally, a lieutenant will come in and check to make sure you are still chained. Medical will pop in and pretend to check on you. They'll tell custody staff that, yes, you are still capable of enduring this torture.

You will try to find any bit of comfort. Trying to rotate a little to the right or left, or trying to flex your hands and wiggle your fingers. Nothing helps. You are being horizontally crucified. Nothing could possibly help. You have no idea how long this will last, but you'll have known others who have had to endure this for fifteen, twenty, twenty-eight hours. You know of people who have spit at the guards when they came to check on their cuffs, people who have verbally resisted until the BOP had no choice but to legally get them out of the cuffs and off the slab. Whatever gives you strength and motivation to endure the pain is a good thing. There is no wrong way to survive.

You start to feel something in your bladder, a dreadful feeling you cannot escape. This is hell. You have to piss. They are supposed to uncuff your arms and allow you to sit up so that you can hold a bottle to relieve yourself in. Sounds good, right? This is a myth. They will not let you sit up. What your body needs to do is not their concern. They control your body, not you. You attempt to hold it for an hour, maybe two, but it burns. Eventually it will hurt so wretchedly that you'll have no choice. You try to rotate your hips, but bodies can only achieve so much while chained to a steel slab. You piss yourself. You feel the urine stream over your legs and pool underneath you. And you will be stuck lying in this pool of piss for however long they leave you there. They want you to feel shame and humiliation. They want you to feel disgraced, that you weren't man enough. That you deserve this. But you know the truth. Their torture reflects on their character, not yours. This is who they are, not you.

Staff is also supposed to feed you. Much like using the restroom, they are supposed to unchain your upper half and allow you thirty minutes to eat. I have never heard of this happening *once* in the Bureau. Sometimes they will come and try to force bread into your mouth, violently rubbing a sandwich all over your face. Do not think for one second that they will lose any sleep if you choke on that bread. Most of the time, you will eat nothing, not even a forced sandwich. You will lie there and have absolutely no comfort.

I was four-pointed for seven and a half hours. It was the worst physical seven and a half hours of my life. All my strength came from willing myself to not let them break me physically or mentally. I conceptualized my torture as a battle between two enemies, and I wasn't going to fold. All you can do is find a way to get through it with your mind intact. You are alone with only your thoughts and your pain. Everything else fades away. This is when you learn that there is pain that exists whether you want it to or not. Pain that exists without even an iota of relief. It swallows you like a Big Gulp and won't spit you out. You're the god of this universe, and you are on that cross.

In the last year or so, four-pointing policies have slightly changed. Arms stretched above the head during four-pointing is rare now, though not unheard of. Thomas Smith, a Blood from Missouri and a habitual resister, was once four-pointed for twenty-eight hours. His body was absolutely decimated. He had to have emergency reconstructive surgery on his shoulder. As soon as his surgery was complete, he was sent directly to ADX.

Nowadays, while being tortured you are more likely to have your arms chained near your waist. You are still chained to a concrete or steel bed, unable to move at all for hours. While chained, you will be punched, choked, spit on, sometimes pepper-sprayed. They will say every horrible thing they can think of to try to make you feel small. Their insults reflect their weaknesses, not yours. Four-pointing can physically break people. You hear the shrieks of raw agony as muscle is torn from bone and stretched to its breaking point. You hear people expressing all their hurt and rage toward the guards. The screaming is nightmarish and visceral. Hours of pain and fear and devastation. Their words and their anger are the only cure for the pain. It's never enough, though. No amount of screaming or wailing stops the pain. Your curse will insist on being felt during every second of your forced chaining. The goal is to ensure that your entire world revolves around a sun of agony. You will suffer through this orbit until they feel you've had enough.

You never hear staff admit they have done anything cruel or wrong. They never admit to pulling out dreadlocks. They never confess to beating and abusing a defenseless person. You never hear the BOP admit that maybe chaining humans to hard surfaces in stress positions for hours on end isn't the best tactic. That's because to them it *is* the best tactic. Remember, the goal is to shatter your entire reality. The first step toward doing that is burying your rebelliousness under your own agony.

I didn't need any further reason to hate the BOP. I didn't need further proof that I was dealing with some of the worst humans and institutions ever to exist. But after having to piss all over myself and having captains attempt to suffocate me, I was able to ascend to newer levels of disdain. I was able to find further reasons to hate them. They made it easy. Years later now, I still can't feel many parts of my hands and arms. I still have radiating pain and suffering in my shoulders, neck, and back. I still have the trauma resulting from the powerlessness of not being able to stop them from doing this to me. No matter how hard I tried, I couldn't save myself. I can still feel the cold shears slicing my clothes off. I can still feel the air abandoning my lungs. I can still feel their taunts.

But I never begged them to stop. I never let them see how bad it hurt. When they came to unchain me and place me in soft restraints, I mocked their attempt to shatter the anarchist spirit. That wasn't me being tough or macho; it was self-preservation. It was what I had to do in order to survive and keep my faculties intact. I leaned into my sarcasm and bravado. I leaned into the mantras. *I will get through this. They cannot break me.* I got through it, but I haven't shaken their claws out of my psyche yet. Trauma has a powerful and determined grip. Its desire to be felt is insatiable. No matter, though—we'll shake those bastards out of there someday. But before then, getting through it is all that matters, and however you manage is the absolute right way. Once you survive this torture, they know they cannot break you. You've stolen their power.

Range 13

Have you ever heard of Range 13? No? I'm not surprised. Neither has anyone else. It is the most secretive part of the most secretive prison in America. What little is known comes from vague commentary from Thomas Silverstein and Ramzi Yousef when they were placed back there together for years.

Range 13 is the SHU within the SHU within the ADX. Range 13 is a very weird place. The secrecy of it implies it's the scariest place imaginable. Why wouldn't they talk about it if there wasn't any funny business going on? What is going on back there that keeps it completely under lock and key?

I learned a lot about Range 13 by meeting several people who had done time there. Range 13 is held in the back of C-Unit, the disciplinary range. On Range 13, there are only four cells, and they are positioned and sorted in a way that makes it nearly impossible to speak with anyone else on the range—if there is anyone else there. On Range 13, you are still allowed your TV unless you're on other restrictions or you *really* pissed the cops off. In the BOP, there are only two places that have permission to have cameras within the cells: 10 South, the SHU at MCC Manhattan that houses the most infamous prisoners in the United States before they arrive at ADX, and Range 13.

Inside the cells, there are multiple cameras watching your every move. They are pointed at the toilet, at the shower, at the bed. All the places you may want a little privacy. This and the absolute silence are the actual punishment of the unit. You are removed from all your property except the TV, you are removed from any routine you had on your range, you are removed from any communication you may have had. It is psychological torture at the highest level. There is not much time for mental peace when your enemy is watching you at all your most vulnerable moments.

Range 13 isn't easy to get to, but it isn't all that difficult either. If you are bucking on your range, you will be placed in C-Unit. You will have to start fresh in C-Unit, which has the worst cells, the worst mattresses, the worst rec cages and rec times, and the worst amenities. This is for people who run the team, people who piss off staff. Range 13 is for staff assaults, continual staff abuse, or serious threats to staff. If you put a hand on staff, you will end up doing three to eighteen months on the range (this is after all the beatings, four-pointings, and property restrictions). It is not used often, but I met seven different people who confirmed they had been on Range 13.

The secret torture cells on Range 13 got a bit of publicity a few years ago when one prisoner on the range managed to kill another. In the most secluded range in the most secluded prison in the entire country, someone managed to catch a body. The facts are blurry, but it was reported to me that a DC convict was either beefing with or got tired of another person back there. Because the range is so secluded, it has its own tiny rec cage that is attached to all four cells. The DC inmate and the other inmate were planning an escape to either get off the range or out of ADX, I don't know which. They came up with a foolproof plan: DC would tie a noose, and the other prisoner would put it around his own neck. They would pretend that DC was taking the other man hostage, and the guards would have no choice but to open the doors to negotiate with them.

In prison, your number one responsibility is to keep yourself safe. No one else will do it. It is entirely up to you. You should never put yourself in positions that may lead to you being hurt or killed. This is why I didn't drink inside. This is why I didn't do drugs inside. And this is why I would *never, ever* put a rope around my neck, especially one that was in the hands of another prisoner. How DC convinced the other man to partake in this plan will never cease to boggle my mind. The other prisoner put the rope around his neck, and DC did the rest.

All of this developed in a unit that has multiple cameras in every cell and multiple cameras in the rec cage. It's almost as if the guards saw what was happening and didn't view these people's lives as valuable enough to step in and save. They witnessed a murder that could've been easily prevented and made a conscious choice to do nothing. In the presence of death, they didn't lift a finger. The pigs do not care about our lives or our safety. No officers were found culpable for this mishap. The deceased wasn't as valuable as someone like Jeffrey Epstein, so there was no internal review or widespread media coverage. Just another dead prisoner, perpetuating the view that we are all violent and need to be locked down. He could have been saved. A thousand things could have happened to prevent this murder from happening, but *they do not care*. They will not protect you.

When I was leaving ADX, there was only one person on Range 13, and it was the guy who had hidden in the vestibule and dropped onto the cops when they opened his door. The cops are taught to not speak about Range 13. But those gossipy bitches still love feeling important for having sought-after information. You hear the dentist talking, you hear the RN talking, you hear the guards chatting among themselves as they walk you to the visiting room or medical. They love being the keeper of knowledge.

I have run the team three different times. I have been placed in an empty cell for months because of it. I have been pepper-sprayed, pepper-balled, concussion-grenaded. I have been held in shackles for hours. I have been violently four-pointed. I have been starved, and I have been starved of all communication (including paper mail). I've had my head cracked open by officers and my body sexually assaulted. I've been dragged out of my bed at 3 a.m., been served food covered in pepper spray and pubic hair. I have had guards slap me, spit in my face, tear my mail into shreds right in front of me. I've had my wife locked in the visiting room and held for over thirty minutes. These are the things people inside face when they decide to resist. To stand up for yourself within the prison walls is to automatically put your life in danger.

I am not unique or special. Everything I have experienced, someone else has experienced, and probably much worse. I wasn't allowed mail for two years, but I know people who haven't been allowed social mail for decades. I was held in solitary for years, but I know people who have been held for decades. I was attacked by cops, and yet Tom Manning was debilitated by pig bastards who shattered his legs. I was sexually assaulted by cops inside, and countless women and femme people in *every single prison* have experienced horrendous examples of this. Prison is abusive. Prison is a hellhole. If you are rebellious or fight back against their torture, you will experience some or all of these things. If you are left-wing and you fight back against the fascist system, you will experience many of these abuses. The prison system absolutely despises left-wing people, but especially those who dare to go against the grain.

If you decide to resist, you will also need to decide what is worth that sort of punishment. What is important enough to you that you would be willing to go through all of this? What will you stand up for, if anything? Consequence awareness is important on the streets, but it's equally important inside, where making the wrong move can cost you years of lost communication with your family, or years more inside prison. You cannot take resistance lightly. You cannot casually put your life on the line. There are certain things you will have to step back from. You cannot wage every battle. Well, you can, but you have to know what forces will be coming back at you. They have every advantage, and you have your determination. Which is more powerful?

Why would someone take these risks? What is the point? If you know you won't win, why put yourself through that hell? Resistance is seldom the first option. When I have bucked against the pigs, it has come on the back of months and months of direct harassment. There were times when it was just death by a thousand cuts, when a ton of small things added up and I had just had enough. I tried being a good little prisoner so I could stay under the radar, but that only made things worse. I tried being respectful, and that was interpreted as weakness by prisoners and staff alike. Sometimes you need to either stand up for yourself or just deal with being treated like you are less than dirt. I was small, very vocal, openly antifascist and anarchist, openly a race traitor, and openly an ally to the entire queer community, inside and out. These things all made me a target at one point or another, and after a while you just get tired of being a sitting duck.

At other times, I was just riding with other prisoners. You see Muslim or gay prisoners facing so many shenanigans from the staff that you cannot in good conscience quietly accept it. Or you can, if you decide those issues are not what you want to risk your neck on. There were times my comrade Smiles would go on a hunger strike and I would join in just so he could have some backup, so the administration would see he wasn't alone. On the flip side, there were multiple times when I went on hunger strike or ran the team and he would join in with me. That is how you show love and solidarity in prison:

by showing that you're willing to put it all on the line for your homies. There were times in the Englewood SHU while pretrial when I was fully fed up and not allowing an inch of disrespect from the guards to fly. If they disrespected someone on my range, I was on them. If they played silly games with our recreation or food or mail, it was time to go. I'd reached my limit, and it hadn't taken much.

But why at ADX? Why, when everything is already so horrendously restricted, would people risk making it even worse? I believe it's because there are things more important than worldly comforts. There are things more important than being seen as "lying down." When you have been placed in such a horrible prison, and then the officers add more to it, it is insulting on a level that reaches beyond mere rudeness. When you are already in the worst mental prison in America and the officers attempt to pile on top of it, you can quickly reach your point of no return. Guards habitually screwing with your mail, staff openly lying about your prison programming or good time, guards playing games with your already very limited time outside of the cell, guards talking recklessly about your family, medical completely gaslighting you about serious medical or dental issues, guards playing games with your family during visits. Which of these would set you off? How many times could you endure any of these before you struck back?

There is a level of pride and self-gratification when you make that choice to engage in combat on your own terms. The administration expects you to be timid. ADX was built to keep people timid. They expect you to be so afraid to lose your TV that you will accept any amount of abuse and stay quiet about it. The admin wants to create an atmosphere in which you constantly whine about your issues and are then constantly gaslit that they will be looked into. All the while, nothing ever gets done, and you eventually get too tired or exhausted to care anymore. They are a customer service line always placing you on hold until you eventually hang up. When you finally say no, declare that "I am now in control of what happens next," it feels amazing. It is likely one of the few times in your entire prison bid that you will have a sense of power or autonomy. You get to provoke their reactions for once, you get to take their sense of safety away for once, you get to make them feel powerless and pathetic for once.

Standing up to your bully is a truly delightful feeling. There were times my resistance felt revolutionary, and there were times it was spectacularly reactionary. But it always felt euphoric. Like kisses from an angel. What the elders in prison, and ADX specifically, taught me is not to waste your rebellion. Don't waste your rage on a missing pack of sugar when the real issue is them holding your mail longer than necessary. Don't let them see that they have the power to get you worked up—and messed up—by doing a couple of small things, because then they own you.

If they see you're easy to rile up, they will never stop doing those small things. Getting the reaction is what they seek, and they'll know you're an easy target. Fight to win. Don't let them hurt you or take away your joy over nothing. Learn when it is time to resist and when it is time to breathe out the rage. Or don't. Go to war over everything if that provides the sense of joy and purpose you need. But that is a long road to travel.

The reality is that every single day some dark-souled cop will give you a reason to go off on them. Every day of your life, something will happen that is enraging and disgraceful enough to throw your entire future away. You cannot rebel every day and maintain any sense of mental well-being, safety, or togetherness. You will lose your mind being in constant fight-or-flight. You will lose the ability to regulate and understand real threats when they happen. You must find your cause. You must decide what means the most to you and what you are willing to lose to defend it.

I saw some resistance at ADX that was awe-inspiring. Folks doing all they could to disrespect and humiliate the cagers walking around wearing badges. There were also more peculiar forms of resistance. There were people who refused to leave their cells, ever. They refused to cell-rotate, they wouldn't go to medical, and they wouldn't go to rec, *ever*. Eventually staff had enough of it and had to force them out. Those prisoners would end up cuffing up before the team got called, but that's still resistance. That still disrupted the officers' day. The cops still had to stop what they were doing, go get all dressed up in their riot gear, go have their little preattack meetings, walk all around the prison, and then those prisoners would make it all for nothing. That is still resistance. Hilarious, anticlimactic resistance.

Every act of rebellion within prison is justified. I may not agree with every tactic. I may not agree with every move. But I will never judge someone for any act of prison rebellion. I think it is brave. I think it is honorable. I think it throws a wrench in their system and shows them that what they think they're accomplishing isn't the case. They are so confident about how to break spirits, so confident they know just what it takes to smother the individualism and dignity of the hardened convict. To stand up to them is to say, "Fuck you and fuck your program!" I love that. I love everything about it, and I would laugh to myself all day seeing the disgust and anger on their faces. Sometimes the agony of your enemy can feel better than the joy of your own life. That isn't a place you always want to be mentally, but while you're there it feels delightful.

That doesn't mean you have to buck to be a solid prisoner. That isn't what I'm saying at all. Some people just want to exist without any extra problems or dilemmas. They want to get their mail, watch their shows, and do their time. They've seen it all and have no desire to see more of it. Sometimes these people will talk down about those standing up for themselves, essentially taking on the persona of their captors. Sometimes they try to offer advice or a cool head. There is nothing wrong with sitting out, but there is something deeply wrong with bashing those who don't. Certain prisoners feeling morally superior by looking down on the resistance of others offends me to my core. I totally understand wanting to lie down and have your time be as stress-free as possible, but we should never side with the enemy.

III CHAPTER 12

The Control Unit

> I have 18 months left in Control Unit, Insha Allah (God Willing), if I don't get my time ran up.... But most likely these crackers are going to keep me here in ADX a while longer. I've been here 12 years. I refuse to kiss these crackers' asses or compromise. It's death before dishonor for life with me.
> —Wayne "Silk" Perry

Joe is pissed. It seems like he just got unpacked and already he is having to cell-rotate. *Again*. Every thirty days Joe is forced to pack up all his belongings, roll up his mattress, and do a deep clean of the entire cage, all to move one cell to the left. The person who just left his new cell was breathtakingly filthy. He never cleaned up after himself, left piss stains all over the toilet and food crumbs all over the floor. Joe would love to put a knife in his throat. The person behind Joe is no better. Loud as hell all night, banging on the shower and trying to keep everyone awake at all hours. Disrupting the lives of the other prisoners because he can't get at the guards. To Joe, he's a dirtbag bastard. Joe is sandwiched between two of the worst people in the entire goddamn unit, and there is nothing he can do to change that. Joe has been on this unit for forty-five months. Sadly, he has gotten two disciplinary write-ups, and he knows what that means: There will be no early exit from this hell. Joe knows that he must endure for at least another twelve months, and he is pissed.

This is life in the control unit. It is miserable. By design, the control unit is the most exhausting unit in the entire prison. It is disruptive to any sense of joy you may have, built to ensure you cannot get comfortable in your surroundings. The control unit is the largest unit in the ADX, holding approximately eighty people at a time. Although every single cell in the ADX is a control unit cell—twenty-three-hour lockdown, no physical contact, two-man staff hold—you have to be specifically designated to this unit during your referral process. Joe isn't a delicate flower. Joe murdered someone at a penitentiary, and this was his reward. Joe was young and wanted to make a name for himself, and for a short while people spoke about him with fear and respect. He had a solid rep, which is more than he ever had in the free world. After a while, though, like most people in prison, he was forgotten. Time slows down for no one, and Joe became just another homie with a body to his name. One of hundreds.

Joe had his ADX hearing after pleading guilty and receiving life in prison. Life in the federal system means life. There is no good time; there is no parole. You will die in prison. He would've been free two years ago, though that is a reality he long ago let go of. His original sentence was only sixty months—that's five years—and he had already done three years. He had one foot already out the door and had plans to live with his mom until he could find a job. Joe made a choice, though. He would rather feel respected and valued in prison than feel like a worthless nobody in the free world. At Joe's ADX hearing, the regional officer told him that instead of going to the ADX GP (general population), he would be sentenced to the control unit for a period of sixty months minimum. It's been almost four years. Joe won't say it out loud, but he desperately regrets his decisions.

This is how the control unit works at ADX. During your referral hearing, the prison will specifically request the control unit instead of GP, alleging some need for extra discipline due to your level of violence or your perceived power. People in the control unit are sentenced to a specific amount of time that they must serve, a minimum time. Everyone in the control unit is there for an action that occurred within a separate prison—typically some sort of violence, usually murder, but also if you've annoyed the Bureau badly enough within your "leadership" role. The more severe the violence, the longer the time you will spend in the control unit.

Life inside the control unit is similar to life inside anywhere in ADX, just slightly more annoying, and those annoyances add up. In the normal GP units, prisoners cell-rotate every three months. Cell-rotation day is the most annoying day in prison (besides shakedowns). You pack up everything you own, clean your cell extensively for the person coming behind you, move into a new cell, and clean that one equally extensively *just in case* that person didn't show you the same respect. Only then can you begin to unpack all your stuff and try to get comfortable. I've never had a cell rotation that didn't cause me a minor panic attack. In the control unit, you barely have time to get your bearings before you're already having to move again. Many people in that unit prefer not to unpack. Instead, they will just get their essentials out, leaving everything else put away.

Control unit convicts have the same amount of limited recreation time as everyone else, but the guards make it slightly more cumbersome. Instead of just handcuffing you behind your back and having the two guards walk you out, they also handcuff your legs, ensuring awkward shuffle steps to get wherever you need to go. Considering this prison is one long, circular maze, it is a major burden to have your ankles chained. But you are so dangerous that the admins couldn't imagine just having two armed guards on you and just having your hands cuffed behind your back. They need more safeguards. They are very delicate.

The biggest difference, though, is the behavior reports and the hearings with the director. During officer walk-throughs in the control unit, the pigs are instructed to observe the prisoner in their natural habitat and document what they see: "Tuesday, 11/19/23, Prisoner Jones was reading a book, 8:30 a.m." Every thirty minutes, these clowns do this performative work for every prisoner in the unit. It is degrading to be documented this way. Some prisoners will stand at the door masturbating or touching themselves so that the guards have to watch and write it down. Prisoners will do whatever it takes to reclaim any sense of power or control over their lives. When you have nothing, you'll do whatever it takes to get something.

Once every three to four weeks, the regional director will get off their lazy fascist ass and fly to Colorado just to conduct hearings with every person in the control unit. These hearings are attended by the director, the warden, the captain, and usually some prick from SIS. At the hearing, they go over your behavior report—what the guards have documented you doing, what psych says you're doing, what SIS reports about you, all the profiling they've done to determine what type of person you are and where you are at mentally. If this sounds disturbing and psychologically invasive, that's because it is. The entire point of the control unit is to change your mindset and behavioral patterns, to make you more compliant. The feds intentionally take away every comfort or stability you have so that when they start giving it back due to "good behavior," you will see them not as the punisher but as the rewarder. If you are a good boy, you get your head scratched and some treats. If you are a bad boy, you get whipped.

The director will go over all these invasive things and ask you a few meaningless questions: "What books ya reading?" "You about ready to get out of here?" "You're still gonna roll with your homies when you're out?" SIS takes notes, documenting things they may be able to use against you later, and once this charade is all over, you are shuffled back to your cell. These hearings aren't mandatory, as in they won't roll up on you if you refuse to go, but they are mandatory if you want to get out of that unit. The control unit has a maximum time mandated by Congress of ten years. If you do not go to those meetings, there is a good chance you will be stuck in that particular hell for the full decade.

While I was in ADX, I heard that only one person was anywhere close to the ten-year mark. You've never heard of this person. They killed someone in USP Canaan a decade or so ago. Now they were refusing to comply, to bend the knee to the director. An act of resistance: "I would rather suffer than allow you to dictate my behavior or mindset." No one's going to stop you from being miserable and right. The BOP doesn't care if you suffer. They are not concerned with our righteous dignity. This person will do the ten years and then be placed in ADX GP for another ten or so, if they are lucky.

Beefs within the control unit can be mentally soul sucking and damaging. They are a swamp that devours you. Small things that are meaningless can become the most important aspect of someone's life. I've met and heard horror stories about people who became unhinged because of a control unit beef from seven years ago that they still haven't been able to let go of. The hooks sink into their consciousness and can never be ripped out.

Imagine: You have been in the control unit for four out of five years. You are desperate to get out, and you are praying the director sees things in your favor at the next hearing. Something is itching in your brain, though. Every night for the past few months, at around 1 a.m., the piece of rubbish living below you begins tapping on their stainless steel shower. The noise reverberates up through your shower, an audible Chinese water torture tactic meant to drive people insane.

At first you tried to laugh it off. *This fool downstairs is a punk.* During outside rec, you complain about it to anyone who will listen, and they offer solidarity. "Yeah, that dude's a fool, brush it off." And you try. God knows you try, and you'll continue to try.

Over the following days and weeks, it begins to take over a portion of your mind, occupying space once reserved for fond memories or old songs or jokes. Sometimes you lose it and start smashing the shower back at them, trying to drown out their taps. You think you've succeeded, but after a few peaceful moments of sleep, the tapping begins again. Turning up the TV doesn't work at all; you can *feel* the taps. The shower is right next to the bed, so you cannot escape it. You yell down the shower drain, "You fucking bitch! I'll fucking kill you, you punk bitch!" Your torturer doesn't go to rec. They sleep during the daytime and attack your brain at night. You can't figure out why this is happening; it makes no sense to you. You've never done anything to this person. You don't even know them. No one at rec has any idea who they are. Someone says they are a "bug" (a derogatory term for someone with mental health issues) who has been inside too damn long. Someone says they are a check-in from Victorville, a dropout, someone who eats their own waste. You begin to visualize what they look like, smell like, talk like. Your fantasies of hurting them become your only source of dopamine.

They never yell back, they never tap harder, they never engage except to worm into your brain. You try speaking with the admins, who tell you, "Sorry, we don't do cell relocations." You ask lieutenants, you ask guards, and they all laugh it off. They tell you to deal with it, to quit being a pussy. Speaking to these people can put your life on the line, but you are so goddamn desperate. You can't stand it. Why is this bastard doing this to you? Why is staff allowing this to happen? You've been lying down, not causing any problems. You've always been respectful; you always honor other people's routines and sleep schedules. You never do anything to bother anyone else in their cells. Why you? What is this dude's problem?

You begin to snap. All you can think about is them. All you can talk about is them. You spend all day thinking about hurting them. You fantasize about putting a knife into them. You aren't a violent person. You've done what you had to do in the past, but you don't worship violence. But they are summoning all your demons. You try pleading with your abuser through the shower. "Come on, man, I'm trying to sleep!" You try finding out when they will get out of the control unit. You learn that they are not going to the director's hearings, that they aren't trying to get out at all. They want to be in there; they want to torture you. They thrive on torturing you. All they want in life is to make sure your life is miserable. People out at rec are tired of hearing about it, and they start ignoring you when you bring it up. You become the annoying pariah; your laments fall on the deafest of ears.

You've run out of options. You hate this bastard, and you hate yourself for thinking about them nonstop. You know you've become boring—you're boring yourself even—but you can't shake this. You have spoken with psychology, begging them to move you, but they've said no. You've spoken to lieutenants, who laughed in your face. You've been gaslit by the captain and warden, who both said they would "look into it." You have no other options. You pack up all your things, you wrap towels around your face, and when the guards come to pass out trays, you throw water right in their faces. They go crazy, screaming, pressing the alarms, emptying their pepper spray into your cell. Within twenty seconds, there are about ten guards outside your cell screaming at you to "Cuff up!" Threatening you, ready to beat you. You immediately cuff up. The point isn't to buck or cause trouble; you've wanted desperately to avoid having problems. The goal is to get out of that goddamn cell. To get moved to a cell where you can sleep, where you can think, where you can function as a human being.

You will be charged with a 203—assault on staff not causing serious bodily injury. You will lose twenty-seven days of good time, lose your phone and visits for a year and canteen for six months. The guards will ignore you on rec day for several months. However, you will be in a different cell. They have to move you once that cell is contaminated. Your body will be burning from the pepper spray, and you will be aching from the casual beating you received. Blessedly, though, for the first night in months, the angels of solemnity will grant you a peaceful night's rest. You can't remember a time when you've ever felt so calm. You will know that you did what you had to do for your own mental well-being. There is no guilt or shame involved, and there is no remorse, because you tried things their way. You tried going through all the official channels, and you were ignored. You put your mental well-being first, and that is nothing to wag your finger at.

At your next meeting with the director, he will bring up your unprovoked violence against staff. How you went out of your way to assault a helpless, innocent staff member who was doing nothing but trying to feed you. How that sort of behavior is the entire reason the control unit exists. That *clearly* you have not learned your lesson yet. All the times you begged for help will be meaningless in their eyes. All the times you tried to handle things in an appropriate and respectful manner will be forgotten. You will bring up the countless times you tried speaking with psych and the administration. The director will patronize you, treat you like a spoiled child, and tell you that this is no excuse, that there are other options available and that you were immature and unreasonable. It will not matter to you at all. You will have seen this word vomit coming a mile away. The director will determine that you need *at least* two or three more years in the control unit. That your previous four years of great behavior are not nearly as important as your one moment of desperation. You'll go back to your cell disappointed but relieved. You'll finally feel like yourself again.

There are people who have gone through this rotation multiple times. Some folks can withstand the barrage of torture, but others need to change their situation or risk losing their minds. They have seen what can happen to people inside this prison, and especially inside this unit. They have seen people snap, seen people reach the point of no return. You can feel it coming up on you. You felt the personality change, when you started waking up and thinking only of revenge. You eat and taste nothing but rage. You didn't want to be that person, you didn't want to live that life, but the prison gave you no other option.

So many of the horrors of prison occur because the administrators leave no other options. People cannot transfer to get away from violent predators, and people cannot leave their gangs without putting their lives on the line. There is no escape from the brutality, because the administration needs it to maintain control. Even the most violent people inside prison are still victims of toxic prison culture. The creators and holders of this culture are not the men who exist within it but the people who propagate and benefit from it. Control units aren't a symptom of prison violence, they are a cause of it.

CHAPTER 13

Little Guantánamo

> H Unit is another level of hell altogether. It's a prison within a prison, yet that doesn't quite convey the unique conditions of confinement there. It's been called the only known black site on American soil, but it's more like a black hole, a void where men are slowly buried alive in layers of isolation until they vanish entirely.... Out of 156,000 prisoners in BOP custody, there are an estimated forty to fifty prisoners under the SAMs restrictions. Nearly all of them are in H Unit. The first rule of SAMs is that nobody involved can talk about SAMs. The entire process is so shrouded in secrecy that it's difficult to ascertain even the names of the SAMs prisoners.
>
> —Alan Pendergast

> Five years ago, if someone told me some of the things I hear in H Unit, I would have thought they were crazy and wouldn't have listened to them. Now I'm listening. Some prisoners tell me to shut off my cell light and never use it because it emits harmful radiation and the TV screen emits the same. These prisoners live in dark cells day and night. Now I wonder if what they say is true. Some say that hot water is poisonous and harmful. Some believe the SAMs will be on us until we die.
>
> —Nidal Ayyad, former ADX prisoner on SAMs who was convicted for involvement in the 1993 World Trade Center bombing

> The longer I spent in this period of segregation, the worse it gets on my efforts to survive, to maintain my state of mind and my mental capacity. I lost fifty pounds from being on hunger strike in H-Unit, and hunger strikes became a regular occurrence in

the unit, with medical staff coming every weekend to weigh each inmate. This was the first time in my life that I experienced the brutality of force-feeding.

—Mahmud Abouhalima, held under SAMs in H-Unit at ADX since 2005

All units in ADX are oppressively restrictive, but some more so than others. The most restrictive unit within the most restrictive prison in the entire country is H-Unit, also known as the SAMs (Special Administrative Measures) unit. SAMs are a type of communication restriction that can only be placed on a prisoner by the US attorney general, the most powerful cop in the nation. H-Unit is only for people on SAMs restrictions, and these are some of the most notorious and infamous prisoners you have ever heard of—or a lot of times never heard of.

SAMs restrictions are personalized and may vary by person, but all of them are unbelievable in their scope and contain certain ugly similarities. Every person on SAMs restrictions is prohibited from writing letters to anyone outside their lawyers and their immediate family: spouse, parents, siblings (in some circumstances), and children. Some cannot even write to their stepchildren or stepparents. These letters take ages to reach their recipients, due to having to be read directly by an FBI agent. This applies to books and media as well. Any books or magazines must be approved by an FBI (or sometimes CIA) officer and can be rejected on a whim without cause. One Egyptian on SAMs was not allowed to receive one of Jimmy Carter's books about Israel and Palestine. These same restrictions apply to phone calls. They are only allowed two or three phone calls per month, and these phone calls are live monitored by the agents and or interpreters. Same for visits, which are live monitored by an interpreter or FBI agent, or both.

SAMs restrictions are powerful and overtake any other designation within the prison system. The Boston Marathon bomber is technically on death row and should be held at USP Terre Haute; instead, because he is on SAMs, he must stay in ADX until the restrictions expire. Only once that happens will he be moved to Indiana to potentially be murdered by the state.

The point of SAMs restrictions is to cut off the prisoner totally from the outside world. SAMs exist to bury the prisoner and limit any influence they may have on the free-world population. The only person who can apply SAMs is the attorney general, and the only person who can remove SAMs is the attorney general. In theory, the SAMs have to be reviewed every six months, but in reality these restrictions can last for decades. Oftentimes prisoners will sue the US government to get their SAMs modified or removed, and sometimes these lawsuits will work, only for the government to immediately place them right back on the prisoner for some frivolous reason. Many of the people on SAMs at one point in time were incredibly infamous for their actions: 9/11 planners and fighters, the Boston bomber, Ramzi Yousef, El Chapo. Those are the big names that everyone associates with ADX.

That isn't the entire story of H-Unit, though. This unit is rife with brutality, racism, and disregard for human life. The majority of people on SAMs restrictions are Muslim. The US government says it doesn't discriminate regarding these measures, but the population of H-Unit strongly disagrees. Many of the people in H-Unit are not American and had never been to America prior to being stolen from their home countries and placed in our prisons. They were fighting either their own governments or a military invasion of their own country. Many of them speak little to no English. This unit is the American-soil Guantánamo Bay. People are taken from their nations, tortured brutally, and then dropped in a box for the remainder of their lives.

Some of the men in this unit have committed—or have been accused of committing—actions that are hard to fathom. Some, however, were accused of the vague charge of "providing material support to a terrorist organization." This charge allows the government to imprison people for anything they perceive as benefiting *any* organization the government designates as terrorist. This charge is incredibly hard to defend against in court, because you must prove you *didn't* know something or intend to do something. The law was established to ensure easy convictions and long sentences. Men accused of letting a friend borrow their car or donating money to a food-support organization end up with decades in prison with the harshest communication restrictions imaginable.

Most of the people within H-Unit are there for fighting against the US military machine in one way or another. The term *terrorist* does not adequately describe someone who was fighting against an invading military force or fighting in solidarity with those under siege. It may be hard for people who have never met a jihadi to understand, but that is an act of privilege. Most of those who would judge have never had to face down the brutality of the US military. It is a privilege to exist outside of that repression. If you cannot understand where they were coming from, then you most likely cannot begin to grasp what it would be like to live under those conditions. The pain it must cause to witness a military brutally eradicating people you consider family. While far-right Christians cry that their faith is under attack, Muslims have seen their families bombed and invaded in dozens of countries for generations.

It isn't my place to judge those who have fallen victim to the US war machine. I may not agree with all the tactics or targets of these fighters, but I can hardly condemn them for fighting back. I am not going to look at the victims of US imperialism and criminalize whatever tactic they used to resist. The US drops countless bombs with drones and billions of dollars' worth of weapons; the jihadis fight with whatever they have access to and pick out the targets they have in proximity to them. War is an ugly game, and when you wage a war you cannot blame the victims for having the audacity to fight back rather than submit.

H-Unit can be a truly awful place to live. The men in that unit do not have showers in their cells and are only allowed to shower three days a week. Shower availability is controlled by staff, who walk each prisoner to the shower in their underwear, time them, and then walk them back. It is degrading. Often, staff will claim that the men can't shower that day because the prison is understaffed or too busy. This is a tactic by those who control everything to degrade those who have nothing.

Outside and inside recreation is often delayed or just flatly denied by staff, and canteen is incredibly limited in H-Unit. They do not have access to the same food, drinks, or clothing, and they are not allowed to spend nearly as much as other ADX prisoners. Mail is delayed for so long that men have found out they have grandchildren before ever finding out their daughters were pregnant. This creates an atmosphere of sadness and loneliness, but also of solidarity among one another. A solidifying of ideology. They are reminded daily that the enemy they fight is disgusting, vile, and worthy of opposing. Many of the officers in ADX were the same soldiers bombing and occupying the Middle Eastern and African nations that the H-Unit prisoners call home. This is not a safe environment for anyone, let alone Muslim freedom fighters.

Although most prisoners in H-Unit are Muslims, there are others who have fallen victim to the government's most restrictive measures. Brand members who once sent out murderous hits from within ADX, writing in urine to hide the messages, were held in H-Unit until their deaths. A mob boss who allegedly tried ordering hits from within prison after his conviction was there for three to five years. A Black gang leader who ordered a firebombing that led to the death of seven key witnesses in his trial was also being held there. Most famously, both the Boston bomber and El Chapo are being held on this range. Others have included cult leaders, someone who filed way too many lawsuits and liens against prison officials, and other high-ranking gang and cartel leaders. But these other folks all get filtered out, doing only a short time on SAMs and then moving on to ADX GP or other penitentiaries.

Only El Chapo, the Boston bomber, and a few others will ever serve the sort of time the foreign jihadis will. The federal government does not care about their family structures, about whether their cousins or aunts are the only family they have access to. They will not get to speak with them. The government does not care that they will never see their grandchildren or hear the voices of their nieces and nephews. They committed an unthinkable act: They went against the war machine. Terry Nichols, one of the orchestrators of the 1995 Oklahoma City bombing, was never placed in H-Unit. Ted Kaczynski was never in H-Unit. Eric Rudolph, the 1996 Olympic bomber, never sniffed H-Unit. They weren't Muslims and their targets weren't military.

Although these men are under restrictions designed to isolate them from their entire world, and break their spirits in the process, the highest concentration of resistance within the ADX comes from H-Unit. Hundreds of lawsuits against the BOP and the federal government have come from within H-Unit. Some of these men were in Guantánamo Bay or in black-site prisons in Poland or Jordan before being flown over to the US and placed into this nation's most restricted prison. They have seen and experienced the worst torture our government has to offer and have lost all fear of retaliation or punishment. You can no longer break someone who has experienced hell on earth. Considering they have literally all day to sit and think and talk among themselves (if they feel like yelling), these men are voracious litigators.

There is a misperception about jihadis that they are these uneducated, backward men who crawled out of a cave. (Some of them did crawl out of a cave, but it was with a machine gun in their hands, firing at invaders.) In my experiences with them, that wasn't the situation at all. These men had been mechanics, doctors, farmers, scientists, and teachers. Fathers and husbands. They picked up the gun not because they were bored but out of desperation and necessity. It is foolish to believe the US government's narrative about who these fighters are. The government wants us to believe all these men are barbaric savages. I believe those flying the drones and loading the tanks are the savages.

When we obsess over alleged crimes, we no longer focus on the *why* of it all. *Why* were they committing those actions? Richard Reid, the "shoe bomber," would point out in good nature that Americans are all frustrated that we have to take off our shoes at airports, but not as frustrated as the parents who watched their children die in indiscriminate bombings. Our minor inconvenience doesn't really add up to the major inconvenience of having a brutal occupying military destroying everything you've ever known or loved. Those of us in Western nations sit on a pile of privilege when it comes to these issues. We have never had a foreign military parading its tanks down our streets or had to hide when a thousand missiles were falling on our suburbs. I cannot judge resistance to occupation.

Richard was one of the men resisting in H-Unit. He filed lawsuits, appealed to the British government, and got international attention. After seven years, his SAMs were removed and he was placed in K-B Unit, the lifer and elder unit. By then it had been seven years of silence. He had no one left. His family had moved on, and his community was too afraid to support him. He sits in the lifer unit with little to no support. That's how SAMs work. People get tired of waiting, get tired of being rejected and denied access to you, and then eventually they move on and you are left all alone. It is exhausting to continually be denied any chance of speaking to your loved ones. Your spirit and hopes can only take so many letdowns before it simply becomes too painful. This is just what the government intended.

Lawsuits aren't the only resistance in H-unit, though. Many of these men have dedicated their lives to their cause, and they were all willing to die in the jihadi struggle. That doesn't just go away the moment you are locked up. You don't suddenly decide, "Well, hey, maybe the murderous fake Christians were right, time to pick up the Bible." Absolutely not. When you have dedicated your life to a cause,

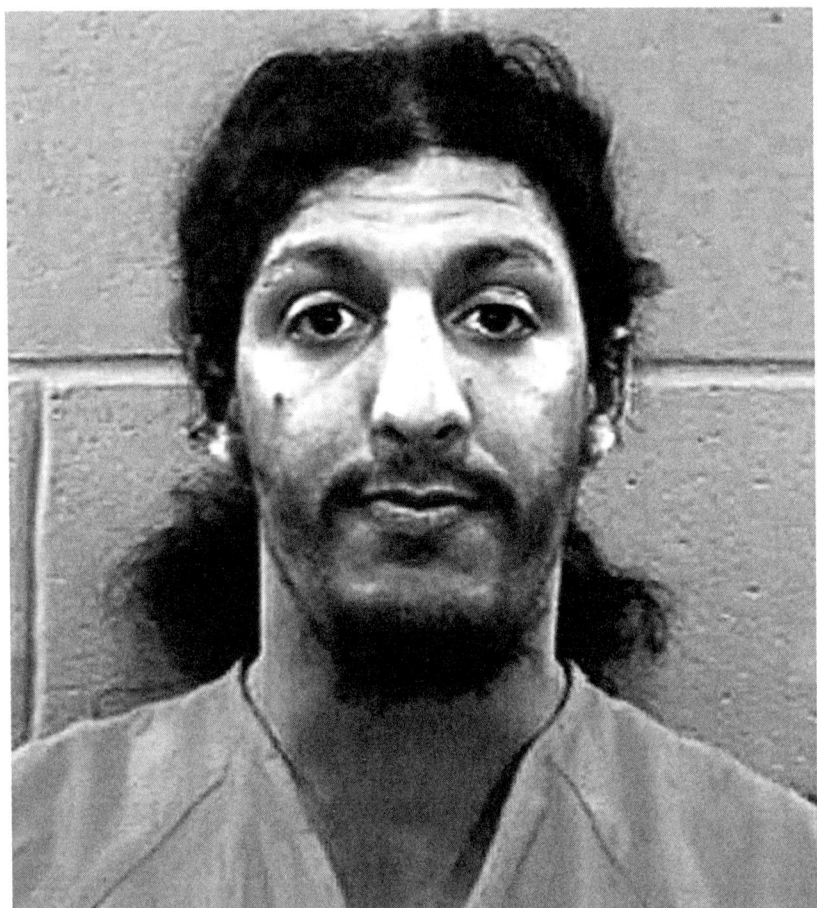

Richard Reid, known as the "shoe bomber." He did seven years on SAMs (Special Administrative Measures).

every act of resistance is an act of life or death. There have been some extreme hunger strikes within the ADX, and almost all of them have come from within H-Unit.

When the prison took away communal recreation, thus preventing group prayer, the men went after it. They tried first to talk with administrators, and then they tried to use the internal BOP grievance forms. After that, they attempted lawsuits against both the BOP and the US government for denying them access to their religious rights. When that was shut down, they took it to the next level. Dozens of men went on hunger strike with no intention of giving it up. In some instances, they achieved their goals, but then the government would go back on their agreements and everything had to start over. There have been countless large and minor hunger strikes, and whether the men achieved their goals or not, they still won. They won by not capitulating to the pathetic humans who lock the cages.

These strikes didn't garner as much attention as the 2013 Pelican Bay hunger strike in California, mostly because there was no way for anyone to find out. The lawyers of the prisoners were not legally allowed to talk about the conditions or what was happening in the prison. In 2005, radical attorney Lynne Stewart was found guilty and sentenced to ten years in federal prison for discussing the conditions of Omar Abdel-Rahman, the "Blind Sheikh," who was on SAMs. That is one of the most devastating aspects of these restrictions. Not only can the prisoners not speak with anyone or seek help, but their lawyers legally can't either. This breeds vile lawlessness and violence by the officers, knowing that no one will ever hear of their brutality. Fortunately, when lawsuits are filed the information becomes public knowledge, and that is the only way we were able to learn what was happening (before some of them finally started getting off SAMs). What we were able to find out was sickening. The filthiness of this government never ceases to disgust me.

The men took their hunger strikes very seriously. When you hunger strike in the feds, they have a policy they are supposed to follow:

- After three days of you refusing every meal, the prison is supposed to report your hunger strike to the Regional Office. At that time, medical is informed, and they should begin to weigh you and check your vitals at least once a day.
- The pigs will offer you food at every meal and will use that time to try to diminish you for what you are doing. They will say every nasty thing, make fun of you, and mock your religion or whatever cause you are standing for. The lieutenants will then try a different routine, to convince you that if you just eat, they will work with you. They will say that this isn't the way to go about things (which is the indicator that this is absolutely the only way to go about things).
- After nine days of refusal, the strike must be reported to the national BOP office. If you have outside support, this would be the time to raise a lot of awareness, do call-in campaigns, and

really try to get attention on the hunger strikers. For the men in H-Unit, that wasn't always possible, so they continued on their own, every day being harassed and belittled for having the gall to stand up for themselves. Guards will begin refusing to allow you recreation, making up excuses that you are going outside to eat, that you are sharing food with one another. Any nonsense to prevent you from having any quality of life.

- After about five to ten days on the strike, your hunger stops. You no longer feel hungry but instead feel tired, restless, subdued. You may think about food and dream about your favorite meals, but you no longer feel the aching pain in your stomach as your brain tries to convince you to eat. The men in H-Unit took strength from one another, from their united struggle, and from all the torture they had already endured. This was just the next step.
- The guards will come with medical and weigh you every day, along with checking your vitals. They will comment on how you are fading away, how you could die any day now if you aren't careful. Medical will use scare tactics on you, commenting on how your kidneys are probably about to shut down, saying that you should eat if you care about your family or yourself in any way.
- If you are one of the few people to make it past a month, things will begin to escalate quickly. The national office will be tired of you and will want this to end as soon as possible. Forced feedings happen in the BOP, and it is as sickening as you can imagine. In the BOP, they do not force-feed you to keep you alive, they do it to end your strike. They do it to break your spirit, and the process is what nightmares are made of.
- After thirty or forty days of not eating but still drinking water, the Special Operations Response Team (SORT) will arrive at your door and tell you to cuff up. Seven guards with batons and weapons telling one starving person that you need to come to the door and get handcuffed or they will beat the living hell out of you. I've never heard of someone refusing.
- They will then walk you to medical, where you will sit in a chair and have your chin placed on this weird head-holder thing. They will have a long rubber straw and a tub of some liquid trash that is supposed to mimic the nutrients you are missing out on. If the

guards are especially cruel and hate you, they will have left the tube in the freezer so that it burns and tears while going down.
- The medical people will give you one last chance to eat, which you will refuse. They will then gleefully insert the hose through your nose, down your throat, and into your stomach. Sometimes (oftentimes), the tube will go into your lungs and not down your esophagus. This is because they are cruel, sick bastards, but also because they are not trained in doing this. Force-feeding is a form of physical torture. Doctors and nurses are not taught how to torture people in medical school; for this type of abuse, they learn on the job.
- The hunger striker will feel like they are drowning, like they are being suffocated, and experience stomach cramps and agonizing pain. Sometimes people vomit violently; other times they get so gassy it's unbearable. They will then be led back to their cell to suffer all alone, and the next person will be grabbed to go through the same process. This will continue until the striker caves in and relents to the torture. Or dies.

During some of these hunger strikes, dozens of people went through this process. For months and months, every single day they were subjected to forced feedings, all because they wanted to be able to pray together. One person ended up being force-fed for three hundred days. It never made the news; it wasn't all over CNN or even on the local Denver stations. The guards still brag about this as if they accomplished something big and interesting. As if they aren't sick and desperate for finding glee in someone else's misery.

After enough time, everyone ends up relenting. Your body can only take so much, and your comrades on the range will console you and let you know that you didn't fail, you didn't give up. You went up against the full power of the US federal prison system and didn't blink. You gave it your all, and they had to resort to sadistic torture to try to break you. These men have steel resolve, and I am constantly stunned by their refusal to bend or yield to the pigs.

I have met many jihadis throughout my time in the BOP. Some of them were just kids who were disgustingly entrapped by the FBI. Here's how it works: Loners with learning disabilities, feeling hopeless and sad, suddenly have a friend who loves them and supports them.

This friend spends time figuring out the deep inner workings of the loner's psyche, then uses all their vulnerabilities and fears against them. The friend encourages, plans, plots, and pays for "terrorist" attacks. Then, when the time comes, the FBI swoops in and arrests the violent, wild, anti-American terrorist! The news broadcasts the major FBI score in crushing another Muslim terror plot, never mentioning that the FBI created this plot, inventing it out of thin air just to boost their arrest numbers and keep their funding flowing.

Other jihadis I've met were assholes. Just like in any other subgroup, there are people who will rub you the wrong way. They can be snotty, shortsighted, rude, misogynistic, homophobic, and overall just gross people. Humans are humans. Most I've met, however, are just people who cared too much. People who had seen enough and didn't feel there were any other options available to prevent the slaughter of their families. There is severe trauma that comes with witnessing horror after horror without being able to do anything about it. After a while, some people decide that there absolutely is something to do about it, and those are some of the people I met.

Regarding those in H-Unit, I feel a deep pit of sadness in my stomach. These are the most infamous jihadis still alive and in custody. Those who bombed the embassies in Kenya and Tanzania, those who planned attacks on US ships in Yemen, those who fought Russians and Marines in Afghanistan. Fighters from the '80s who took on the Palestinian struggle for freedom, those who didn't bow to US firepower. Those who brought the fight to US soil in whatever form they felt best emphasized their rage and heartbreak. I do not see monsters. When I talk about these people, I am often met with questioning gazes or confused glares. People cannot understand my empathy toward these people. But they are facing a unique form of imprisonment, and the enemy of my enemy...

Can you understand an action without necessarily feeling positive about it? Do I want to be blown up by the underwear bomber? No. Would I have celebrated that action had it been successful? Not at all. But can I understand the desperate need to strike back at the US war machine? Hell yes I can. I can imagine how devastated and enraged I would be if a bomb fell on my community and killed hundreds or thousands of people I consider family. I can picture that rage. When the cops killed Michael Brown, I was so sad and angry that I put my freedom on the line to express what I felt was righteous rage. What if the military had dropped a bomb on the community of Ferguson? What if my family had been under that bomb?

Taking the moral high ground gets us nowhere. If we are not willing to understand why these actions happened, then we can never move forward. H-Unit is not acceptable in any way. It is a weapon for political posturing. It is a device used to beat these men's psyches every single day. It is abusive on micro and macro levels. From the small indignities, like having to strip naked before recreation, to the massive pain of losing almost all contact with your family, it is the absolute worst that ADX has to offer, and if it weren't for the prisoners and lawyers filing those lawsuits, we would never know of the horrors happening there.

Today, there are only thirty or forty people still on SAMs, and I pray that number never increases. I, as an anarchist, can never stand by quietly as the government destroys this community of fighters. If we continue to remain silent on this and let these things stay under the radar, we cannot complain or play the victim when H-Unit is filled with our fighters, when the Stop Cop City people or antifa fighters or Palestinian activists fill those cages. We have to say that government brutality is never okay, even if the actions of the fighters are hard to comprehend. Abolition only works when it is hard. It is easy to want the peaceful protesters to not be held in prison or tortured, but this must apply to everyone. I want Ramzi free. I want Abdulrahman El Bahnasawy free. I want an end to US imperialism, and I want its resisters to breathe free air once again in their lives. All means all.

||| CHAPTER 14

Those Who Stay and Those Who Go

> i use the word "spiritcide" to describe the dehumanizing and pernicious existence that i have suffered since i have been a prisoner, particularly the years that i have been in this dungeon (labyrinth). It is spiritcide because the death and annihilation of the spirit are what the jailers are seeking by keeping me in such deleterious conditions.
> —Oscar López Rivera

J-Unit

J-Unit is for men who are being allowed to step down and reenter normal custody penitentiaries. The Bureau cannot, despite its most desperate desires, keep every single person in ADX. Some people have to be allowed to leave, or it will become overcrowded. The administration decides who is worthy of stepping down and who isn't, and like most things in ADX, this is arbitrary. Some of the people stepping down have been doing prison programs their entire stay and are desperate to be out of the dungeon. Others haven't touched a single work packet and refuse to participate but are also equally qualified to leave.

Stepping down is a long process. Typically, you will do two years within the ADX GP, and then, if you have been well behaved, the admin will move you to J-Unit. In theory, you will be placed in a group that doesn't have any social or gang rivals in it. This rarely happens. Men are often placed in direct contact with people they want to kill and who want to kill them. Once the inevitable happens, they will be placed back in GP and ridiculed for throwing away their chance at escape. Blamed for existing in the world the BOP created and maintains.

After six to twelve months in J-Unit, prisoners are moved to the USP Florence Step-Down Unit. I was terrified they would send me there at first, before I was hip to the policy. In this unit, prisoners get a bit more time outside their cells. This is supposed to prepare people to be more social, to learn how to get along with others and play nice. Yet this place can often be a bloodbath. Just because you are leaving ADX does not mean that you are leaving behind all the experiences you have absorbed throughout your incarceration. Those beefs and fears and pains do not just disappear. Further, just because you are leaving ADX does not mean the administration wants you to leave. The ADX admins answer to the regional officer, and there are often disagreements about who should stay and who should go. If the admins disagree with the regional officer, they will simply place you around someone you aren't safe to be around. There will be violence, and the ADX admins will be justified in showing that you shouldn't have been stepped down in the first place.

Stepping down is a goal for many people, but it is also a scam. Your step-down can be revoked at any time for any reason. All it takes is one officer saying you looked at them funny or threatened them and you will be back in GP. Even once you make it to the USP Step-Down Unit, any disciplinary write-up will result in you being sent back to GP.

Randy Platt was in the control unit for approximately three years for slicing an officer before he was sent to GP. After being in GP for a year, the SIS officers came and asked him if he wanted to step down. This was unheard of. There was absolutely no way that someone who had committed that type of violence would be allowed to step down so quickly. Randy wanted it badly. He desperately wanted to be able to smell fresh air and walk around a yard again. His desperation clouded his judgment. He enthusiastically agreed to head over to J-Unit. During his first group recreation, a small Italian attacked him with a prison-made hammer. The guy was a member of a group that SIS knew Randy couldn't be around. They had set him up. Randy ended up "dog-walking" (severely beating) the hammer-wielding clown and then was promptly and predictably sent back to GP. He was admonished for not taking his opportunity to step down. No one will ever hold that SIS officer accountable. No one will ever care that these bastards tried to get Randy severely hurt. After all, he deserves it; otherwise he wouldn't be in ADX.

K-A, the Prerelease Unit

Before being placed in the ADX prerelease unit, I had no idea it existed. You never hear about all the people being released from ADX, and it never crossed my mind that they would have an entire unit to help people "transition" to the free world. This unit exists to prepare people for the culture shock they are about to experience, to reacclimate them to being around other humans again. This is bureaucratic nonsense.

The prerelease unit is called K-A, and it is in the same general area as K-B, which is the lifer and elder unit. K-A is split up into four different groups of cells. Each group has seven cells at most, although they are typically only filled with two to five people. I went into K-A with four months left in my sentence and was placed into Group 1. There were two other people in my group: a gang dropout who had been in ADX for four years, and the supposed brother-in-law of El Chapo. Whenever someone would get released, SIS would fill their cell with another person so that there was a continual rotation of people coming and going.

K-A has a few notable differences from other units. The showers are no longer in the cells. Instead, they are in the back of the unit, with two showers upstairs and two downstairs. The cells only have one door, so staff and other prisoners (during their rec time) can walk up directly to your door and have a chat or pass notes or do whatever they want to do. The biggest difference, of course, is being let out of your cell around other people again.

Having "group rec" made me incredibly nervous. I had a lot of experiences with staff—especially the fascist Florence staff—trying to set me up to get demolished. You never forget these moments. They are experts in this depravity. When you control all the movement, you can control all the violence. Every drop of blood within that prison was entirely on their hands and happened under their watch. I was 100 percent convinced that they were going to put someone around me who I would have to deal with one way or another. Either me getting hurt or me having to hurt them to *prevent* me from getting hurt. Thankfully, that never happened, but it did get close. Being around even two or three other people made me wildly uncomfortable. You cannot let your guard down or trust other people in these situations, even if they are about to get out of prison. Assuming that you are always safe or that they won't try something is a fool's game. I had my guard up for four straight months while in that unit, even when around people I generally liked or got along with. Everybody was nervous. Everybody was trepidatious about being around other people, other egos and weirdnesses, not to mention what the future held. We had no idea what it was going to be like being transferred, released, and placed in the halfway house. It was terrifying.

Every day, the doors automatically open at 6 a.m. for your group, and you walk out to get breakfast at the front of the range. The entry to the range is a big row of prison bars with a slot for staff to pass food trays through. Staff never comes into the unit while any group is outside their cells. You will see medical, talk to your unit team, and get your food and cleaning supplies through these bars at the front of the range. The guards stand on the other side of these bars and pass your tray through, you walk back to your cell, and then the officer in the control room automatically closes your door. Then, when it's time to return the trays, the doors will automatically open and you will walk your tray to the front of the range, drop it off, and return to your cell. When someone wanted to cause problems in the unit, they would refuse to return to their cell. This would not only get them beaten up by staff but also get them removed from the unit and placed back in GP. People who were too nervous about being in a group would often do this on purpose, just to go back to their solitude. Isolation can be extremely difficult to shake off. I still struggle with this today.

There was a very confusing schedule in K-A for when we would come out and when the other units would come out. Every other month, either Group 1 or Group 2 would get to eat their dinner outside their cells in the unit. There were two tables placed in the units, and one of these groups could sit together and eat and chat or go and talk to the other cells. (Groups 3 and 4 were dropout/PC groups, and they were not allowed to eat outside their cells ever.) Every other day, we would come out for inside rec at 7 a.m., 9 a.m., 11 a.m., or 1 p.m. In my four months there, I never fully figured out the schedule. Stupidly, although we were allowed around our group for inside recreation, for outside rec we were placed in cages that resembled oversized dog kennels.

Guards would often try to intentionally antagonize people by abusing the rec schedule. Folks would be standing at their doors, ready to get some desperately needed time out of their cells, and the guards would wait . . . and wait . . . and wait . . . taking away five, ten, fifteen minutes of precious rec time. This infuriated people, as intended. But if we got mad or yelled too much, the pigs would just cancel rec altogether, blaming our behavior instead of their purposeful incompetence. Win-win for them. Guards would also delay allowing us to grab our trays of food, waiting until the food was cold before opening the doors. They played all sorts of small-time games to try to get under our skin, and it often worked.

K-A Unit did nothing to prepare me for returning to the world. I wasn't allowed more phone time, I wasn't allowed email, I wasn't allowed more visits. The big preparation for freedom was that I got to be in a room slightly bigger than a cell with two other people who often had their headphones on and were doing their own things. Everyone focused on their own release dates.

At one point, they brought a new guy, N, into our group. He had been at ADX for five years, following a series of "self-defense" violent attacks. Eventually the Bureau just got tired of the habitual "self-defenses" and dropped him in the unit. He was dangerously paranoid. He constantly felt like folks were talking bad about him, constantly felt the need to tell everyone how much he had it together. Bro needed to keep assuring folks that he wasn't like everyone else, that he was going to be a success once he was free.

The amount of trauma he had from his upbringing and youth, plus life within federal prison, was severe. He hated me. He hated that I got mail, that I had legal visits, that I had a family to return to, that I had a successful relationship with my wife and kiddos. I never flaunted these things or bragged about them, but their existence was enough for some people to get really bothered by and preoccupied with. They would ask invasive questions or make passive-aggressive, rude comments. My visits were an affront to N. Who did I think I was, having people come to see me? Every visit I had was one he didn't. This is what being cut off from the world can do to some people. It can magnify every self-doubt or insecurity. All the things you feel are lacking in your life become the only things you're able to think about. This is from trauma and abuse. It also wasn't just me he felt this way about, but I wasn't worried about everyone else's safety, I was worried about mine.

He would randomly say things like, "You think you're the only one with a girl? I've got lots of them. You aren't the only one, ya know." He would start telling me out of the blue about the child who would presumably be his stepkid whenever he was released. He would often talk about the gifts he was buying for her and how he was a *real* dad, "not like the rest of the scum in here." I couldn't tell if I was a part of the scum or not. He never told me I wasn't. Everything was a competition. Every workout he did was to prove that he was in the "best shape out of anyone in the unit." When I quietly disagreed and said that maybe the cartel guy was in better shape, he stewed on this slight for weeks, growing silent and cold. I'd often find him glaring at me randomly when we were out at rec.

After a couple of weeks, he came and told me, "I really want to hurt you right now." When I asked where this hostility was coming from, he pointed out that I was disrespecting him, that I thought I was better than him, that I thought I could just belittle anyone and get away with it. This interaction happened because a few days earlier I had implied that maybe someone else in the unit was in equally good shape as him. KC had asked me if I had heard N saying he was in the best shape out of everyone in the unit. I'd said I had, but thought it was a bold thing to say. Something so stupid and small, something that didn't matter to me in any way. Meant nothing to life, did nothing to add or subtract from my day. Yet to N it was a violent attack on everything he had dedicated his life to. He needed to be the best; otherwise how would he have value? He had serious trauma and had no idea how to handle it without violence.

You are not taught how to deal with this in foster homes or in prisons. They do not teach impulse control or how to regulate emotions when you're feeling triggered. Prison teaches you violence as the only solution to every problem. I had to navigate that situation very delicately. It wasn't a time to be a tough guy or puff up my chest. In no way was I going to let my ego take control and ruin everything I was working toward. There's a solid chance I would have lost the fight, and Rochelle would have had to hear that not only was my good time pushed back but I was also in the hospital. We were too close to the door, and she had been through enough.

It was in K-A Unit that I met Shahid from DC. Shahid had been inside ADX for approximately nineteen years and was a constant source of fascinating prison history. His entire adult life had been spent in twenty-four-hour lockdown, and hearing his stories about how the prison had been, and how it had changed, never ceased to captivate me. Shahid would later almost die after staff allowed the wound from his knee surgery to become infected and then had to race him back to the hospital for emergency surgery. The Bureau hates influential DC Black prisoners, and Shahid had been a part of a riot at USP Florence that had left a couple of prisoners dead. The BOP partially blamed him for this violence and placed him in ADX as his reward for having too big of a voice behind the walls.

Not everyone in K-A Unit was being quickly released. Some people had been in that unit for years and still had years to go. The policy that the Bureau spouted to us was that if you had less than two years left on your sentence and you weren't being sent to a lower custody level, then you could qualify for the unit. Shahid still had four years left; others still had three to five. All the prison's policies are arbitrary and can change on a whim. The reality was that ADX received extra funding for transitioning people out of the prison, for providing us with the skills to make it in the free world. They had to keep people in that unit to avoid losing funding.

K-A Unit was strange. Not only was I around a gaggle of people from different backgrounds who had all been inside ADX for several years (some for decades), but we were also around all the outside visiting dignitaries. Prior to coming to the Alcatraz of the Rockies, I was not aware of the number of tourists who walked through these halls. Visitors would walk up to the outside gate and gawk at us, stare, and hold discussions among themselves. We would be trying to enjoy our inside rec and some group of assholes would show up outside the front bars. Escorted by the warden, they would sometimes even try to speak with us.

There were tours with South Korean prison officials who were learning how to model their most severe prisons on ADX. Brutality is America's most profitable export. There was the convention of intelligence officers from around the country who came to see how ADX handles isolation and communication restrictions. Twenty to thirty cops just standing outside the range, staring like they had never seen something so interesting as the three men standing in the rec cage. There were federal judges who were given tours to see how gentle and kind ADX is, that we were being pampered and spoiled and there was no need for any more oversight by any judge or government official. There were also journalists. They would come and walk around with their notebooks in hand, taking notes and asking questions of the warden or the captain. The admins who controlled our lives in essentially every way, who diminished us at seemingly every turn, were answering to some five-foot-two person with a notebook. It astounded me how normalized this was. Part of the job of being a warden in ADX is also being a tour guide, apparently.

ADX is potentially the most famous prison in the world, and a part of that is the PR campaign. ADX only works and maintains its notoriety if the public and government continue to believe that the people held at the prison are grotesque abominations, truly vile creatures. If folks begin to see us as humans, the whole sham falls apart. There is no justification for keeping humans locked down for twenty-four hours a day. If you truly feel that some prisoners need significantly more restrictions or guidelines, fine. But how do decades of solitary confinement play into that? You could have the entire "terrorist" contingent of ADX in its own unit, without any lockdowns, and you would still have the same amount of control on the prisoners' outside restrictions. They could have the normal amount of time out of their cells, yet the administration could still restrict all their calls, visits, mail, and so on. The lockdown does nothing to increase "the safety and security of the institution." It exists only for the pain it causes and the lie it sells to the public. It is all to convince the people in power that continuous lockdowns are necessary and that without them there would be murder and chaos.

K-B, the Lifer/Elder Unit

Right next to the prerelease unit, oddly, is the *never*-release unit: K-B, the lifer or long-timer unit. K-B is meant to house people who have been in ADX for an exceptionally long time, have a long sentence remaining, and will never be released from ADX. We call it the lifer unit even though not everyone in there has a life sentence (although 95 percent do). K-B is an even weirder unit than K-A, but it's also a glimpse into what ADX could be. Structurally, K-B is set up exactly like K-A. There are four groups, you get an hour and a half out of your cell every day, and you are locked down twenty-two and a half hours a day, every day of your life, for the remainder of your life.

The differences, however, although few, are truly massive. K-B prisoners are given access to comforts and opportunities in a way that is hard to comprehend in ADX. They are not handcuffed when walking around the staff on their way to or from recreation, like we are in other units. The gates are opened, the group walks through an outside metal detector, they grab whatever basketball or football they want, and they head to rec. This leads to the second difference: They have group outside recreation. They are allowed to be around their group inside and outside, which is shocking. They also have a real rec yard. There is a basketball court, a track to walk around, and as of 2024, small gardens to tend. All this space is built into the ground under the surface of the prison. The area is still surrounded with a chain-link fence on the roof, but just having access to grass and plants is an unreal blessing—although it shouldn't have to be. I've never seen a report showing that removal from nature is beneficial to rehabilitation. There are no peer-reviewed papers going over all the bonuses of ensuring that humans never see grass again. This should be the bare minimum. Instead, it is the extreme exception to the rule.

Another huge difference is that folks in K-B are given fish for pets. Because they have been in prison for so long, and have been in ADX for so long, and have no chance of ever being released (mostly), they are given the option to have betta fish in their cell. These brightly colored fish with large, flowing fins are also known as Siamese fighting fish. I have no idea how the men feed the fish, if they need to buy anything from the canteen, or if it is just a psych program for everyone. Apparently, the administration found out that keeping people in extreme solitary confinement for decades on end without any hope of release may be torture. That it may be inhumane to destroy the psyche of someone every day for years and years and years. Betta fish are, I guess, one way of combating that.

Sadly, much like how K-A only exists for people who are getting released and who have not caused any problems in other units, K-B is similar. There are many people who have been in ADX for over fifteen years and who have decades left on their sentences who will never get close to K-B unit. You have to have shown a willingness to "lie down," to stop being so resistant or active in prison politics. It doesn't take much to be sent back to GP. Jeff Fort was sent back for having a casual conversation on the phone. They accused him of trying to lead his gang. If you are considered a leader and you ask your wife how her day is going, you are automatically guilty of plotting. The administration is cruel and pathetic. Within K-B there are also some of the most infamous people in the entire prison. All the big names from the '90s have aged and are now lying low in K-B, including:

- **Wayne Perry**, aka Silk, is currently in K-B. Wayne is a DC Black prisoner who had a high level of power and respect within prison and was infamous for his multitude of bodies. Wayne was allegedly a hitman in DC who made many enemies and had many snitches. He is a very serious person, although every time I heard him interact with people he seemed respectful and kind. His family was super chill as well, even interacting with Rochelle at visitation. Wayne has a revolutionary mindset and could almost be considered a politicized prisoner. He is a polarizing person, with folks from DC either idolizing and respecting him or finding him to be the lowest scum on earth. One man's hero...
- **Larry Hoover** and **Jeff Fort**. I've spoken about these two elders previously, but they were both in and out of K-B. When I was last inside, Jeff had been removed from the unit after being accused of talking gang politics on the phone with his family. This is a tactic used by SIS to remove influential people from open units.
- Scumbags **Eric Rudolph** and **Terry Nichols**. Rudolph orchestrated the 1996 Olympic Park bombing in Atlanta, and Nichols helped in the 1995 Oklahoma City bombing. Two people about whom I have nothing positive to say and who are seeing out their days with betta fish.
- **Richard Reid**, the previously mentioned jihadi.
- **Ted Kaczynski**. Ted was in this unit before he was transferred to USP Butner to live out his last days. Apparently he did not enjoy interacting with other prisoners all that much. He was known for skipping rec and preferred to stay inside his cell. He didn't want to be around people in the free world, so naturally he would prefer his solitude in the carceral world. He was considered deeply strange for this behavior.
- **Michael Swango**, the doctor who killed approximately sixty people through lethal injection, is housed in this unit. He also carries himself like a proper piece of human waste. He is not imposing and does not have any special characteristics. But he is capable of doing things I cannot imagine. Somewhere in his

childhood, he needed help. He needed someone to pay attention to his hurting or what his brain was up to. The consequence of the capitalist approach toward mental health is Michael Swango. People slip through the cracks, end up doing unspeakable damage, and then rot away in prison because they couldn't exist properly. He has done horrific things, but horror doesn't exist in a vacuum.

- **Luis Felipe**, aka King Blood, is the founder of the New York chapter of the Latin Kings (ALKN). After twenty years of totally restrictive isolation, he is now allowed to walk a yard for an hour and a half per day.

It is strange to think that the most "humane" unit in the prison is available for those who are "too dangerous" to ever be released. The people who are considered unremovable are the same people who get to walk around staff without wearing handcuffs. This shows the completely farcical nature of this entire prison. The BOP has labeled certain people as too powerful or influential, or too famous, to ever be released from ADX but then also lets those people have the most freedom in the entire institution. It is completely bewildering. Thank goodness those men receive *something* decent, but it shouldn't have to happen this way.

One of the most effective and honest aspects of the campaign to free Leonard Peltier was pointing out how spine-chillingly disturbing it is to keep an elder in a prison where he doesn't have proper access to mobility or medical care. People truly cared that Leonard could be locked down for a couple of weeks at a time. That point stands for every single elder in ADX. Our feelings about the prisoners' actions should not be the determining factor in how we allow them to be treated. We shouldn't be holding these men in concrete cages on twenty-four-hour lockdowns. We shouldn't be holding them in a prison where they cannot communicate with their families or share any physical connection with them. Some of these prisoners have grandchildren they will never hold or touch. Some have *children* they've never held or touched.

This is diabolical, and it is symbolic of the entire Bureau. They label someone as dangerous, and then the person's life as they know it is over. All of us are allowing this to happen. Not a single person in the United States is innocent of participating in this abuse, because we haven't done nearly enough to stop it. We have allowed the most sadistic arm of the federal government to have carte blanche over men who can barely walk. Imagine your grandfather never being able to hold your hand. Imagine his fear as his health begins to fade and there is no one to comfort him. Imagine his terror as his breathing becomes labored or his joints begin raging in pain and not a single staff member gives him any care or kindness. Imagine the person you love most, a human you hold so tenderly in your heart, dying alone. Dying while surrounded by people who hate his guts and hope he burns in hell. If we wouldn't want that for our grandparents, we shouldn't want it for anyone else's.

K-B Unit isn't some delightful treat served up by the BOP's kind heart. It is the aftermath of countless lawsuits and battles and legal interventions. These small benefits are not life-generating gifts, they are scraps. They are hand-me-down comforts. They are not even the bare minimum of how people should be treated. But within ADX these prisoners are considered almost spoiled. Guards hate that they are allowed to see grass or toss a football. These are the worst of the worst, those who will *never* see freedom. The BOP doesn't want to provide them with a single thing. The BOP gets to then destroy you in every way possible and also blame you for the treatment: *If you weren't such a threat, then we wouldn't have to come down so hard on you. Why do you make us treat you this way?*

III CHAPTER 15

Before the Devil Knows You're Gone: Walking Out of Hell

I was released after sixteen months of ADX imprisonment. There had been many problems leading to my release, most of which revolved around probation and my case manager inside. In prison, even the simplest things can become massive burdens.

When you are being released from prison, you are typically released to the same state or region where your original crime occurred. Because my action had taken place in Missouri, that is where probation wanted to send me. This was a major issue. My wife and kids were in Colorado. My job was in Colorado. My lawyers were in Colorado. My home was in Colorado. All the things in my life that are supposed to lead to a successful transition were in Denver, and yet they wanted to send me to Missouri, where I would be nothing but a target for police and a burden on any support system I had. Typically, getting transferred to a different state wouldn't be a big deal. The "home" state and the receiving state exchange some paperwork, you sign some forms agreeing to let the receiving state have power over your probation, and that's it.

Like every other aspect of my imprisonment, however, the people in charge had to make it as complicated, annoying, and stressful as imaginable. After I had submitted the probation transfer request the first time, I was told it had been approved and I would be released in September. Fantastic! This joy only lasted two days before my case manager came to my cell to let me know that for it to actually be approved, I had to agree to certain special circumstances requested by the state of Colorado. You can imagine my rage and disappointment. The special conditions were unacceptable and made absolutely no sense. They included:

- I would have to submit to urine tests in accordance with the rules of my receiving state. This was normal and not an issue at all.

- I would have to allow tracking devices to be placed not just on my electronic equipment but on every piece of electronics in my entire home. My teenagers, my wife, and my little one would all have to have a digital tracker that recorded every single button pressed, every search, every call. The government would record and keep all of this. Usually, this sort of draconian guideline was reserved for sex offenders with internet charges, hackers, or those engaged in computer fraud. The internet had absolutely nothing to do with my action, and this made no sense whatsoever. I did not feel comfortable submitting my children to participate in my punishment even further.
- Probation would determine whether I had to see a mental health doctor, and I would be forced to take any medication that this person requested, whether I wanted to or not. I would have to submit to weekly random blood tests to prove I was taking the medication that the state required. This was a stunning request. Giving the enemy the power to have control over how my brain acted and responded was terrifying and unprecedented.

I refused. I refused because I believed that it would be an easy task to get a judge to overturn it or to get probation to step down. After ten years inside, I still can't believe I was so naive. My lawyers contacted probation and the courts and received nothing positive. We tried to file motions, but everything was stalled and we were starting to get desperate. Why did every single aspect of release have to be littered with difficulties?

After a few months, my wife got tired of waiting. She wanted me home and was willing to call and talk with anyone necessary to get some damn information. After weeks of trying, she finally got a hold of the head of the US probation office in Colorado. Rochelle's vulnerability, openness, and vast understanding of the situation led to the first positive conversation we'd ever had with probation. We would agree to certain terms, and others would not be enforced as severely as they sounded on paper. Rochelle would have to allow a home visit from probation officers and would have to get a landline telephone installed. It was agreed, though. Rochelle pulled it from thin air. After ten years of imprisonment, after five and a half years of no-contact, twenty-four-hour isolation, I would finally be coming home to my family. I was not used to receiving good news. I was not used to things falling in our favor. It was a dream.

Being released from ADX is not a straightforward process. As part of their contract with Congress, the BOP states that no one is ever released straight from ADX to the free world. All prisoners are given a chance to rehabilitate, get acclimated to being around people, and prepare for freedom. We all know this is not even close to true, and they know it as well. It's all performative rehabilitation. Here is what happens when you are set for release:

- You must have an address to be released to. If you are homeless, your case manager will put the halfway house as your address, but they need to have a location to send you. This address will be verified over and over. You will sign countless forms confirming you are going to this address, and you will sign an itinerary created by the prison stating exactly how you will get to the address. My itinerary stated that my family would pick me up at the prison on December 12, 2023, between 8 and 9 a.m. and that I would then have four hours to get from the prison to the halfway house in Denver.
- You are given a chance to mail your property home so that you don't have to transfer with all your possessions and have the potential to lose them. At other prisons, you are required to pay for this, but at ADX the mail officer was shockingly respectful and considerate and mailed it home free of charge.
- If you are being released to a state outside of Colorado, about a month before your release date you will be transferred to a prison or jail in that state, or whatever prison is closest to your release state. People being released to Florida are sent to USP Coleman or USP Atlanta; people being released to Kansas City are sent to Leavenworth. This is supposed to make your release as smooth as possible, but all it does is add the additional stress of another transfer. Once you land at your last prison, you will immediately be placed in the SHU. You are still an ADX prisoner, so you will still be escorted by three guards and you will still not be placed around other prisoners. In transit, this is especially annoying. If you are going across the country from ADX, you will often have two or more facilities to stop at along your way. People being sent to the Northeast must stop at both the Oklahoma City Federal

Transfer Center *and* Allenwood in Pennsylvania before making it to the SHU of their final location. Transferring like this is a mess, and it exhausts you mentally and physically.

- I wasn't flying across the country, thankfully. I was being released to a city right up the road. The Regional Office could have sent me to FCI Englewood, the scene of so many of the worst days of my life. That prison was only thirty minutes from my final location. Instead, they decided to place me at USP Florence, the scene of so many of the other worst days of my life. The day before my release I would be transferred to USP Florence, which is in the same complex as ADX and the medium-security FCI. This is where my family would pick me up and I would finally breathe free air. They told me that my family would be able to pick me up at the prison gates, that they could meet me there and welcome me with a hug. This was just another in a long line of bald-faced lies, and they knew it. They have absolutely no shame.

On the day of my transfer to USP Florence, I was supposed to leave ADX at 8 a.m. The hours slipped by, and I began to get increasingly nervous. By 10 a.m., I figured something must have gone wrong. Something always goes wrong. Finally, at 10:30, I was told that I had a legal call. This was highly unusual, to have a legal call two hours after you were supposed to have already left. My legal team was justifiably worried. I was being sent back to a prison filled with guards who had beat me senseless, who had literally tortured me. Those guards were all still there. The son of the lieutenant I fought was still working as a guard at that prison.

Being sent there, even just for an evening, was terrifying. It felt the same as my arrival to ADX had felt sixteen months prior. Was this another setup? Was this more of the same? The BOP isn't opposed to having people hurt or killed. They get their revenge. I assumed something terrible was happening and panicked when I got on the phone with my lawyers. The first thing I said to my team was, "What's wrong?!" Nothing was wrong. They were just calling to make sure I was doing okay. It was a safety check, a mental health check-in. The phone call lasted twenty minutes, and then I was taken back to the cell. Then, immediately after I made it back to the cell, I was told to get packed up—I was leaving.

Leaving the dungeon is a similar process to arriving. You are handcuffed and walked the long trek back to R&D, where you are placed in a holding cell. This is where you will sit. And sit. And sit. In my case, it took about an hour and a half before the transport crew started arriving. I had to strip out for them, show them my rectum, lift up my penis, make sure I wasn't hiding anything in my mouth or cavities. Then, after all that humiliation, I had to go through the X-ray machine, which would have shown them anything I had on me. I then changed out of my ADX clothes and into my transport clothes. Then I waited... and waited... for another hour.

When the transfer crew was ready, I was handcuffed, walked outside, and placed in a transport vehicle. There were two officers inside the car, both armed with pistols. There were also three officers walking around the vehicle, all with rifles and handguns. We drove approximately two miles per hour to the USP. The guards walked around the vehicle the entire time, just in case someone got beyond the security checkpoint and all the cameras and then managed to get to us. The amount of security and precaution is all theater. They know there is zero threat to me besides themselves, and I was incapable of being a threat to them. The drive to the USP, which would have normally only taken about two minutes, took more than twenty. Everything felt off. Surely getting released from ADX wouldn't be so weird? Surely it wouldn't be five guards escorting me to the Florence penitentiary. I did not and do not have any trust for these people. I have been hurt by them, and I have seen what they have done to others. It isn't a game. It isn't a joke. These people get folks killed or severely hurt. It's not a "few bad apples," it is a functional policy, and I will never forget what they are capable of. This was at the front of my mind for the entire snail-paced drive.

On arrival at the penitentiary, I was walked inside their R&D, placed in a holding cell, and left there for another two and a half hours. While I was arriving, another prisoner was going back to ADX from the Step-Down Program. All of this was oddly casual and low-key. On the drive there it seemed like I was headed to death row, but once I arrived it was like I was forgotten. After getting my arrival clothes (more khaki pants and a stained white T-shirt), I just sat in the holding cell by myself while the prison went about its business. I was freezing. I was exhausted. I still wasn't sure that they weren't going to dump me in a cell with some fascist sociopath. These things happen. One thing you learn in prison is to "hurry up and wait." You are rushed somewhere, told it is so important, and then forced to sit for hours and hours at a time doing absolutely nothing. This is the life of a prisoner, especially one who is transferred on a regular basis. Your time is meaningless.

Eventually, they moved me to another holding cell, this one in the SHU. It was dark and freezing (it was December), and the only thing to sit on was a four-point table—the same type of table I had been tortured on five years prior. I arrived in that holding cell at approximately 2:30 p.m., and I was in there until 8:30 p.m. These sick schmucks sat me in this torture room, doing less than nothing, for half a day. I tried walking laps, but the cold floor was painful on my feet. I tried to meditate, but being right next to the SHU units, all my thoughts were drowned out by the screaming, rapping, and door banging. Prison SHUs may be the loudest places on earth. Every sound is magnified and enhanced by all the steel surrounding us. The SHU orderly slipped me a book under the door at some point, a *True Blood* book. The orderlies brought me Crocs slip-ons around 5 p.m. and then a blanket at six o'clock. Dinner at 7 p.m. was beans, rice, bread, salsa, and a piece of tofu. I was not given a spoon or spork, so I just shoveled the horse food into my starving mouth. I was shaking with nerves and needed anything to help me settle.

After several hours of having terrible thoughts take up residence in my brain, all the fear transformed into severe boredom and apathy. I knew the mental game that was being played, and I was over it. They could have put me in a cell thirty minutes after arriving, but this is how those pukes play. This is business as usual. At approximately 8:30 p.m., they came and asked, "King, you ready?" I almost mocked them and said, "No, I need a little longer," but I have seen what happens when you lay snark on these people. Instead, I just rolled up my blanket, placed it under my arms, and got cuffed up behind my back.

I was taken to the upper unit of the SHU, where the cells were run-down, filthy, and isolated from the rest of the SHU. I believe this was a PC section, but I couldn't confirm this. One other person was moving cells at the same time, an older Black dude. He was placed in a cell with water covering the floor and no shower curtain. He yelled and yelled, and the guards assured him that they would return with a mop and a curtain. There was a better chance of him being freed than them providing him with a mop. By the time I left the next morning, they had not brought him as much as a towel, let alone a mop.

I tried doing the cleaning routine I did on entering any new cell, but I was so worn down. There was a small bottle of clear "soap" in the cell, so I used my washcloth to at least wipe down my sleeping area and the toilet. There are things you can accept mentally, but that doesn't mean you have to, and I don't accept living with dirty floors and a putrid toilet. Once this cleanup was taken care of, it was time to lie down. Every prisoner who has ever transferred knows this feeling. You've been through an exhausting hell, and there is nothing left to give. At the end of this misery, sleep is a necessity. My mattress was tolerable. My sheets were only partially covered in stains, and I was given a "blanket." That's all I needed. As soon as the pigs turned off my lights, I was out.

The next morning, I was up and ready at six o'clock on the dot. I was told that I would be taken down to R&D at 7 a.m. and that my family wouldn't have to wait for me to get released. I should have known better. I waited. And waited. And waited. At 8:30, I was at the door, harassing the guards walking by, asking what was going on, why wasn't I leaving? They seemed confused. "Oh, you're leaving today? Well, let me check. I haven't heard anything." Steam was coming from my ears when they came to my door and cuffed me up. Then I was finally walked down to R&D.

In R&D, I was given the clothes my wife had mailed to the prison months earlier for me to wear on release. Being able to put on my own normal street clothes again for the first time in ten years was a surreal feeling. It felt so natural and so foreign at the same time. She had sent my lucky socks and underwear from trial. I had a Kansas City hat and a really meaningful shirt. I had spent my entire prison bid refusing to buckle on my ethics. This had often led to violence from staff and other prisoners. But you have to stand for what you believe in. Being able to walk out of prison wearing a "Protect Trans Kids" shirt felt important to me. I went in with my solidarity and I walked out with it as well. Of all the things they stole from me and my family, they were never able to strongarm me out of my ethics.

Leaving R&D, me and two other prisoners were walked down through the administrative portion of the prison. We had to sign more forms and confirm who we were, and then we were led to the entrance of the prison. I had previously been told my family would be able to pick me up at the door, but of course this wasn't true. Not even flirting with the truth. Everything in this process was about misdirection and waiting. What should have been one of the most joyful moments of my life was intentionally turned into one of the most stressful. This is on brand for the BOP. Why give you joy when they can give you uncertainty and agitation?

The wait was a unique and horrid ordeal. What was really going on? What madness were they trying to pull? Prison trauma is a serious matter, and the feeling that everything good is a trick and everything bad is a certainty gets etched in your psyche. I became convinced that they were going to cancel everything, that this was actually a trick and they were going to rearrest me for something I had completely forgotten about. I had let myself feel hopeful, and they were going to shove that hope right down my throat.

The three of us were waiting in the front lobby of the penitentiary. The other two were both getting flights to the East Coast. I was two hours from home. I was waiting to see my family. I asked to use the phone so I could let Rochelle know what was happening and was told this wasn't going to happen. Policy said I couldn't use the phone. I asked when we were leaving and was told it was none of my business. Policy said I didn't get to know when we were leaving. I hate these people now, and I especially hated them at that moment.

After about twenty-five minutes of sitting and waiting, a USP counselor came down and let us know that he would be dropping us off at the front gate. Once all the paperwork was sorted, we three now-former prisoners were loaded into a van and driven to the main entrance of the prison. My family wasn't allowed to park near the prison. Instead, they were forced to park on the side of the busy road that runs beside the prison. This is where I was headed. Once I was off the prison's property, I saw them. I saw my wife running to me. My future was racing toward me. There were two cars full of people who had come to welcome me to freedom, to rescue me from this nightmare. My little one was trailing my wife. I saw everything that had ever mattered. Then she was in my arms. Gasping. Then I was holding her. Then I was hugging my daughter Penelope. Then I was hugging S, one of my lawyers, and Z, S's friend and my comrade and current boss and friend. My dear friend Alex from Unicorn Riot came down and was recording the entire thing.

An assortment of other friends and comrades had made the trip, and it was amazing to see that many people there to support me. Hugging people for the first time in so long. Then we loaded into an SUV with Z driving, herding us toward home.

My case manager had lied about giving me four hours to get to the halfway house. Probation had decided we only needed three. By the time we were actually on the road, we had a little more than two and a half left to get to the halfway house, which was approximately two hours away. I was handed my new phone, a red iPhone. I was handed coffee and a box of oatmeal creme pies, of which I could only eat two. I was free. I was sitting beside Rochelle. I was, for the first time in my life, controlling a phone that was connected to Bluetooth, and I was playing music and chants and everything. I was free, and Rochelle was beside me. My friends were around me. My future was in front of me. I was free.

CHAPTER 16

First Breath of Freedom

I am one of the privileged ones. There are a thousand reasons for this, but luck or fortune was always on my side. I had a release date, a date that provides hope and purpose and is denied to tens of thousands of people. I was a cis-hetero white male. I had made it out alive. No one is guaranteed to make it to freedom, and to do so felt like an unlikely blessing.

I had support—family, friends, work, comrades. I had things that made my release as bearable as it could possibly be. And it was *still* hard. You do not just shake off prison the second you walk out of the gates. All the talk about the day you're released being the best day of your life is make-believe, a fairy tale. It is scary and confusing. You go from prison to freedom to a different type of prison at the halfway house. The halfway house isn't there to assist you, it's there to house you until you can either find a place to live or they feel you cannot get adjusted to free life and you get sent back to prison. Although some of the reception staff can be really helpful, they are not your friends.

There are many people who will never get out of the ADX and many others who will never get the ADX out of them. I was there for almost two years, and I think about it every single day. I watch YouTube videos about it. I wrote this book about it. I think about the powerlessness and lack of control every single day. Maybe one day I won't think about the ADX, but I doubt it.

Prisoners need help. We need therapy, we need access to doctors, we need communication, we need empathy and kindness and accountability. We need to be treated like humans while also being treated like someone who has experienced something truly awful. I found myself bottling up my emotions. I would have conversations in my head that I would then assume were clear to others, though I had not actually said a word. I had spent five and a half years talking to myself, and now I had to free my words.

Prisoners struggle with emotions. I couldn't handle even a tiny bit of kindness. When Rochelle did something kind, I would sob. When Erika and Z bought me lunch, or gave me a goddamn paycheck, I would sob. When Josh answered the phone, I would sob. Kindness is scary. It is unpredictable, and you never feel as if it's deserved. Anger is deserved. Tension and suspicion make all the sense in the world. You can predict those emotions, and you know how to counter them. How do you counter someone giving you love that you 100 percent know you don't deserve?

Love is a two-way street. Not only do we need help after prison, but we need to be able to help others. At least I did. I needed to feel productive, helpful, and essential. I was desperate to show that I wasn't a charity case and that I could contribute to the movement that had kept me alive. I was released on December 12 and was working by the 20th. I had to. I had to do something to feel complete. Small things would make me feel so stupid and worthless. I didn't know how to download apps or use Bluetooth. Those things had existed when I was free, but I'd never used them then, and now you couldn't escape them. I had to figure out how to handle all the codes you receive on your phone for confirmations, how to handle texting. I had to learn that people can love you and still not immediately respond to texts. I had to learn how to accept friends and how to be a friend.

There are people who will leave ADX after having done ten or twenty years there, and I have no idea how they will survive on the outside. I cannot imagine the mental toll, and I cannot imagine what will be necessary to help them make it in the "free" world.

Sometimes it feels like succeeding post-ADX isn't a tangible thing, it's a mental victory. It is being able to accept kindness and know that I deserve it. We are taught that we are trash, that we will never be loved and never deserve love, and that what is happening to us is our fault. Even if you intellectually know this isn't the case, it can get ingrained within you.

Success is being able to take off that cloak of misery and know that you are not what they say you are. We are not our enemies' definition of us. We are human. We are deserving of love and support and kindness. And hopefully there will be people there to provide those things when we set foot outside the walls.

||| CHAPTER 17

When One Door Closes

As of this writing, in February 2025, I have been out of federal custody for a year and two months. Life is both beautiful and shockingly difficult. When inside, I told Rochelle countless times that I would survive. I would not need mental health help, I would not need trauma help, I would be fine. I had read books inside and I had braced myself. Oh, how wrong I was.

I was released from the halfway house in January 2024. I was placed on an ankle monitor and was permitted to move in with Rochelle and the kids. We had not touched hands in almost six years, and we were now living together as a family. There were times that were exceedingly difficult. We had ten years of separate and conjoined trauma to work through, and we put in the work. We still are putting in the work. When I first got out, we lived an hour from Denver, so Rochelle would drive me an hour to work, stay there with me, and then drive us an hour home. It was not sustainable. There were times when it was hard to be touched, hard to be around cats, hard to hear people raise their voices. It was beautiful, though. It was beautiful being able to hug my soulmate. It was beautiful getting to go on walks with my family. It was beautiful hearing them complain about putting away dishes. These are blessings.

By the grace of the goddesses, I was able to gain access to EMDR therapy. I'd never heard of this before and it sounded ridiculous, it is anything but ridiculous. EMDR stands for Eye Movement Desensitization and Reprocessing, a type of treatment that helps you cope with and reprocess traumatic memories. S helped introduce me to my therapist, A, and since then I have gone twice a month, every month. I work through trauma and I sob uncontrollably. We go over all the hurt I have been through, all the hurt I have caused, all the insecurities

The day Eric was released from the federal halfway house on home confinement.

I have developed, and we work through them. Since the day I met them, A has been one of the most important people in my life. I also have a psychiatrist. At first this was a court-appointed thing, but I now see the benefit of it. I am on certain mood-stabilizing medicines that help prevent manic, uncontrollable sadness or anger. I should never want to stab someone for bumping into my cart at the grocery store, and I should never have to have two knives by me every time I am near the front door. Trauma will do that to you, and thanks to the doctor, I am getting to a place where that is no longer needed.

There have been times when readjusting has felt almost unattainable. There have been long periods when any act of sincere kindness has

Eric and his younger daughter the day they had their first offer on a house accepted. (It was later rescinded due to the inspection.)

broken me down. I have sobbed almost uncontrollably at kind words or gestures. Rochelle making a nice dinner or saying she is proud of me. My bosses giving me appreciation or tokens of respect and support. I did not expect this. I never expected that after years of being mistreated, being treated as a human would have such a profound impact. I have cried more in the last year than throughout the decade before that. I had been repressing hard emotions as a survival technique. My brain felt that if I let the soft in, I would not be able to make it through so much hard. Now it is being released, and it feels wonderful and scary at the same time.

Since getting out, I have been absolutely floored by the amount of rudeness I see in everyday life. While inside, you can learn to expect and anticipate inconsideration from guards and prisoners alike. I knew *exactly* how certain guards would act, and that made it feel safer. But I cannot anticipate when someone will honk at me while driving, cut me off in line, or just give me a bad glare. A bad glare in prison is a 100 percent sign that something horrible is coming your way. Bad glares are a threat and a trigger, and people in the free world do not hesitate for one second to dish them out. Staring, shouting on their phone, blaring music, not moving out of the way—all of this feels like an odd

Eric holding Rochelle as they drive away from the prison and toward freedom. Image by Alex Binder.

lack of civility that I naively never expected to find when returning to the free world.

This has affected me in my home life as well. Trauma does not just go away on its own. Just because you are living somewhere safe does not mean that you can shake off a decade of routine and hurt. When my daughters leave their drink glasses out on the counter, it feels like an attack. When dirty dishes are left in their rooms, another attack. When things are just thrown on the ground or not picked up, well, friends, that is an attack. Even when they talk rudely it feels like an attack—and they are children, teenagers. My wife is so patient and helpful with this. We are completely honest with them and try to be as open as possible so that when this happens they can understand and contextualize my reaction. It is confusing for a child to see someone upset over a dish on the counter. I never yell, never even raise my voice. But there have been times when I am clearly annoyed and I don't express it the right way. My brain tells me it is a personal affront to me, and A and Rochelle have helped me learn that it is the exact opposite. Disproportionate responses to small things that are normal to every child. Thank the goddesses for the patience of the people who love me. I spend a lot of time working out how to be a better dad, how to

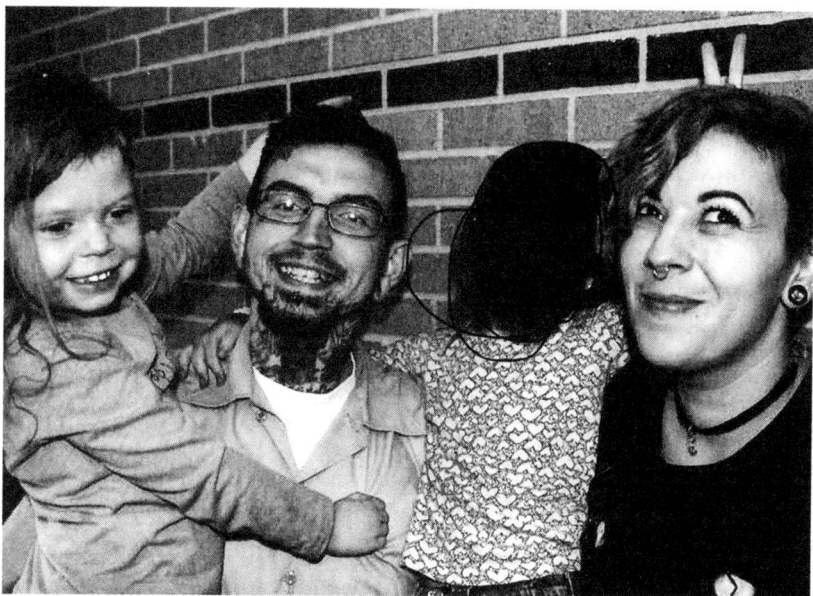

Eric and his family while visiting at FCI Florence in 2017. This would be their last family contact visit for the next six years.

feel worthy of them and this family. I feel immense guilt all the time at what I put Rochelle and these little defenseless kids through. I cry. I cry a lot.

Thankfully, I have been supported as much as any person on earth has ever been supported. My family has been there for me in every way possible. I have been loved, and I have people who care for me and want me to feel whole and healed. They understand that these things take time, and they have given me that time and space. I am encouraged to do things that provide happiness. I am encouraged to find joy and to express myself in ways that I have been denied in the past. Rochelle happily paints my nails, gently holding my hands and giving me love in the form of art. There is not a time when I do not feel loved.

My mom and stepdad have been there for me also. After my brother passed away at the hands of a slumlord while I was imprisoned, my mom looked out for me and my family to ensure that we had transportation and a place to live. So many people struggle with this when they are released, and it is a stress and fear and panic that I have been able to avoid. That is a huge blessing that I still do not feel I deserve.

I have a fantastic relationship with Dev, one of my best friends, and that is something I do not take for granted. We do not talk every single day, but I also do not feel like we need to. We have both grown up and both have lives, but we are also still there for each other in any and every way. Dev never left my side. From the first day I was arrested until the day I was released, I knew I could count on them without any hesitation. They do not make people like Dev very often.

Another difficulty that recently released people face is employment. Finding a job when you are fresh out is a serious pain. We are often relegated to low-paying, low-advancement, and unstimulating jobs. Before I had even stepped foot outside the ADX, though, I had a career, because Z Williams and Erika Unger had committed to hiring me at Bread and Roses Legal Center, first as a legal assistant and then as a paralegal.

It took about eight months of daily thoughts that I would be fired or would be abandoned before I was able to accept that something so amazing could be real. That this could be my life. I take this job seriously, because it is a blessing. I have been looked out for, given space, pushed forward. I have been taught a skill that I can use for the rest of my life and have been put in a position to succeed in any way I choose. I get to watch and help Erika do everything possible to keep people out of prison. It does not get better than that. I have a mentor named Courtney who teaches me how to be the best paralegal possible and how to generally be a living adult. My gratitude for them as people is only surpassed by my appreciation and passion for the work we do. I've met so many good people through this profession. People who are fighting the abolitionist struggle in multiple different ways. Social workers like Amber, lawyers like Ashley and Joey. I am stunned at the amount of love I see from my colleagues. Keeping people out of prison and fighting for trans dignity are things I wake up every morning thanking the universe I have a chance to participate in. I wake up with pride and hope and joy, and that is a true gift.

The radical community has also been there for me in ways I never thought possible—or thought that I deserved. Josh Davidson pushed our book *Rattling the Cages* to the public and put me in a position to promote it relentlessly after my release. He has been a constant source of immense friendship, inspiration, and motivation. Every podcast I do, every speaking event I attend, and every single book that is sold is down to his commitment to raising up those in need. So far, I've gotten the opportunity to speak in Seattle with Jake Conroy, and I've given talks in Sacramento and Oakland with fellow organizers. I've spoken in Chicago with Jeremy Hammond, in Portland with Bonzo, in Eugene, Oregon, with Josh and D, and in Gary, Indiana. I spoke in Oakland with Claude Marks and Donna Wilmott, two inspirational elders. Sharing this time with my revolutionary elders and making new friends along the way has been amazing. I have gone to colleges to speak to students about the brutality of the carceral system, and I have spoken to letter-writing events about strategy and how best to communicate. I'd never had friendship in the radical community, and now my cup runneth over.

Things are not always easy, but they are always sweet. My worst moment being free so far has been better than my best moment inside. I have not missed nor longed for prison for even a second after my release. I have been stunned by the capitalist attacks on the poor in my community, and I have been saddened by the horrific treatment of trans and immigrant people. I have also been inspired by the amount of mobilization and commitment to liberation displayed in the streets, in infoshops, and online, like seeing organizations like Midwest Books to Prisoners giving countless hours of time and work to show love for those still locked down. It is amazing. Inside, I was surrounded by people who hate everything we stand for. It can convince you that the world is a hateful, dark place. But this is not the case. Love flourishes in the free world, even when it is hard. My struggles are still blessings. When I get scared and feel dumb because I am not sure how to use my phone to navigate the TV, or use an app for my banking, I recognize it is still a privilege to have access to these things.

The capitalist world is a scary and hard place, but there is beauty all around us. There is beauty in kindness and mutual aid. There is beauty in the friendships we make, whether virtual or in person, and in the family we choose. There is sun shining, there is grass to feel, there are flowers to smell. This may sound like hippie nonsense, but after you have been in a concrete box for a decent amount of time, these things will start to feel like speculation. You will start to wonder if they were *ever* real. Well, they are. I have been amazed at what the world has to offer. I understand that this comes from a place of privilege. But when I get to pet lambs with Alex at an animal rescue or eat gluten-free vegan doughnuts with Jake and Josh, I thank the goddesses for this existence. When I get to hug my kids, or argue with them, or talk with my mom

Eric walking off the Florence complex holding Rochelle's hand and wearing a "Protect Trans Kids" shirt. It was important to him to wear clothes in solidarity with the trans community. Image by Alex Binder.

freely, or see Dev when I visit KC, or call Josh every time I have even half a thought in my head, I thank the goddesses. Every time I get to talk trauma or watch football with wonderful Tyler. And when I get to go home and see Rochelle, see her smile, see her crafting or walking around or just *being*, I understand what freedom is.

Kuwasi Balagoon said that "freedom is a habit." You have to develop your freedom, nurture it, appreciate it. You have to find out what your freedom means to you and cultivate that world into existence. Government officials do not care if we are happy, and they do not know what freedom looks like. Their blinders allow their vision to exist only as far as their lobbyist paychecks. We have a beautiful opportunity, though. We have the chance to resist. We have the chance to say *no* to evil. We have the chance to extend love to those who are in need and a fist to those who are deserving. Every single breath is an opportunity to do something great, big or small. The revolution starts between our ears, and we have to determine what world we want to live in and how we are willing to raise it up.

I honor every person still locked up, specifically those in ADX. I honor those who have given my life a sparkle and those who refused to let me drown. I honor those who fight, especially those who came before us and still have not given up. I honor every abolitionist, anarchist, revolutionary, feminist, and every other "ist" who is standing up to fascism and government domination. I am with you. Thank you for reading my story. Please write a prisoner.

Toward Liberation!

Acknowledgments

This book would've never happened without my wife, Rochelle Bricker. Throughout my entire bid, she was a constant source of joy, happiness, growth, and survival. She allowed me into her family, and that gave me hope and purpose. I am now a father of two amazing kids, and that is an indescribable blessing. There are not enough words in the dictionary to describe the impact she has had on me and the love that I have for her. She is my everything, and I thank her for every good thing in my life. My best friend, my soulmate, my Cabbage.

This book also would've never happened without Josh Davidson. Josh wrote to me all those years ago, and since then he has been a constant in my life. His dedication to the abolitionist cause is unparalleled. He is so consistent and so thoughtful, a man who keeps his word and is always there when you need him. It is a blessing to be his friend and comrade and to put out another amazing project with him. Anarchism would be unstoppable if it was full of Joshes.

Joey Paxman is an amazing human. From our first conversation to today, I have felt trusted, believed in, and "worth it." Joey has made sure I never felt bullshitted or disregarded. He has had my back and given me permission to believe in myself. The combo of Joey and Courtney has been such an amazing and beneficial addition to my life. This team at PM Press has made me feel unstoppable, and getting to know and work with them is nothing but a blessing. Thanks also to all the PM people who have worked on this book or shown love, including Wade, Brian, Steven, and Ramsey.

Dev is my best friend and has been there for me before prison, during prison, and after prison. Her entire family is top shelf and I consider her a part of mine.

My mom has been through a lot. It is hard to lose so many people you love. It is hard to raise two bad kids by yourself. It is hard to work countless hours to provide a good life for yourself and your children. My mom is a warrior. My mom taught me how to be kind and to always show up for those who need it. I love you, Mom.

To all the people and organizations who have had a beautiful impact on my life, in absolutely no order: Mom and Bill, Dev, Andrew, Carissa, Annie, Little E, Jake, Dirty, Grandpa, Jim, Alex and Micah, Danni and Mica, Elisa, Badger, Brian, Josh and D and their entire families, Courtney and D, Z and their entire family, Erika and their family, Amber, Paul, Ashley and Joey, Kristin, Anna, Ann R., Cindy, Olivia, Isabel, Todd, the Ritters and Blancks, Amanda, Sara Wild, Artxmis, Big J, Sean, Frankie, Hannah, Claire, Calvin, Parrott, dequi kioni-sadiki, susie day, Dr. Samanski, Claire, S, Rachel, Jamie, Gloom, Trish, Goh, Max, Bonzo and W, all the organizers in Portland and Eugene, Ev, Ian, Heather, Kristin, Jon NZ, Rob and B, Sam, Sara Falconer, Wes, Colin, Emma B., Smiles, Cueta, Richy and Paul, Corinne, Marissa, Melissa, Liberte, Chad, Josh Fernandez and family, all the Sacramento folks, Matt Hart, Denver students, Tyler and Maria, Chad with *Blood on the Razor Wire*, Pepe at *Back on the Grind*, Jules, Nick Wright, Margaret Killjoy, Jude, Jenny, Sebastian, Danika, Libby, Myles Bullen, Ed O'Keefe, Dave B., Maggie R., Sean, Taylor and Tyler, Holly, Zane, April H., Wildes, Brad Thomson, Sean O'Hearn, Hailey, Neon Rose, Dan and Hollie, Monterrey Stephanie, Ella, Ryan Harvey, Pat, Pam, Marci M., *The Sit Down* with Jeff, Apes of the State, Pigeon and Moth, Looms, Pigeon Pit, Lomes, all the Food Not Bombs chapters, every ABC and ABCF chapter, every abolitionist organization, Black and Pink, Calpoppy, Pilsen Community Books, Midwest Books to Prisoners, Stephanie, Bloomington ABC, Pushing Down the Walls, Philly ABC, the Fire Ant Collective, Conspiracy Cells of Fire, AEK Antifa Ultras, Trans Protection Party, Representative Garcia, Representative Cori Bush, the Jericho Movement, Broken Records Radio, Tamarack, Joy Bomb, In the Belly, the Green Brigade, In the Mix, 7th Circle, AMOD, Lowell ABC, Peter and Cripple Punk Alliance, Potted, all of Stonewall Self Defense, First Things First, Warzone Distro, *The Dugout*, Firestorm Books, LAABCF, NYC ABC, NYC Books Through Bars, Blue Ridge ABC, all Irish Republican freedom fighters, and all the Palestinian people fighting for their freedom.

ACKNOWLEDGMENTS

To all the political prisoners who came before me, both living and dead, on whose shoulders we stand: David Gilbert, Kathy Boudin, Ray Luc, Susan Rosenberg, Laura Whitehorn, Donna Willmott, Linda Evans, Marilyn Buck, Mark Cook, Janine Bertram, Alan Berkman, Claude Marks, Herman Bell, Thomas Manning, Ed Mead, Ashanti Alston, Lorenzo Kom'boa Ervin, Jeremy Hammond, Jason Hammond, Jake Conroy, Josh Harper, Kuwasi Balagoon, Anne Hansen, Zolo Azania, Nicole Kissane, James Kilgore, Harold Taylor, John Brown, Michael Kimble, Jennifer Rose, Bill Dunne, Kojo Bomani Sababu, Joe-Joe Bowen, Oso Blanco, Xinachtli, Marius Mason, Casey G., Sasha and Emma, Jalil Muntaqim, Eric McDavid, Alex Stokes, Tall Can, David Campbell, Dr. Mutulu Shakur, Mumia Abu-Jamal, Sundiata Acoli, Jamil Al-Amin, the SLA, Russell Maroon Shoatz, Kamau Sadiki, Veronza Bowers, Sekou Odinga, Seth Hayes, Oscar López Rivera, and all Puerto Rican freedom fighters.

III

Glossary

Communications Management Unit (CMU): These units were built post-9/11, when the BOP decided that they needed to better monitor and restrict the communications of certain prisoners but not everyone in ADX. Early in its existence, the CMU held people the government considered terrorists: jihadis, ELF/ALF (Earth Liberation Front and Animal Liberation Front), sovereign citizens, white power militants. As the years went on, the BOP started filtering those prisoners out, and the units became a holding place for undesirable prisoners: sex offenders, scam artists, older jihadis, militia members, and so on. They have monitored calls and visits, and letters need to be read before being sent. They get to have their own single cells and have normal out-of-cell times, but the units are self-contained and they cannot interact with prisoners on the normal yard.

Federal Correctional Camp (FCC): Camps are for low-level nonviolent prisoners. Dirty politicians, bankers, snitches, low-level drug offenders, prisoners with less than ten years inside. Camps are barely prisons. These institutions often do not have fences around the compounds, and prisoners are allowed to leave the compound for work. There is usually just one guard on shift for the entire camp population. Campers have access to outside food, phones, and drugs. There are some amazingly cool campers I've met in different SHUs, but they are scabs. When the higher-custody prisons are locked down, it is the campers who do all the compound work—thus allowing the prison to stay locked down longer.

Federal Correctional Institution (FCI) Low: These prisons are for first-time offenders, sex offenders, rats, white-collar criminals, and gang dropouts. Jared from Subway was at a Low. I started at a Low for a couple of months. Many modern political prisoners have started or ended at Lows. They usually have the best environment. They have the best food, libraries, classes, jobs, and activities. There is little to no racial politics at Lows and little to no violence. Because of the lack of violence, there is a lot more time to have fun and do things that can lead to a productive bid. There is a lot of pettiness at these yards. Both the guards and other prisoners will pretend they are at a higher custody level while doing everything possible to avoid those levels. I had very rough times with the guards while at a Low.

Federal Correctional Institution (FCI) Medium: The quality of medium-custody-level facilities varies. Some of them are very serious, with a lot of violence and lockdowns. They are run on racial politics, enforced with violence or intimidation. You will not see as many serious stabbings or life-threatening attacks as you would see in the USP prisons, although they can happen. Other Mediums are just as soft as low-security facilities. They are never locked down, and they have a lot of "quality" jobs and programming to pass the time. At most Mediums, you are not allowed to walk the yard if you have any snitching or sex offense charges on your record. You cannot cross the racial line without repercussion. Some queer or trans prisoners may be allowed on the yards, but they will be isolated or continually at risk.

Special Management Unit (SMU): This unit no longer exists now that USP Thomson has been converted to a low-security facility. These were programs at different penitentiaries at different times that were used for short-term "behavior modification." SMUs were used to isolate prisoners who had committed severe acts of violence but didn't qualify for ADX. They had their own referral and acceptance process that was very similar to ADX. If you stabbed someone and they didn't die, you'd go to the SMU. SMUs were very dangerous places. Guards would often set up prisoners to have gladiator fights or to be killed by each other. Recently, before the administration shut down Thomson, the guards had placed a Jewish prisoner in a recreation cage with two white skinheads. For over twenty minutes, the skinheads stomped the Jewish prisoner to death while the guards ignored all the cameras and screams for help. Political prisoner Oso Blanco has navigated three separate stays in the SMU.

United States Penitentiary (USP) High: Even the "softest" USP yard features much more tension, paranoia, intensity, and violence than even the hardest FCI yard. These are violent places filled with serious people, where actions have severe consequences. They have the worst food, worst living conditions, worst SHUs, and most militant staff. These yards are on lockdown for several months out of the year. Any rats, sex offenders, dropouts, race traitors, or thieves will be severely punished and possibly killed. All programming at the USP level is limited due to the constant lockdowns. All the benefits from programs like RDAP (Residential Drug Abuse Program) or the First Step Act are negated. These are not yards to play games at.

Abbreviations

ACE	Adult Continuing Education
ADX	Administrative Maximum
BOP	Bureau of Prisons
CMU	Communications Management Unit
FCC	Federal Correctional Complex
FCI	Federal Correctional Institution
FDC	Federal Detention Center
FMC	Federal Medical Center
FTC	Federal Transfer Center
GP	general population
PC	protective custody
R&D	Receiving and Discharge
SAMs	Special Administrative Measures
SHU	Special Housing Unit
SIS	Special Investigative Services
SOMP	Sex Offender Management Program
SORT	Special Operations Response Team
STG	Security Threat Group
USP	United States Penitentiary

About the Contributors

Eric King is an anarchist who was imprisoned in 2014 for acts of solidarity with the uprising in Ferguson, Missouri. While in federal custody Eric was indicted for a self-defense incident at FCI Florence. Eric took it to trial and is one of the few people to ever win a federal trial. After his victory Eric was sent to the federal supermax, ADX, where he spent most of the final two years of his prison bid. During his time in prison Eric coedited the political prisoner anthology *Rattling the Cages: Oral Histories of North American Political Prisoners*. Eric survived years of documented physical and psychological torture and made it out of prison with heart and soul intact. Eric is an activist, antifascist, and loving father and husband. He lives in Denver.

Ray Luc Levasseur was born in 1946 of working-class, Quebecois blood. Labor history: farm worker, construction laborer, tannery worker, forklift operator, janitor, logger, factory worker, carpenter, plumber, soldier. Political activism: Southern Student Organizing Committee, Vietnam Veterans Against the War, SCAR/Red Star North, Mainers Against Solitary Confinement/Maine Prisoner Advocacy Coalition, Free Palestine. Underground resistance: 1974–1984. Imprisoned: 1969–1971, 1984–2004.

Josh Davidson is an abolitionist, a member of the Certain Days: Freedom for Political Prisoners calendar collective, and a part of the Children's Art Project with political prisoner Oso Blanco. Josh coedited *Rattling the Cages: Oral Histories of North American Political Prisoners* with Eric King. He works in communications with the Zinn Education Project, which promotes the teaching of radical people's history in classrooms and provides free lessons and resources for educators.

ABOUT PM PRESS

PM Press is an independent, radical publisher of critically necessary books for our tumultuous times. Our aim is to deliver bold political ideas and vital stories to all walks of life and arm the dreamers to demand the impossible. Founded in 2007 by a small group of people with decades of publishing, media, and organizing experience, we have sold millions of copies of our books, most often one at a time, face to face. We're old enough to know what we're doing and young enough to know what's at stake. Join us to create a better world.

PM Press
PO Box 23912
Oakland, CA 94623
www.pmpress.org

PM Press in Europe
europe@pmpress.org
www.pmpress.org.uk

FRIENDS OF PM PRESS

These are indisputably momentous times—the financial system is melting down globally and the Empire is stumbling. Now more than ever there is a vital need for radical ideas.

In the many years since its founding—and on a mere shoestring—PM Press has risen to the formidable challenge of publishing and distributing knowledge and entertainment for the struggles ahead. With hundreds of releases to date, we have published an impressive and stimulating array of literature, art, music, politics, and culture. Using every available medium, we've succeeded in connecting those hungry for ideas and information to those putting them into practice.

Friends of PM allows you to directly help impact, amplify, and revitalize the discourse and actions of radical writers, filmmakers, and artists. It provides us with a stable foundation from which we can build upon our early successes and provides a much-needed subsidy for the materials that can't necessarily pay their own way. You can help make that happen—and receive every new title automatically delivered to your door once a month—by joining as a Friend of PM Press. And, we'll throw in a free T-shirt when you sign up.

Here are your options:

- **$30 a month** Get all books and pamphlets plus a 50% discount on all webstore purchases

- **$40 a month** Get all PM Press releases (including CDs and DVDs) plus a 50% discount on all webstore purchases

- **$100 a month** Superstar—Everything plus PM merchandise, free downloads, and a 50% discount on all webstore purchases

For those who can't afford $30 or more a month, we have **Sustainer Rates** at $15, $10, and $5. Sustainers get a free PM Press T-shirt and a 50% discount on all purchases from our website.

Your Visa or Mastercard will be billed once a month, until you tell us to stop. Or until our efforts succeed in bringing the revolution around. Or the financial meltdown of Capital makes plastic redundant. Whichever comes first.

The Warehouse: A Visual Primer on Mass Incarceration

James Kilgore and Vic Liu

ISBN: 979-8-88744-042-2
$24.95   208 pages

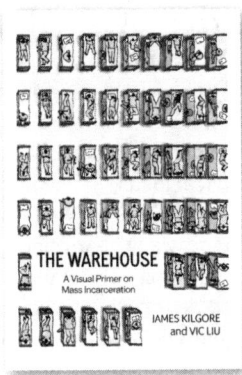

Mass incarceration is a lived, sensory experience.

The most eye-popping statistics alone cannot relate the enormity of its psychological and societal impacts. This concise, illustrated primer is a collaboration between one of mass incarceration's sharpest opponents, James Kilgore, and information artist Vic Liu. It brings to life the histories and means of daily survival of the marginalized people ensnared in this racist, ableist system of class-based oppression. The book elegantly weaves together the most insightful activist scholarship with vivid testimonials by incarcerated people as they fight back against oppression and imagine freedom.

Those targeted for incarceration do not simply submit to a monochromatic existence behind bars. *The Warehouse* showcases the abolition futures being crafted from the inside as people resist through direct action and artistic expression. This book is designed to inform, enrage, and ultimately inspire the same radical hope propelling incarcerated underminers of the carceral state.

"This book vividly activates the senses in its sharp, accessible, and principled analysis of the scope and scale of the carceral state. From cops to cages, from 'get tough' politics to the economics of phone calls, e-carceration, and rural prison building, and from incremental legislative reforms to the visionary organizing of abolitionists, Kilgore and Liu break down the contours of this warehouse and illuminate our paths toward dismantling it."
—Judah Schept, author of *Coal, Cages, Crisis: The Rise of the Prison Economy in Central Appalachia*

"A visually stunning primer on how the US became the world's incarceration nation. Read it and learn how the criminal punishment system works, whom it affects, and what we, as a society, could be doing instead."
—Victoria Law, author of *"Prisons Make Us Safer" and 20 Other Myths about Mass Incarceration*

"James Kilgore is one of my favorite commentators regarding the phenomenon of mass incarceration and the necessity of pursuing truly transformative change."
—Michelle Alexander, author of *The New Jim Crow*

Oscar Lopez Rivera: Between Torture and Resistance

Oscar López Rivera with a Foreword by Archbishop Desmond Tutu and an Introduction by Matt Meyer

ISBN: 978-1-60486-685-8
$18.00   160 pages

The story of Puerto Rican leader Oscar López Rivera is one of courage, valor, and sacrifice. A decorated Viet Nam veteran and well-respected community activist, López Rivera now holds the distinction of being one of the longest held political prisoners in the world. Behind bars since 1981, López Rivera was convicted of the thought-crime of "seditious conspiracy," and never accused of causing anyone harm or of taking a life. This book is a unique introduction to his story and struggle, based on letters between him and the renowned lawyer, sociologist, educator, and activist Luis Nieves Falcón.

In photographs, reproductions of his paintings, and graphic content, Oscar's life is made strikingly accessible—so all can understand why this man has been deemed dangerous to the U.S. government. His ongoing fight for freedom, for his people and for himself (his release date is 2027, when he will be 84 years old), is detailed in chapters which share the life of a Latino child growing up in the small towns of Puerto Rico and the big cities of the U.S. It tells of his emergence as a community activist, of his life underground, and of his years in prison. Most importantly, it points the way forward.

With a vivid assessment of the ongoing colonial relationship between the U.S. and Puerto Rico, it provides tools for working for López Rivera's release—an essential ingredient if U.S.-Latin American relations, both domestically and internationally, have any chance of improvement. *Between Torture and Resistance* tells a sad tale of human rights abuses in the US which are largely unreported. But it is also a story of hope—that there is beauty and strength in resistance.

"In spite of the fact that here the silence from outside is more painful than the solitude inside the cave, the song of a bird or the sound of a cicada always reaches me to awaken my faith and keep me going." —Oscar López Rivera

"Listening to Oscar's voice in this book makes something clear that one such as Nelson Mandela would know well: his sense of liberty has not been extinguished by the jailers' bars or the torturers on call."
—Celina Romany-Siaca, former president, Puerto Rican Bar Association

Resistance Behind Bars: The Struggles of Incarcerated Women, 2nd Edition

Victoria Law with an Introduction by Laura Whitehorn

ISBN: 978-1-60486-583-7
$20.00   320 pages

In 1974, women imprisoned at New York's maximum-security prison at Bedford Hills staged what is known as the August Rebellion. Protesting the brutal beating of a fellow prisoner, the women fought off guards, holding seven of them hostage, and took over sections of the prison.

While many have heard of the 1971 Attica prison uprising, the August Rebellion remains relatively unknown even in activist circles. *Resistance Behind Bars* is determined to challenge and change such oversights. As it examines daily struggles against appalling prison conditions and injustices, *Resistance* documents both collective organizing and individual resistance among women incarcerated in the US. Emphasizing women's agency in resisting the conditions of their confinement through forming peer education groups, clandestinely arranging ways for children to visit mothers in distant prisons and raising public awareness about their lives, *Resistance* seeks to spark further discussion and research into the lives of incarcerated women and galvanize much-needed outside support for their struggles.

This updated and revised edition of the 2009 PASS Award–winning book includes a new chapter about transgender, transsexual, intersex, and gender-variant people in prison.

"*Victoria Law's eight years of research and writing, inspired by her unflinching commitment to listen to and support women prisoners, has resulted in an illuminating effort to document the dynamic resistance of incarcerated women in the United States.*"
—Roxanne Dunbar-Ortiz

"*Written in regular English, rather than academese, this is an impressive work of research and reportage*"
—Mumia Abu-Jamal, death row political prisoner and author of *Live from Death Row*

"*Finally! A passionately and extensively researched book that recognizes the myriad ways in which women resist in prison, and the many particular obstacles that, at many points, hinder them from rebelling. Even after my own years inside, I learned from this book.*"
—Laura Whitehorn, former political prisoner

Lucasville: The Untold Story of a Prison Uprising, 2nd ed.

Staughton Lynd
with a Preface by Mumia Abu-Jamal

ISBN: 978-1-60486-224-9
$20.00   256 pages

Lucasville tells the story of one of the longest prison uprisings in United States history. At the maximum security Southern Ohio Correctional Facility in Lucasville, Ohio, prisoners seized a major area of the prison on Easter Sunday, 1993. More than 400 prisoners held L block for eleven days. Nine prisoners alleged to have been informants, or "snitches," and one hostage correctional officer, were murdered. There was a negotiated surrender. Thereafter, almost wholly on the basis of testimony by prisoner informants who received deals in exchange, five spokespersons or leaders were tried and sentenced to death, and more than a dozen others received long sentences.

Lucasville examines both the causes of the disturbance, what happened during the eleven days, and the fairness of the trials. Particular emphasis is placed on the interracial character of the action, as evidenced in the slogans that were found painted on walls after the surrender: "Black and White Together," "Convict Unity," and "Convict Race." An eloquent foreword by Mumia Abu-Jamal underlines these themes. He states, as does the book, that the men later sentenced to death "sought to minimize violence, and indeed, according to substantial evidence, saved the lives of several men, prisoner and guard alike." Of the five men, three black and two white, who were sentenced to death, Mumia declares: "They rose above their status as prisoners, and became, for a few days in April 1993, what rebels in Attica had demanded a generation before them: men. As such, they did not betray each other; they did not dishonor each other; they reached beyond their prison 'tribes' to reach commonality."

"Mr. Lynd is a masterful storyteller and he has a hell of a story to tell. [He] has written a definitive history of one of the longest prison riots in US history and its aftermath. That alone is worth the price of admission.... What makes the book unique in the historical sense is the remarkable range of primary and secondary sources; Lynd writes with a lawyer's pen but a poet's ear.... This book is a reminder that prisoners—even death row prisoners—are human beings, too. Lucasville is a resounding affirmation of our common humanity."
—Michael Mello, author of *The Wrong Man: A True Story of Innocence on Death Row*

Shadows in the Struggle for Equality: The History of the Anarchist Red Cross

Boris Yelensky, edited by Matthew Hart, illustrated by N.O. Bonzo

ISBN: 979-8-88744-087-3
$19.95   160 pages

From Cop City to the Dakota pipelines and Jane's Revenge to numerous struggles worldwide, anarchist organizers are relentlessly targeted by the state today as they have been for over a century.

Shadows in the Struggle for Equality is the firsthand account of Boris Yelensky, an activist of the Anarchist Red Cross (later the Anarchist Black Cross), during the Russian revolutionary movement from 1905 through 1917, and the subsequent Leninist/Stalinist repression.

Written with great humility and compassion, Yelensky recalls his fifty years of tireless organizing to aid victims of state oppression and injustice, beginning with a vivid sketch of the history of the Russian revolutionary movement and the critical role played by anarchists. He then provides the rich history of the Anarchist Red Cross spanning the time from the Revolution to his settling in the US, where he dedicated his life and his book "to the Fighters for Freedom, Humanism and Justice, to those who endeavored to help these fighters by applying the principle of mutual aid."

In telling why an anarchist relief organization became necessary, he calls attention to a neglected aspect of revolutionary history—the sabotage and discrimination of many social-democrats against their fellow prisoners and in the outside relief organizations. Of the vast sums collected all over the world, from czarist times up through the 1950s when the book was written, very little reached the anarchist prisoners.

With newly translated material, and over a dozen beautiful illustrations by N.O. Bonzo, this stunning edition of *Shadows in the Struggle for Equality* will serve to inspire a continuation of solidarity and support for those who are incarcerated in the struggle for freedom, humanism, and justice.